A Black Soldier's Story

Ricardo Botrell Oviedo

1900

A Black Soldier's Story

The Narrative of Ricardo Batrell and the Cuban War of Independence

RICARDO BATRELL

Edited and Translated by Mark A. Sanders

University of Minnesota Press
Minneapolis
London

This text is a translation of *Para la historia: Apuntes autobiográficas de la vida de Ricardo Batrell Oviedo,* by Ricardo Batrell Oviedo, published in Cuba in 1912. The frontispiece photograph is from this publication.

The map of Matanzas was drawn by Philip Schwartzberg for Meridian Mapping.

Published by the University of Minnesota Press
111 Third Avenue South, Suite 290
Minneapolis, MN 55401-2520
http://www.upress.umn.edu

Library of Congress Cataloging-in-Publication Data

Batrell, Ricardo, b. 1880.
[Para la historia. English]
A black soldier's story : the narrative of Ricardo Batrell and the Cuban War of Independence / Ricardo Batrell ; edited and translated by Mark A. Sanders.
p. cm.
Translation of Para la historia : apuntes autobiográficos de la vida de Ricardo Batrell Oviedo. Habana : Seoane y Alvarez, impresores, 1912.
Includes bibliographical references and index.
ISBN 978-0-8166-5008-8 (hc : acid-free paper)
ISBN 978-0-8166-5009-5 (pb : acid-free paper)
1. Batrell, Ricardo, b. 1880. 2. Cuba—History—Revolution, 1895–1898—Personal narratives. 3. Blacks—Cuba—Biography. 4. Soldiers—Cuba—Biography. I. Sanders, Mark A., 1963– II. Title.
F1786.B3313 2010
972.91'05—dc22

2010026454

Printed in the United States of America on acid-free paper

The University of Minnesota is an equal-opportunity educator and employer.

18 17 16 15 14 13 12 11 10   10 9 8 7 6 5 4 3 2 1

Dedico este libro a mis hijos,
Isaiah Anthony Wallace Sanders
y Joshua Allen Wallace Sanders:

que siga yo descansando debajo de la sombra de sus sonrisas . . .

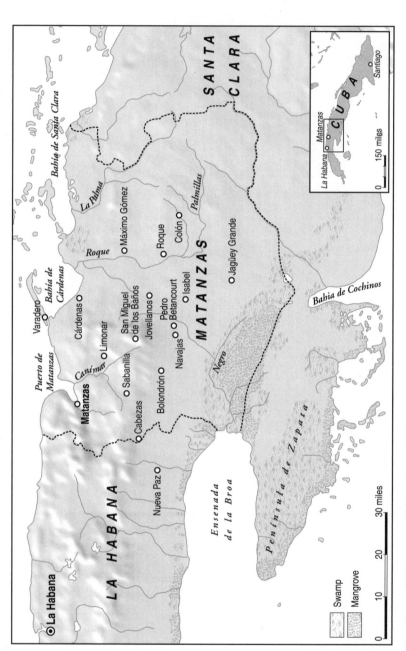

Province of Matanzas, Cuba, circa 1896.

CONTENTS

RICARDO BATRELL AND THE CUBAN RACIAL NARRATIVE

An Introduction to *A Black Soldier's Story*

Mark A. Sanders

Antes que la paz quiero la libertad de la patria y la conservación de los ideales revolucionarios; y si para defenderlos contra los agresores hay necesidad de combatir en las calles o aspirar el aire puro de las montañas, sabré cumplir con mi deber . . .

Before peace, I want liberty for the country and the preservation of its revolutionary ideals; and if in order to defend them against aggressors, it is necessary to fight in the streets or to take to the mountains and breathe its pure air, I will do so knowing that I have served my country . . .

—Juan Gualberto Gómez

La República es la realización de las grandes ideas que consagran la libertad, la fraternidad y la igualdad de los hombres: la igualdad ante todo, esa preciada garantía que, nivelando los derechos y deberes de los ciudadanos, derogó el privilegio de que gozaban los opresores a título de herencia y elevó al Olimpo de la inmortalidad histórica a los hijos humildes del pueblo . . .

The republic is the realization of the grandest ideas that consecrate the liberty, fraternity, and equality of all men; equality above all else, that precious guarantee, makes equal the rights and obligations of all citizens, revokes the privilege that the oppressors enjoyed as titled inheritance, and elevates our humble native sons to the Olympus of historical immortality . . .

—Antonio Maceo, *El Pensamiento Vivo de Maceo*

ON FEBRUARY 2, 1896, an illiterate black field hand, just five days shy of his sixteenth birthday, went to war for the independence of Cuba. Though poor and uneducated, Ricardo Batrell (he would add Oviedo after the war) fully understood the broader implications of his contributions to the rebellion. He believed in Cuba Libre, a vision of a democratic and egalitarian Cuba, and thus he believed in the full participation of Afro-Cubans in the national struggle for independence and the creation of a new republic. Indeed, for Batrell and his compatriots, Cuba's fight for independence was an intensely racial one, a struggle not simply to throw off the yoke of colonial rule but to replace its social and political hierarchy, largely defined by race and caste, with a society founded on Enlightenment ideals: liberty, fraternity, equality.

Yet by the time Batrell published his manuscript in 1912 (just ten years after the founding of the republic), he was acutely aware of how far short the young democracy had fallen in achieving these ideals. Political corruption was rampant; economic resources and political power were concentrated in effectively the same hands as before the war; the promise of land reform had been reneged; blacks were largely excluded from private schools and social clubs; black veterans found it increasingly difficult to reap the same benefits for their military service that their white counterparts did; racist stereotypes were still commonplace in popular culture; and perhaps worst of all, blacks who criticized the government or the society at large for its assaults on black civil rights were called racists themselves, a devastating manipulation of José Martí's vision of a society free of racial discrimination.

Despite this increasingly hostile political and social environment for Afro-Cubans, Batrell entered the fray, continuing his struggle for racial equality. Soon after the war, he taught himself to read and to write, and began to compile notes for his autobiography: *Para la historia: Apuntes autobiográficos de la vida de Ricardo Batrell Oviedo*. Also, he wrote letters to government officials and coauthored a manifesto protesting discrimination and calling for a return to the ideal of Cuba Libre. In a sense, Batrell exchanged his gun and machete for literacy, thus arrogating to himself the power to recount the birth of the nation in a new rhetorical battle over the definition of the state and therefore over its future. And it was the narrative of his own experiences in the war that served as his most potent weapon in the struggle for racial democracy. Indeed, in the Liberation Army, which was between 60 and 80 percent black,[1] he was the only black soldier, as far as we know, to write and publish his own narrative account.[2] In a context of postwar memoirs, written almost entirely by white officers, the interjection of this black voice is of enormous significance. Where the other narratives either minimized the issue of race or ignored it altogether, Batrell placed it at the center of this memoir, indeed at the center of the national narrative, and ultimately judged the success of Cuba Libre by it. That Batrell focused on race in his account of the final war for Cuban independence was by no means a distortion of the historical record or a manipulation of the facts. Part of his argument, in fact, is that to ignore race, either in politics or in historical accounts of the war, is a crime against the nation. Or, put another way, his text asks us what happens to Cuban history if we posit race as its very engine. Here, race means more than the mere presence of Europeans, Africans, Native Americans, and their respective and collective descendants, but the racial categories—white, black, Indian, *mulato,* mestizo, and so on—wielded in the ongoing struggle over resources, wealth, and power. What happens to our understanding of Cuban society if the African slave trade, slavery, and race relations figure as pivotal elements of Cuban history from its earliest moments, and particularly across all three wars of independence? How is the history of the entire region ultimately transformed if we take the implications of Batrell's narrative at face value—that black Africans and their descendants have played crucial roles in the greater history of the Caribbean and the Americas, indeed laying the foundation of democracy perhaps for the entire hemisphere?

This introduction addresses the central roles Batrell and the larger concept of race play in Cuba's struggle toward democracy, first by reviewing the history of race in Cuba through the colonial period, the three wars of independence, and the early years of the republic leading up to Batrell's publication. The introduction will then consider Batrell as author and historical protagonist in order to examine his specific role in Cuba's early history as a republic, to assess his political and literary legacy, and to read his text in light of extraordinary political circumstances.

Introduction

Race and Revolution in the Late Colonial Period

Although the history that concerns us most begins in the late eighteenth century, needless to say, phenotypic, cultural, and linguistic differences were of central importance at the first moment of European contact with the indigenous population of what would become Cuba. Columbus and his Spanish cohorts immediately identified the indigenous Arawak, Taino, and Sub-Taino groups as populations ripe for domination and exploitation. They were the first groups to be enslaved, and when their numbers plummeted as a result, they were replaced by black Africans at a moderate yet steady rate through the sixteenth, seventeenth, and eighteenth centuries. By the last decade of the eighteenth century, the enslaved African population had exceeded fifty thousand, and the black population overall amounted to approximately 42 percent of the island's total population.[3]

It is at this point that the Haitian Revolution set in motion the titanic changes in Cuban economic and political history that led directly to Batrell and the overwhelmingly black racial makeup of his Liberation Army. In 1791, the beginning of the rebellion, the French colony was the economic gem of the Caribbean, as far as Western European moneyed interests were concerned. Saint-Domingue generated more revenue through the production of sugar, coffee, indigo, and cotton than did any other Caribbean colony; as for sugar, Saint-Domingue produced more than did Brazil, Jamaica, and Cuba combined, accounting for 30 percent of the world's production.[4] When the French Revolution erupted, the Jacobins were in a quandary as to the extent to which the Rights of Man should be applied in the colonies. Would the Revolution abolish slavery in the colonies, or should the new republic continue to profit from slave labor? While scholars still debate whether the Haitian Revolution was fomented first by small landowners seeking to wrest power from *grands blancs* (wealthy whites) or by enslaved Haitians themselves, it is quite clear that blacks striking for freedom quickly took up the rhetoric of the French Revolution and sought to claim the newly won freedoms in France for themselves.

As testament to the Haitian revolutionary resolve, one of the insurgents' chief strategies was a scorched-earth policy in which they burned cotton fields and sugar and coffee plantations to the ground, forcing moderates on the island to choose sides and depriving France of the revenue necessary to promote the war to reconquer the colony. As a result, by mid-decade Haitian sugar, coffee, and cotton production had plummeted, creating an opportunity of which Cuba took full advantage immediately. Because of late-eighteenth-century transformations in Cuban society, the island was well positioned to fill the production void created by the Haitian Revolution. The larger Cuban population in general, the rapidly growing free and enslaved black population in particular, and the modernization of sugar production set the stage for the events of the last decade of the eighteenth century and the beginning of the nineteenth. Specific to sugar, Cuba's newly modernized plantations were able to increase production dramatically. For example, in 1790 Cuba exported only 15,423 tons of sugar; by 1829 it was exporting 84,187 tons (Pérez, *Cuba*, 77). New lands were cleared for greater sugar production; former tobacco and coffee plantations were also converted to sugar; and more and better railroads lowered the price of transportation. Indeed, the entire Cuban economic profile shifted; where, in the eighteenth century, farms had produced foodstuffs and supplies for domestic consumption primarily, by the turn of the nineteenth century, sugar had replaced a major percentage of domestically produced materials. In the span of barely twenty years, Cuba had gone from a relatively self-sufficient colony with healthy exports to one fully committed to the production of sugar (and thus one dependent on the importation of basic foodstuffs) (ibid.).

Needless to say, slave labor was the engine that drove Cuban economic expansion. As the world demand for sugar continued to rise in the wake of the Haitian Revolution, and as Cuban planters tried to keep pace, the demand for slave labor increased as well, and thus the population of free and of enslaved blacks. Between 1763 and 1862, approximately 750,000 Africans were imported for slavery; by 1827, more than half the population was black (roughly 56 percent), a combination of free and enslaved black Cubans. And though the percentage of blacks in the greater population began to decline by the 1830s, by 1862, just six years before the first war for independence, the black population was still slightly more than half, approximately 52 percent (85–87).

At the same time, the general population of the island grew exponentially. Where in 1791 the total population was only 272,300, by 1862 it was well over one million: 1,396,470 (85). Spaniards emigrated from Florida after its sale to the United States in 1819, while planters and displaced military personnel came from newly independent countries across Central and South America. Consequently, these white immigrants tended to have a vested interest in Spanish colonial rule and thus its chief moneymaking institution: slavery. At the same time, white criollos (native-born Cubans, usually of Spanish descent)—planters, farmers, shopkeepers, laborers, artisans, merchants, and so on—chafed under the privileges new Spanish émigrés enjoyed, particularly their control over finance capital and access to peninsular markets. Tensions between Cuban growers and Spanish mercantilists over pricing, financing, and access to global markets continued to increase throughout the period, an element that would play a major role in all three wars for independence.

Yet, while Cuban economic and social elites resented Spanish colonial rule, they continued to invest in slave labor, even as prices for slaves rose dramatically as a result of the banning of the slave trade, first in 1817, again in 1835, and in 1845. These elites invested in a particularly brutal form of slavery, in a region known for working slaves to death. Enslaved blacks often worked eighteen-hour days and six-day workweeks, first under the tropical sun cultivating and harvesting sugarcane, then in overheated boiler rooms to complete the sugar-refining process. They were beaten and tortured in efforts to coerce them into greater productivity; many collapsed and died of exhaustion. Indeed, prior to the great rise in prices, planters debated the economics of working slaves to exhaustion and death over a relatively short period of time, or of caring for them and thus extending their lives and productivity over time. Either way, the death rate for enslaved blacks exceeded births. Disease, epidemics, malnutrition, and backbreaking work contributed to a life expectancy for blacks of less than seven years after their arrival on some plantations (98). And although the majority of enslaved blacks suffered under brutal conditions on plantations, often slaves hired out to work in urban centers fared little better. Subject to the whims of their owners or employers (or both), they too had little choice over working conditions, and no defense against physical abuse. Also, taking into account the separation of families by sales at the master's whim, and the omnipresent threat of sexual abuse for both female and male slaves, it becomes clear that Cuba's was one of the most oppressive forms of slavery in the long history of human bondage.

In response to such conditions, enslaved Afro-Cubans engaged in numerous forms of resistance throughout the eighteenth and the nineteenth centuries. Men and women committed suicide; women aborted pregnancies; and black workers slowed the rate of production by breaking tools, burning crops and buildings, hobbling animals, and feigning sickness. Furthermore, large numbers escaped to the rugged mountains in the interior of the island where they formed communities (*palenques*), grew their own crops, and even staged raids on nearby plantations to take livestock and to free family members.[5]

Also, enslaved Africans and their descendants staged outright rebellions against planters and eventually against colonial authorities. During revolts in 1812, 1826, 1830, 1837, and 1840, blacks fought to take possession of the specific plantations on which they were enslaved. Such rebellions erupted across the island on sugar, tobacco, and coffee plantations alike, but because blacks had limited arms, organization, and support, these insurrections were quickly and brutally suppressed, most often by local authorities and property owners.

At the same time, blacks undertook more sophisticated and widespread revolts with the ultimate goal of abolition in mind. For example, in 1812, a free black carpenter named José Antonio Aponte organized a slave uprising based in Havana, but involving slaves as far away as Puerto Príncipe and Oriente province. Some whites and free blacks participated as well, inspiring well-founded fear on the part of both criollo planters and Spanish-born financiers. Although the rebellion was crushed in relatively short order, it was followed in 1825 by another large-scale revolt in the province of Matanzas, resulting again in the destruction of plantations and in the execution of slaves and collaborating whites alike.

In 1843, hundreds of slaves from more than fifteen plantations in Matanzas effectively formed an insurgency but were eventually defeated by Spanish armed forces; and later that same year, again in Matanzas, the largest and most famous Cuban slave conspiracy took place.

Authorities claimed that hundreds of slaves and thousands of whites and free blacks from across the island were in on the plot, later dubbed "La Escalera" for the ladders used to torture suspected conspirators. Accusing thousands of plotting rebellion, the Spanish implemented widespread repressive measures, including censorship of the press, and executed nearly a thousand slaves and free blacks.[6] In fact, Cuba's most famous black poet, Gabriel Concepción Valdés (Plácido), was executed as a conspirator; Juan Francisco Manzano was also accused, though later exonerated.

La Escalera, in particular, both reflected and exacerbated the criollo planters' and the Spanish elites' fears of the growing black population and its portents for Cuba. For the landed gentry, the Haitian Revolution already loomed as specter—the threat of unbridled black rage and retribution, and the resulting black nation erected on the bodies of white slave owners. True enough, Toussaint Louverture had gone to considerable lengths to secure the property and the personal safety of *grands blancs* willing to stay in Haiti and lend their agricultural and manufacturing expertise to the newly reformed colony. Nevertheless, upon Napoleon's invasion and Louverture's subsequent death in prison in 1803, the emerging regime took a decidedly different approach to landed whites. Reports of massacres of *grands blancs* quickly traveled to Jamaica and Cuba, as Jean-Jacques Dessalines's legendary philosophy for black insurrection— "Koupé têt, boulé kay!" (Cut off their heads and burn their houses!)[7]— became the ultimate nightmare for slaveholding whites across the Caribbean, not to mention North America.

La Escalera also helped to spawn in whites an antiblack hysteria that would shape Cuban history well into the twentieth century. The widespread reprisals against free and enslaved blacks revealed an underlying paranoia that blacks were not simply inferior human beings, but a real threat. Prevailing sentiment associated discernible African cultural traits with being at best uncivilized, if not essentially savage. Blackness was often associated with bestiality, unbridled sexuality, and criminality; and thus African-derived cultural practices and their practitioners were deemed suspect relative to requirements of civilization and citizenship.

More specifically, African-derived religions, such as Santería or Palo Monte, were regarded as prime examples of black atavism. Religious rituals that involved chanting and singing in African or African-derived languages, energetic if not frenetic dance, African drumming, spirit possession, and animal sacrifice appeared to the outsider often as throwbacks to a precivilized era. It followed that the *babalao* or *santero/a* (a priest or priestess who presided over religious ceremonies) was regarded as deviant, if not clearly evil. In fact, they were more commonly referred to by the general public by the Spanish pejorative *brujo* (witch doctor or warlock), and their strange practices were referred to as *brujería* (witchcraft or Satanism). In reality, *babalao* helped to organize and maintain the *ñáñigos* (religious and ethnic self-help organizations) and *abakwás* (Afro-Cuban secret societies specific to African ethnic groups), again viewed as sources of alien, quasi-deviant cultural practices. And even though Spanish and Cuban elites encouraged the formation of *ñáñigos* as a means of dividing enslaved blacks along ethnic lines, these organizations helped to solidify and promote religious identity and to sustain cultural connections from one generation to the next. As a result, throughout the late eighteenth and the nineteenth centuries, African-derived religions and religious practices were able to grow along with the ever-increasing black population.

In the eyes of most whites, this ever-growing black population, with its alien languages and strange religious habits, was clearly unfit, indeed incapable of civilization, and thus was best kept under the supervision of slavery. This fear of blacks—black savagery, black revenge, and the consequences of black freedom—would be used by Spain across all three of Cuba's wars for independence and would play a major role in the early republic's struggle over Afro-Cuban civil rights. Ironically, at the very moment when almost all of Latin America struck for independence, and with it the abolition of slavery, Spain and its loyalists in Cuba sought to exercise even greater control over the island. By imposing censorship, regulating commerce to increase profits for Spain at the expense of Cuban planters, and passing laws to control even further the free black population, Spain sought to ensure the fidelity of the allegedly "ever-faithful island."

But by midcentury, the contradictions defining Cuban society helped to foment revolution, just as Spain sought to forestall it. Although Cuba continued to enjoy steady economic growth, because of peninsular control over financing and markets, Cuban planters grew more and more frustrated over their relatively small portion of the growing profits. So too, as the enslaved population increased after 1820, the date at which Spain's 1817 treaty with England to prohibit slave trading went into effect, those Africans imported illegally (some 350,000 between 1821 and 1860)[8] were technically free, if in fact the treaty were enforced. Thus, the instability of the slave system itself, a growing free black population, and increasing frustration with Spain's mercantile system worked to arouse revolutionary sentiments and activities.

Indeed, well prior to the 1868 uprising beginning the Ten Years' War, several annexationist groups had rebelled—in 1848, 1850, and 1851—in an attempt to wrest Cuba from Spanish control and to deliver the island to the U.S. South, where slavery seemed much more secure. Although this attempt to preserve slavery lost much of its allure after the Emancipation Proclamation of 1863, the efforts demonstrated the widespread and long-standing discontent with Spanish rule. Subsequent and effective rebellion on the part of white criollos would not move toward annexation but toward independence, yet an independence that would have to incorporate the rights and interests of Afro-Cubans, both free and enslaved, in a radically reconceived and reconstructed national vision.

The Wars for Independence

The first war for Cuban independence, the Ten Years' War (La Guerra Grande), 1868–78, began with an eastern criollo planter's discontent with Spanish rule and his strategy to win the support of blacks for Cuban independence by championing emancipation. On October 10, 1868, Carlos Manuel de Céspedes addressed his slaves, declaring them free and imploring them to fight with him for the independence of Cuba.[9] Later known as "El Grito de Yara" (the Cry of Yara), this proclamation of Cuban sovereignty effectively wed Cuban independence and black freedom. Although fraught with tension and contradictions, this comingling of Cuban national identity and black civil rights would persist across all of Cuba's revolutions. Other eastern planters quickly joined Céspedes, freeing their slaves, recruiting enlistees, and, by the early 1870s, garnering close to forty thousand supporters.[10]

Yet, despite the rhetoric of universal liberties, planters were deeply divided over the amount of freedom to be accorded blacks. Unable "to reconcile their need to attract slaves, so as to have the soldiers necessary to wage war, with the need to attract slaveholders, so as to have the resources required to finance the war,"[11] planters fomented a decidedly reformist rebellion, one committed to the protection of property and the reestablishment of economic and social hierarchy. Relative to blacks and slavery, for example, the provisional government and army commanders in effect defended slavery, at least in the short term, arguing for gradual emancipation and indemnity for slave owners, both to take place after Cuban independence. Often when former slaves enlisted in the insurrectionist army, for example, they were granted emancipation but pressed into service roles; many African-born enlistees, in fact, were sent back to the fields to work.

In particular, eastern planters sought to allay the fears of their western counterparts in the provinces of Matanzas, Havana, and Pinar del Río, where the largest and most lucrative sugar plantations were located, and thus a higher concentration of blacks. In order to woo western support, eastern planters strove to limit freedoms for blacks and to guarantee property rights. Indeed, across the decade of warfare, factions argued and fought over the meaning of freedom and citizenship for blacks. Vacillating between an absolutist position of immediate abolition and full citizenship on the one hand, and limited rights for blacks on the other, white insurrectionists confronted the historical fear of black retribution and the example of Haiti. Particularly as the infantry ranks swelled with blacks, whites feared a full-scale race war. For their part, the Spanish also understood the importance of the west, not simply that greater numbers of blacks would join the insurrection, but that profits from sugar production were dramatically higher there. Thus, confining the war to the east would preserve the source of revenue necessary for waging war on the insurrectionists. To that end, the Spanish dug a *trocha* (a fortified ditch) across the width of the island at its narrowest point near Puerto Príncipe, in order to prevent the insurrection from spreading to the west.

Within insurrectionist ranks, debate continued over the strategy to attack the west, ultimately a debate between reform and revolution. Stymied by internal division and a buildup of nearly a hundred thousand

Spanish troops,[12] the rebellion remained largely confined to the east, and by the late 1870s had fizzled to isolated guerrilla maneuvers. By 1878, the majority of the insurgent leadership welcomed negotiations and signed the Pact of Zanjón on February 10. The provisional government agreed to local rule similar to that granted Puerto Rico, namely, amnesty for insurgents and legal freedom for former slaves and Chinese laborers who had joined the rebellion. Because the agreement fell far short of Cuban independence and immediate island-wide emancipation, commanders such as Antonio Maceo viewed Zanjón as a betrayal of Cuba and chose to continue fighting. In what was known as La Guerra Chiquita (the Little War), Máximo Gómez, José and Rafael Maceo, Guillermo Moncada, and Quintín Bandera (all of whom would be heroes in the War of Independence) resumed fighting in August 1879 and fought well into 1880. But finally, as a result of casualties, desertions, and lack of arms and popular support, the forces disbanded, many leaving Cuba and vowing to return to renew the battle under more favorable conditions.

Although the two wars for independence ultimately failed to deliver the full range of rights hoped for by so many Afro-Cubans, they did produce moderate yet important gains in black civil rights. Chief among these gains was a plan for abolition. Passed in 1870, the Moret Law, or free womb law, mandated that all blacks born after 1870 were free, regardless of the status of the mother. The law also implemented the *patronato* system in which enslaved Afro-Cubans were made apprentices and obligated to work for a designated number of years for their *patrón*. As a means of indemnifying *hacendados* (plantation owners), the system would gradually replace slave labor with contract labor. According to the original plan, the last *patrocinados* were to be freed by 1888, but because there were so few left by the mid-1880s (approximately fifty-three thousand),[13] slavery was officially ended by royal decree in 1886.

Yet, despite the legal end of slavery, colonial Cuban society in the 1880s remained extremely hierarchical, with blacks, poor whites, and newly immigrated Chinese laborers sharing in few of the benefits of an expanding postwar economy. Indeed, Afro-Cubans still faced pervasive discrimination in access to education, higher-paying jobs, public transportation, housing, theaters, restaurants, and parks. Even after antidiscrimination laws passed, largely because of protests led by Juan Gualberto

Gómez, discrimination remained rampant in education, in labor sectors, and in public accommodations. Perhaps most acute was the fact that chronic unemployment and the lack of access to education rendered many blacks—particularly the still landless former slaves and their children—frustrated, destitute, and in desperate search of immediate and palpable remedies.

So too, the period between wars was one of reflection on the meaning of the Ten Years' War and its impact on national identity and aspirations for independence. Again, with race at the heart of the issue, black, white, and mixed-race intellectuals and writers debated the meaning of the Ten Years' War, as its significance would have a tremendous impact on the hoped-for republic. As Ada Ferrer recounts, such discussions worked to construct a narrative of redemption for the country. Prior to the war, as the narrative goes, Cuba was stained by the sin of slavery. Although lucrative, the institution, in its oppression and inhumanity, had compromised the morality of whites, had assaulted the humanity of blacks, and thus had corrupted the nation as a whole. But white slave owners were able to achieve redemption by freeing their slaves and by fighting alongside them for abolition. For their part, blacks shed the stigma of slavery by fighting for their own freedom and for the independence of their country. Thus, the war washed away the stain of slavery and restored whites and blacks to just fraternity.

Ferrer notes another phenomenon of the period, one that would be particularly important for black *mambises* (insurrectionists) after the War of Independence: the figure of the loyal and trustworthy black insurgent. In response to historical and ongoing fears of black retribution against whites and the creation of another Haiti, José Martí, Juan Gualberto Gómez, Rafael Serra, and others wrote extensively about the black veterans who recognized their former masters' sacrifice and were steadfastly devoted to their former masters and to the country, thus making racial warfare an impossibility. Ultimately, the narrative cast the war as a transforming event through which "blacks and whites became brothers."[14] Fighting and dying together, the former slave and the former slave owner achieved true racial fraternity, a unity that might serve as the foundation of the new Cuban society.[15]

Simultaneously, a much larger set of Cubans, both on and off the island, were becoming increasingly unhappy with post-Zanjón Cuba, and began to renew efforts to secure Cuban independence. Later lionized as the father of a free and independent Cuba and as the chief architect of Cuba Libre, José Martí began to organize separatist groups in the United States, the Caribbean, and Central America. Born in 1853, in Havana, to Spanish and white Cuban parents, Martí was nonetheless an outspoken critic of colonial rule, so much so that he was imprisoned for seven months during the Ten Years' War and then deported to Spain. Afterward, he traveled across Latin America and the United States, writing for various North American and Latin American periodicals on a number of cultural and political subjects. By 1880, he was in New York City writing propaganda for the Cuban Revolutionary Committee (CRP) and working to organize the disparate groups invested in Cuban independence.

In April 1892, Martí created the Cuban Revolutionary Party that helped to unite the previously fragmented revolutionary community. Veterans of the Ten Years' War and La Guerra Chiquita, Cuban expatriates in the United States and across the Caribbean, wealthy whites, poor blacks, and working-class blacks and whites were all resentful of prolonged Spanish rule; but it was through Martí's tireless work through the 1880s and early 1890s that these disparate groups could unite under a common goal, not simply of an independent Cuba, but of a new society, a new Cuban nation shaped by the vision of Cuba Libre.

In stark contrast to the social and economic hierarchy under colonial rule, Cuba Libre promised a truly egalitarian society, not simply a "change in forms but a change of spirit."[16] A country, in Martí's words, "con todos y para todos" (with all and for all), the new Cuba would eliminate racial and economic oppression, unearned privilege, and concentrated wealth; it would guarantee equal political rights for all Cubans, and promote economic egalitarianism through land reform. Ultimately, Cuba Libre would replace social and economic hierarchy with a society of small landowners and farmers, all roughly equal in their ability to compete, to participate, and to prosper.

Of the burgeoning numbers of separatists, two Afro-Cubans are of particular importance in the larger history of race in Cuba and for Batrell personally: Juan Gualberto Gómez and Antonio Maceo. As we have seen, Maceo was a hero of the Ten Years' War and a chief voice of dissent in the Protest of Baraguá that rejected the Zanjón pact. Affectionately known as the "Bronze Titan," by the mid-1890s he had come to embody the cause of a free and egalitarian Cuba. After the end of the Ten Years' War, Maceo had traveled throughout the Caribbean, Central America, and the eastern United States soliciting funds and support for a new insurrection. In New York City, he met with African American writer Frank Webb and conferred with Martí over the activities and progress of the CRP; and in Key West, he won the support of poor and wealthy Cuban expatriates eager to advance the final struggle for Cuban independence. Equally important, Maceo shared with Martí a vision of racial equality for Cuba, a society that would transcend racial differences and forge a new unified identity (*una alma nacional*). Indeed, his often-quoted proclamation—"aquí no hay blanquitos, ni negritos, sino cubanos" (here there are no petty little whites nor petty little blacks, only Cubans)—succinctly collapses racial identity (expressed with the diminutive) into a race-neutral national identity, one decidedly free of the condescending "*ito*."

The journalist and activist Juan Gualberto Gómez also played a large role in shaping Cuba Libre and prewar politics, but with important ideological distinctions and with different tactics. The son of slaves, Gómez nonetheless received an advanced education in both Havana and Paris. He wrote extensively for black periodicals of the day, such as *La Fraternidad* and *La Igualdad,* advocating for equal rights for blacks. Indeed, Gómez's career as both journalist and activist began during a period of growing Afro-Cuban political activity. The post–Ten Years' War period was marked by a flourishing of the black press in which new periodicals engaged the debate over the evolving Cuban national identity and the role of Afro-Cubans in that evolution. New mutual aid societies and black schools, all supported by a growing black middle class, also contributed to a growing sense of political self-awareness and entitlement. And while Gómez was in accord with both Martí and Maceo concerning racial fraternity under Cuba Libre and the image of the loyal black insurgent, he argued that blacks and *mulatos* should create their own organizations and institutions in order to address the specific needs of Afro-Cubans.

For example, in 1892, Gómez created Directorio Central de las Sociedades de la Clase de Color (Central Directorate of Societies of Color) to coordinate the efforts of smaller black and *mulato* organizations in their push for civil rights. One of the Directorio's first efforts was to press for the enforcement of civil rights laws enacted in 1885 and 1887, laws that sought to redress the chronic discrimination of the day, particularly in public education.

Despite the fact that both Maceo and Martí were openly critical of exclusively black organizations and their public criticism of racial discrimination, Gómez's leadership and dedication to Cuba Libre were duly recognized; in fact, Gómez was chosen to lead the rebellion in Ibarra at the beginning of the War of Independence. Ultimately, within and beyond black communities, Gómez was regarded as a leading patriot, and to Batrell he served as a symbol of the race through his devotion to equality and to a free and independent Cuba.

While Martí, Maceo, and Gómez represented the leadership framing and guiding efforts for Cuban independence, Batrell was also very much a part of a larger social and political transformation that helped to set the stage for the 1895 war. By the early 1890s, growing frustration and resentment of Spanish rule were deeper and more widespread than in previous moments of political unrest. Whereas both the Ten Years' War and La Guerra Chiquita ultimately addressed the concerns of planters and their interest to preserve their class privileges, the new insurrection promised real social revolution. Now dispossessed peasants, poor blacks, working-class expatriates, displaced urban professionals, and small shopkeepers looked to the coming revolution as a means of dismantling the social order that historically had ensured their economic and political subordination. Despite the fact that Cuba experienced an economic boom through the early 1890s, in late 1894 and early 1895 the economy virtually collapsed when Spain severed Cuba's lucrative economic ties with the United States, Cuba's largest trading partner by far. Sugar prices in particular plummeted, triggering a recession that pushed the few remaining fence-sitters over to the separatist side. For stakeholders of all political stripes, not only was Spain unable to protect Cuban economic interests, Spain proved to be the source of Cuba's economic ruin.

By early 1895, Martí and the CRP had made sufficient plans for rebellion to break out simultaneously across the island. Accordingly, on February 4, "el Grito de Baire" (the Cry of Baire) was sounded, inciting insurrections in Baire, Ibarra, Bayate, and Guantánamo. And although the leaders for the western rebellion were captured in Havana before they could incite their local uprising, the revolution quickly took hold in the east. Throughout the month of March, insurgents staged skirmishes and raids, mainly in Oriente province, while awaiting reinforcements and the arrival of the acknowledged leadership. José Martí was still in the United States, while Maceo and Máximo Gómez were on their way to Cuba from Costa Rica and Santo Domingo, respectively. Maceo landed near the town of Baracoa on March 31; Gómez and Martí, after having met up in Santo Domingo, arrived at Cajababo on April 10. Thus, with the leadership on the island, the insurgency grew quickly. By April 30, Maceo reported that he had six thousand men under his command;[17] and by the end of 1895, Liberation Army forces had swelled to fifty thousand.

Although the rebellion began in the east, in order for it to be successful—indeed, for it to become a revolution—Gómez et al. would have to take the war to the western provinces, a strategy that failed in the Ten Years' War. The provinces of Matanzas, Havana, and Pinar del Río still possessed the largest and most lucrative sugar plantations, whose production was essential for Spain's financing of the war. Equally important, the *hacendados* of the west, still the wealthiest and most powerful of Cuban elites, perpetually sought protection of their privileges either from colonial rule or perhaps through U.S. annexation. The revolution had to attack their privilege directly. And, more practically, because there was such a dense population of Afro-Cubans in the west, the Liberation Army would swell its ranks through a western invasion. Indeed, as Batrell attests, thousands of local plantation workers joined the Liberation Army as it marched westward.

Accordingly, in December 1895, Maceo led 1,500 men across the Spanish *trocha* near Puerto Príncipe and into the west. Running from Júcaro to Morón, the *trocha* was supposed to have been impenetrable, but Maceo crossed it within forty minutes without losing a single soldier.[18] Maceo's brigade was followed by Quintín Bandera, another black general, and Máximo Gómez's divisions; they engaged in largely diversionary skirmishes with the Spanish, allowing Maceo to continue his march to the western tip of the island. And all three generals led swelling bands of Cuba's poor and disaffected. In terms of the racial makeup of the army, as we have seen, estimates assert a minimum of 6o percent black.[19] In a country that at this point was approximately 6o percent white and 35 to 40 percent black or mixed race, the overrepresentation of Afro-Cubans in the Liberation Army was of enormous significance. Given the historical fear of black rebellion and retribution, much of the white population in the west waited with considerable trepidation for this invading black army, an anxiety that Maceo had to address on an ongoing basis.

But equally, if not more importantly, for blacks fighting in the Liberation Army and for blacks like the young Batrell awaiting its arrival, the revolution was the means by which to enter the country, if you will, to advance from disenfranchised seasonal employee to voting landowner, to move from margin to center. For black men in particular, the revolution was ultimately a fight for personhood, citizenship, and country; for Batrell, clearly, and his fellow black *mambises* (insurrectionists), all three were inseparable, and relied entirely on the destruction of the colonial social order.

Thinking of the war in a strategic sense, *insurrectos* used an array of guerrilla tactics in order to prolong the fight. Vastly outnumbered by the Spanish (at one point by more than two hundred thousand), the Liberation Army merely strove to stay intact and to keep fighting. Thus the insurgency tried to avoid head-on confrontations with larger Spanish columns. Instead, insurgents waged smaller attacks, ambushes, and so on as a means of perpetual harassment without full-pitched battles. For example, the rebels often sent a smaller unit to open fire on a larger column. After a short engagement, the smaller troupe would retreat into a grove of trees or into a mountainous area where a larger force of *mambises* awaited to ambush the pursuing Spanish.

In the case of larger battles, the Cubans were always outnumbered. Therefore, they seldom tried to win such battles outright, but instead attempted to inflict as much damage as possible through frontal assaults and flanking maneuvers; then they would retreat. On occasion, as Batrell recounts with great pride, *mambises* used machete charges to strike fear in the hearts of their enemies. Facing a Spanish regiment, Cuban revolutionaries occasionally charged into the Spanish lines with machetes raised, killing and maiming with the blade rather than the gun—a sign of valor and steadfast dedication to the cause of Cuban liberation. Recalling a crucial battle at Mal Tiempo, Esteban Montejo recounts:

> They [the Spanish] went crazy when they saw us, and they threw themselves into the thick of it, but the fight didn't last long because at almost the same instant, we started to chop off their heads. But really chopping them off. The Spaniards were scared shitless of the machete. They weren't afraid of rifles but machetes, yes. I raised mine, and from a distance said: "You bastard, now I'm going to cut your head off." Then the starched little soldier turned tail immediately and took off.[20]

The chronic shortage of guns and ammunition also forced the Cuban forces to employ guerrilla tactics. A U.S. filibuster prevented the importation of arms from the States, while funds were scarce for buying guns from other Caribbean or Central American countries. Therefore, insurgents relied heavily on arms and ammunition taken from fallen Spanish soldiers and from prisoners of war. Thus, not only outnumbered in the field, but also usually having insufficient ammunition to sustain a prolonged fight, a given unit often fought until its ammunition ran out, then retreated to meet another unit that might be able to resupply it.

In addition to such tactics against the Spanish army, insurrectionists attacked the means of financing the war: sugar production. Soon after his arrival, Máximo Gómez declared a moratorium on the production of cash crops, particularly the cultivation and refining of sugar. Any plantations found harvesting or processing sugar would be destroyed; using the strategy often called *la candela* (literally "the candle"),[21] he ordered the torching of numerous sugarcane fields and the razing of sugar processing plants in both the east and the west.

In fact, the seizing and destruction of estates looked forward to more radical land-reform policies after the war. In July 1896, the provisional government issued a land-reform decree, declaring all confiscated lands property of the Cuban Republic, to be reapportioned among its defenders:

> All lands acquired by the Cuban Republic either by conquest or confiscation, except what is employed for government purposes, shall be divided among defenders of the Cuban Republic

against Spain, and each shall receive a portion corresponding to services rendered as shall be provided by the first Cuban Congress, after Cuban Independence has been recognized by Spain.[22]

The land-order decree and Gómez's scorched-earth strategy were ultimately emblematic of the larger aim of Cuba Libre. These were not simply attacks on Spain's financial means to wage war; they served to attack the entire social order upon which the Spanish rule was predicated.

In response to the devastating success of the western invasion and the very real threat it posed to Spanish hegemony throughout the island, Madrid quickly replaced its hero of Zanjón, Arsenio Martínez Campos, with a new, more aggressive governor: Valeriano Weyler. Arriving in early 1896, along with fifty thousand new troops, Weyler vowed to meet "war with war," and so implemented a policy of "reconcentration," one that would prove disastrous for Cuban peasants and ultimately for the Spanish campaign itself.

Prior to Weyler's arrival, *pacíficos* in the countryside, most of whom were deeply loyal to the insurgency, helped the campaign by supplying food, medicine, shelter, and intelligence concerning Spanish numbers and movements. Free to travel between town and country, they often informed *mambises* of Spanish locations, their strengths, and possible plans for attack.

In response, Weyler implemented his reconcentration policy—the evacuation of the countryside—forcing civilians into fortified towns and cities, and thus cutting off support for the insurgency. Also, Weyler banned all subsistence agriculture, the trade between towns and the countryside, and decreed that all livestock be moved into fortified locations or be slaughtered. Furthermore, reconcentration focused on the families of insurgents, often razing their houses and harassing and murdering family members.

Some three hundred thousand men, women, and children were removed from their homes and held in what amounted to concentration camps. The lack of adequate food and sanitation resulted in rampant malnutrition and disease; and, quite predictably, *reconcentrados* died by the thousands. Estimates ranged between 102,469 and 170,000 civilian deaths as a result of the policy.[23] Reconcentration, in fact, amounted to war against the civilian population, one with unintended consequences for the Spanish. Deprived of homes and a means of making a living, men (and not infrequently women) chose the Liberation Army over almost certain starvation in the reconcentration camps. With mounting casualties and Weyler's failure to put down the insurrection quickly, reports of reconcentration atrocities only served to erode Weyler's support in Spain more quickly. As this January 1897 communiqué aptly illustrates, public opinion in Madrid had turned against him within a year of his arrival in Cuba:

> It is impossible to remain silent any longer. Spain has clearly suffered a failure in the war in Cuba.
>
> . . . Let's confess it although it wounds our pride to do so: we do not know how to defeat the insurrectionists.
>
> Who is to blame for this disaster?
>
> . . . the reality is that we have failed and we know that we are obligated officially to declare our failure.
>
> . . . The situation is unsustainable and critical.[24]

The campaign went so badly for Weyler that by the winter of 1897 the Spanish were confined to fortified cities and towns, and the insurgents roamed the countryside virtually unmolested. By late 1897, insurgents began to take strategic cities, and by April 1898, Calixto García, head of the Liberation Army in the east, began to prepare an assault on Santiago de Cuba, Cuba's second-largest city. For *insurrectos,* Cuban independence seemed to be simply a matter of time.

Unfortunately for Afro-Cubans and all Cubans who pursued the full realization of Cuba Libre, Cuban independence was anathema to U.S. political and financial interests in the region. Long coveted, first by antebellum Southern planters hoping to expand slave territories into the Caribbean, then by post–Civil War industrialists and sugar producers, Cuba loomed as a lucrative prize newly made available by what North Americans regarded as Spanish weakness and mismanagement. Needing authorization to intervene, President William McKinley gained tacit approval from Congress through the Teller Amendment. Passed in April 1898, this amendment authorized North American troops to intervene in order to "pacify" the country, and once pacification was achieved, the resolution stipulated that the troops were "to leave the government and control of the island to its people."[25]

But well before arrival, most civilian and military officials regarded Cubans as a mongrel horde, largely unfit for self-rule. The military governor, General Leonard Wood, wrote back to McKinley dismissing the concept of Cuban independence out of hand, describing Cubans as "a race that has steadily been going down for a hundred years and into which we have to infuse new life, new principles and new methods of doing things."[26] As far as Wood was concerned, Cubans were little better than children in need of constant supervision. Needless to say, North American attitudes would profoundly shape the postwar occupation and Cuban efforts to form a republic; but even before the end of the war, North American disregard for Cubans and their cause was manifested in the first appraisals of conditions on the ground. With the war largely at a standstill, North Americans arrived and reported that Cubans were not fighting. Three years of warfare were quickly dismissed, as U.S. troops took on the final offenses on Santiago de Cuba and other major towns, all of which fell in quick succession. What was quickly dubbed in the United States as that "splendid little war" proved to be so much adventure for the U.S. military, and a boon for North American businesses. Indeed, the North Americans claimed victory over Spain, negotiated bilaterally with Madrid for cessation of hostilities, and in turn took responsibility for shaping the Cuban government. What had been the Cuban War of Independence was quickly transformed into the "Spanish-American War," a transformation that would undermine any real sense of Cuban independence.[27]

Moving quickly to check the populist thrust of Cuba Libre, the U.S. occupation, beginning on January 1, 1899, backed white criollos and Spanish elites, a class historically cool to Cuban independence.[28] The North Americans also sought to restrict voting rights, requiring voters either to own a minimum of $250 worth of property, to be literate, or to have served honorably in the Liberation Army. As a result of the restrictions, two-thirds of Cuban men and all Cuban women were denied the vote, limiting the franchise to 5 percent of the adult population.[29] These restrictions were not corrected until the ratification of the Cuban Constitution, and even then, U.S. officials campaigned aggressively against universal male suffrage.

Furthermore, the United States insisted on provisions allowing for future interventions, in order to protect North American investments. Senator Orville H. Platt wrote what would be called the Platt Amendment, which, among other things, restricted and defined Cuban foreign relations, and authorized U.S. military intervention in order to protect U.S. business interests. When the amendment was met with stiff opposition, the United States threatened a prolonged occupation; as a result, the Platt Amendment was ratified into the Cuban Constitution in 1901. Thus, the early history of Cuba's independence from Spain began not with full sovereignty, but with Cuba as a quasi protectorate of the United States.

The Early Republic, 1902–12

Although the end of the war brought relative peace to Cuba, the North American occupation, Cuban moneyed interests, and long-standing cultural biases against blacks largely prevented the young republic from realizing the promise of equality for all citizens. In a sense, the United States attempted to export to Cuba a post-Reconstruction model of American democracy, one that secured white privilege at the expense of black disfranchisement and economic deprivation. Thus, North Americans favored white Cuban *pacíficos* and Spanish volunteers for government positions and for access to U.S. investment capital. Whites who had sat out the war, who had openly campaigned for annexation, or who had remained loyal to Spain often found well-paying jobs in government service sectors or were able to return to their plantations and revive their production of sugar, tobacco, cotton, or coffee. By contrast, the exclusion from government jobs and the failure of land reform had devastating effects on black veterans and Afro-Cubans more generally.

The North American occupation also inaugurated a longer period of intensified foreign investment in Cuban utilities, manufacturing, and agriculture. By 1905, nearly 60 percent of all rural land was owned by North American individuals or firms. The American Sugar Company, the United Fruit Company, and the Taco Bay Commercial Land Company, for example, bought vast tracts of land for the production or cultivation of sugar, bananas, coffee, tobacco, indigo, and other crops. Furthermore, North American firms bought controlling interests in mines, railroads, and electric and telephone companies, and took control of the banking industry. Further jeopardizing black political and economic inclusion, the Platt Amendment served as a convenient lever for Cubans and North Americans alike to destabilize Cuban politics.

All in all, by the middle of the first decade of the twentieth century, peasants—black, white, and Asian—returned to the land, not as owners but as renters or seasonal laborers. The majority of black *mambises* were again poverty-stricken, struggling to find gainful employment. "When the army was disbanded," Montejo recounts, "the black revolutionaries were unable to remain in the city [Havana]. They returned to the country, to the cane fields, tobacco fields, to whatever, except to the offices. The partisans had more opportunities, even being traitors all."[30] Batrell also documented the situation in a 1906 letter to Juan Gualberto Gómez in which he complained that the only employment he could find was as a policeman in Bolondrón, and that his salary allowed him to do little more for his family than to secure food and shelter.[31]

In addition to the failure of land reform, more racially specific attacks further threatened the promises of Cuba Libre for black Cubans. As we have seen, they were largely barred from government jobs, and were increasingly shunned from civil society. White social clubs began to exclude them, while some public parks were designated for whites only. And while publicly funded education remained open to all, private schools began to exclude blacks. Many American-owned restaurants and shops refused service to blacks, to which public officials responded not with protest but with appeals to blacks to respect American prejudices, so as not to threaten the tourist industry.

The federal government conspired as well, implementing an immigration policy to "whiten" the country. By restricting immigration from other Caribbean nations and by promoting immigration from Europe, particularly Spain, the Estrada Palma administration sought to increase the number of whites dramatically and thus to dilute black political and cultural influence. This policy had widespread support on both the Left and Right, where most Cubans (including many blacks) felt that Cuban society should be shaped primarily by European cultural influences. Furthermore, just as in the colonial period, many white Cubans still felt that blacks were not yet fully civilized. Racist attitudes toward African-derived religions persisted, as did assumptions of black sexual excess and savagery; the increased popularity of *comparsas*—public celebrations often featuring raucous music (often *son*), bawdy lyrics, sexually suggestive dancing, and public drunkenness—seemed to underscore blacks' backwardness. Cuban popular cultural representation of blacks again marked their distance from cultural norms, and thus raised the question of citizenship. Advertising, cartoons in newspapers, literature, and theater all traded on well-recognized stereotypes forged in the colonial period. For example, the *bembón* or *negrito bembón* (thick-lipped darkie)[32] served as a prevalent feature of Cuban poetry and fiction. Poor, uneducated, of limited intelligence, and semantically grotesque, the *bembón* served as the antithesis of culture and refinement, and lacked the acuity necessary for self-improvement and progress in the modern world. He further marked his backwardness through *jitanjáforas*, "nonsense words of highly onomatopoetic and rhythmic effect"[33]—a broken Spanish somewhat analogous to African American dialect of the plantation tradition.

The *bembón*'s female counterpart, the *negrita* or *mulata*, emphasized black female sexuality as a sign of black inferiority. Young, attractive, fair-skinned—usually of mixed European and African descent—poor or working-class (and thus economically vulnerable to the sexual advances of white male elites), the *mulata* used her sexuality as a means of economic and social advancement. A temptress of sorts, she lured rich white men for material gain.

While these two figures were almost ubiquitous across Cuban popular literature of the second half of the nineteenth century and into the twentieth, the popular stage offered additional black stereotypes. In particular, the *teatro bufo* (the comic stage) offered spoofs and burlesques that often traded on exaggerated black figures. In addition to the *bembón* and the *mulata*, the *teatro bufo* featured the *bufo cubano* or the *negrito*, a white actor in blackface, rendering a comic depiction of black life and speech. With its origins in early-nineteenth-century Cuban culture, *negritos* "sang and danced in the style of their nation,"[34] signifying black contentment and happiness under slavery. Furthermore, the *negrito* spoke the language of *bozal* or dialect, a corrupted form of Spanish again marking black difference and inferiority.

The *teatro bufo* also featured the *catedrático,* the black professor, or more generally an urban dandy, with airs and social ambitions beyond his station and education.[35] This figure feigned erudition, but uttered malapropisms, comically portraying the absurdity of black intellect. And finally, another urban figure, the *candela*–the "streetwise, sexually potent black male"[36]–dramatized the threat of blackness through violence or unbridled sexuality. All in all, these stereotypes, much older than Cuba Libre and the rhetoric of racial fraternity, perpetually questioned black preparedness for citizenship, and, at heightened moments of racial conflict, effectively sanctioned attacks on political rights. By 1912, they would sanction state-sponsored murder.

In reaction to the assault on Afro-Cuban political rights during Estrada Palma's first administration, expectedly, blacks became increasingly frustrated. Largely excluded from government jobs, competing for work with new Spanish immigrants, confronting new forms of social discrimination in the public square, Afro-Cubans blamed the Palma administration for deteriorating circumstances and thus opposed his reelection. By August 1906, a campaign year, both blacks and whites, under the command of José Miguel Gómez, staged a liberal rebellion to overthrow Palma's administration. In what was dubbed the August Revolution, Independence War veterans, some twenty-five thousand strong, formed the Constitutional Army, in which Batrell was an officer. And just as with the Liberation Army, the Constitutional Army too was overwhelmingly black. In response to black dissatisfaction, Gómez promised soldiers that if he became president, they would receive officer commissions in the Rural Guard and that he would specifically reward Afro-Cuban veterans.[37] Although the August Revolution did succeed in bringing down the Palma government, it also prompted a second U.S. occupation, which, like the first, thwarted most of the hopes for Afro-Cuban advancement.

Yet, while U.S. political and financial interests partially succeeded in undermining many of the original goals of Cuba Libre, the constitutional convention of 1901 did ratify universal male suffrage (women would win the vote in 1924), guaranteeing "electoral rights to all males regardless of race, literacy, or income."[38] Thus, in an era of eroding black political rights, Afro-Cubans would continue to exercise some influence on electoral politics. As Alejandro de la Fuente points out, because of the franchise, both the Liberal and the Conservative parties had to address Afro-Cuban concerns to some extent; both recruited blacks for membership, and both claimed Martí's vision of racial equality as their own legacy.[39] As a result, blacks continued to have high hopes for the fulfillment of Cuba Libre, as many worked primarily through the major parties to reverse the trend toward deteriorating conditions.

Nevertheless, by 1908 many blacks began to search for additional avenues for the pursuit of equal rights. Frustrated that the Liberal and Conservative parties did not push black civil rights far enough, Evaristo Estenoz, Pedro Ivonnet, Batrell, and other officers from the Liberation and Constitutional armies began to discuss the creation of a black political party. On August 7, 1908, group leaders formed the Agrupación Independiente de Color, soon renamed El Partido Independiente de Color (the Independent Party of Color, or PIC). With a membership of between ten and twenty thousand,[40] the PIC immediately introduced its periodical, *Previsión,* in preparation for the 1908 election, and planned to offer a slate of candidates for municipal, provincial, and national offices. The party's stance was one of patriotic inclusion—"Cuba for the Cubans"—advancing a platform relevant to blacks and to the country as a whole: land reform; an eight-hour workday; priority given to Cubans over immigrants in the labor market; expansion of compulsory education from eight to fourteen years; free technical, secondary, and university education; and the abolition of capital punishment. Specific to Afro-Cubans, party members demanded black access to diplomatic service and other public-service positions, the end of racial discrimination, and an end to the ban on immigration from other Caribbean islands (in effect a ban on immigrants of color).[41] All in all, the party advocated Afro-Cuban integration into "mainstream" Cuban society, and pursued that integration by directly attacking the race- and class-based barriers that prevented black advancement.

Elaborating on the party's platform, *Previsión* focused on issues and themes specific to Afro-Cubans across the island. Concerning politics, the periodical attacked the Platt Amendment and called for its repeal; it directly refuted the claims that the party sought to create a new Haiti in Cuba, and it rejected the pseudoscientific claims of innate white superiority and innate black inferiority, instead insisting on the theological and scientific truth that all humans were of the same species.[42] The newspaper also stressed the record of black patriotism and overrepresentation in the Liberation Army.

Addressing culture, *Previsión* rejected African dance and drumming or other forms of "African atavism" (148), again attempting to promote blacks' entrance into the mainstream. On the other hand, the newspaper promoted racial pride, stressing the African origins of mankind (150). Indeed, as Aline Helg points out, letters to the editor expressed pride in being black, as the newspaper pressed a nationalist message combining blackness and *cubanidad* (ibid.). Emblematic of its agenda, the party's logo, an unharnessed horse rearing up with its mane swept back by the wind, was not simply a nod toward the romance of the War of Independence but a reference to Changó (ibid.), the Yoruba god of lightning and thunder and an orisha in Santería's system of deities. Thus, the party appealed to the specificities of Afro-Cuban culture and addressed Afro-Cuban–specific political issues, while claiming and promoting black access and inclusion in the greater Cuban body politic. Ultimately, the party's "political message," according to Helg, "profoundly challenged the dominant ideology, including the myth of racial equality. And last but not least, it comprised a nationwide independent structure capable of competing with mainstream political parties" (159).

Despite the PIC's position of inclusiveness, the response to the party's focus on race and its platform was quick and vociferous; both the Left and the Right attacked the notion of a party devoted to the redress of racially specific grievances as an affront to Martí's vision and as threat to Cuban polity and civil society. White government officials and liberal and conservative newspapers spread rumors of a black conspiracy to attack whites and to foment a Haitian-style revolution in Cuba. Editorials castigated blacks and the party as racist, antiwhite, and thus unpatriotic. Indeed, liberals and conservatives reiterated the myth of racial equality, insisting that through the war racial equality had been achieved, and thus, to cite racial discrimination and to promote race-based remedies was to be in fact racist.

Perhaps more to the point, as a third party the PIC represented a threat to both the Liberal and the Conservative parties, attracting potential members, revenue, and votes from both. Consequently, both parties supported Senator Martín Morúa Delgado's amendment to the electoral law, "establishing that any group composed of individuals of a single race or color would not be considered a party."[43] Such a composition, according to Morúa, amounted to racial discrimination, a violation of the Constitution. Despite the fact that the PIC claimed black, mixed-race, and white members, the Morúa Amendment was ratified. In January 1910, El Partido Independiente de Color was outlawed, *Previsión* seized, and Estenoz imprisoned. Although he was quickly released, because of widespread protests, mainstream newspapers and official government rhetoric again spread rumors of conspiracy and black revolution, helping to inflame antiblack hysteria. By April, Estenoz was arrested once again, along with more than two hundred party members from across the country, inaugurating a larger government crackdown on the party and its members. This campaign of repression lasted for the rest of the year, resulting in Batrell's detention in April 1910, even though he was not a party member.

By March 1911, the PIC reasserted itself by holding a national assembly in Havana and calling for a repeal of the ban; and throughout the year, members continued to pressure Gómez to repeal the ban so that the party could participate in the 1912 national elections. In February 1912, frustrated with Gómez's unresponsiveness, the party issued an ultimatum: if the Morúa Amendment were not repealed, party members would stage massive demonstrations. Receiving no reply, Estenoz and Pedro Ivonnet led armed protests across the country, choosing May 20, 1912, the tenth anniversary of the founding of the republic, as the date to begin their protests.

Concentrated in Oriente province, but visible across the island, protests first simply consisted of a show of force and threats to American-owned properties. By the early summer, when tensions had escalated even further, *independientes* resorted to isolated acts of arson. Yet, the protests were largely peaceful, and those that did turn destructive were few and did not threaten lives.

That fact notwithstanding, the response on the part of the government, foreign companies, and private citizens was swift and brutal. Days after the May 20 protest, both liberal and conservative newspapers published editorials that again used long-standing racial prejudices and stereotypes to denounce the protests and to inflame antiblack hysteria, and both sanctioned reprisals on the part of the government and private citizens. Led by José de Jesús "Chucho" Monteagudo, a Liberation Army veteran, government troops marched on *independiente* protesters in Oriente province; concurrently, private companies, many foreign-owned, hired and deployed their own militias to protect crops and manufacturing equipment, and private citizens formed their own militias.

By late May, repression and reprisals were widespread. As Gómez suspended constitutional rights in Oriente province, government troops and private militias attacked blacks across the country, as most were suspected of being *independiente* sympathizers and so were subject to arrest, beatings, and murder. In the province of Havana, for example, black sugarcane workers were arrested on suspicion of being sympathizers, while black *mambises* were arrested and accused of inciting a race war. In Ciego de Ávila, blacks were banned from public parks on weekends. Haitians and Jamaicans were prohibited from landing at Cuban ports. In Holguín and Nipe Bay, black bodies were left hanging in trees or lying by the side of the road as a warning to would-be protesters; and in Boquerón in Guantánamo Bay, a captain and militia regulars beheaded a black policeman and killed five black soldiers for allegedly conspiring with Jamaicans.[44] Perhaps the worst atrocity was the massacre at Hatillo, where approximately 150 Afro-Cubans—unarmed men, women, and children—were gunned down in their homes in a display of military aggression against *independiente* protesters.

As the repression continued to intensify, officials hunted the PIC leadership. On June 27, Estenoz was captured and killed; just three weeks later, on July 18, Ivonnet was captured and shot to death while allegedly trying to escape. The deaths of the two leaders marked the effective end of the protests and served as the crushing blow to the party. Final estimates of casualties of the 1912 massacres ranged between two thousand and six thousand dead.[45]

According to the Constitution and to national mythology, Afro-Cubans were full citizens, free to participate in Cuban social and political life as they saw fit. Yet the quotidian political reality was far different in the early republic. Beyond the general cultural predisposition that valued all things European and tended to denigrate all things African-derived, Afro-Cubans faced real and palpable discrimination in education, housing, public accommodations, and access to gainful employment. Furthermore, the myth of racial equality made mobilization along racial lines and protest of racial discrimination extremely difficult in that, according to the myth, blacks could easily be branded as racist themselves. Or, as Helg puts it:

> Cuba's combination of a myth of racial equality with a two-tier racial system confronted Afro-Cubans with an unsolvable dilemma. If they denied the veracity of the myth, they exposed themselves to accusations of being racist and unpatriotic. If they subscribed to the myth, they also had to conform to negative views of blacks. Indeed, the myth made it blasphemous for Afro-Cubans to proclaim both their blackness and their patriotism.[46]

In short, the period of the early republic was a dire one for Afro-Cubans. The August Revolution to protest discrimination and corruption was met with fear of black retribution and thwarted by U.S. occupation; *independiente* protests, largely confined to the single province of Oriente, were met with nationwide repression and brutality, resulting in the deaths of thousands of blacks. While the atrocities raged across the island, few white citizens protested; in fact, the vast majority approved of the assaults either through silence or through active participation. Furthermore, this decade-long period of eroding black civil rights played out against the backdrop of long-standing fears and racial prejudices. The fear of black reprisal and of African cultural roots, coupled with popular cultural representations of black buffoonery and sexual excess, gave license to these more brutal and overt forms of oppression. Such was the context in which *Para la historia* was published; indeed, such were the conditions Batrell hoped to reverse through his account of the war.

Ricardo Batrell and the Cuban Jeremiad

Born in 1880 in Sabanilla, on the Santísima Trinidad de Oviedo plantation in the province of Matanzas, Ricardo Batrell grew up in the center of the province literally at the heart of the island-wide struggle over Cuban nationality. Set between the provinces of Havana and Santa Clara, Matanzas was by far Cuba's largest sugar producer, accounting for more than half of the entire island's sugar production. The two major bays of Matanzas and Cárdenas provided important trading ports, strategic for the economic development of the province and the island as a whole. Just south of the rolling hills near the northern coast, the terrain flattens into a lush green plain that stretches south all the way to the marshes of Zapata and the Bay of Pigs on the southern coast. With some of the island's richest soil, the central plain proved crucial for the expansion of sugar, tobacco, and coffee plantations from Havana. Havana had been the original site of Cuban agricultural production, but by the end of the seventeenth century its productivity had decreased measurably owing to deforestation, exhausted soil, and the scarcity of new land for cultivation. Drawn by Matanzas's flat terrain, forests, rich soil, uncultivated land, and navigable bays, planters began to move east into the new territory. Indeed, as the farming population grew and agriculture production increased, planters sought a port market closer than the city of Havana. And in 1693 a group of Canary Island émigrés founded the settlement of San Carlos y Severino de Matanzas. (The bay and surrounding area had already been dubbed Matanzas [massacre], most likely because of the 1513 killing of twenty-seven shipwrecked Spaniards by the Amerindian locals.)

Just as Cuban sugar production increased through the eighteenth century, so too did Matanzas's production, and with the collapse of the Haitian sugar market, Matanzas met the turn of the nineteenth century with accelerated cultivation and production that far outpaced that of the rest of the island. Of course, with this increased production the black population, both free and enslaved, increased as well. For example, from 1817 to 1841 the enslaved population went from 49.5 percent of the total population to 62.7 percent,[47] while the free-black population doubled in the same period of time.[48]

Because of Spain's ability to contain the Ten Years' War to the eastern half of Cuba, Matanzas had emerged from the conflict with its infrastructure intact and well positioned to take advantage of the postwar economic boom of the late 1880s and early 1890s. Thus, Batrell was born into a sugar-producing province that both before and after the Ten Years' War drove the national, sugar-dependent economy. Nevertheless, workers under the new *patronato* system and local merchants resented the radically inequitable distribution of wealth and Spanish control of the local economy.

Known as "little Africa" because of its high concentration of enslaved Afro-Cubans and their descendants,[49] the area of Sabanilla in particular was known historically as a site of political unrest. In November 1843, for example, a slave rebellion broke out on the Triunvirato sugar plantation, and Esteban Santa Cruz de Oviedo discovered a conspiracy on his Santísima Trinidad plantation. So too the conspiracy of La Escalera, later the same year, implicated many blacks in Sabanilla. And though Batrell was born free (thanks to the free-womb law of 1870), his early life is indicative of the persistent racial hierarchy and economic deprivation that fueled ongoing unrest. Batrell's mother may well have been enslaved in the area; at the very least, she took her name from the Oviedo family.[50] We have no record of Batrell's father, but by the 1850s the Santísima Trinidad plantation had become notorious for breeding slaves. Esteban Oviedo "appeared to have run his three plantations like a Simon Legree," Robert Paquette writes. Oviedo was charged by area planters "with sexual abuse of his female slaves," and he fathered "at least twenty-six mulatto children."[51] Indeed, Batrell himself went by either Ricardo Batrell or Ricardo Oviedo until approximately 1906 when he began to sign letters and public documents with both names.[52]

Because Batrell's mother was too poor to send him to school, he worked from early youth on the Santísima Trinidad plantation as a field laborer. When the Liberation Army finally arrived in Matanzas in the winter of 1896, Batrell and his brother Bernabé enlisted. (In chapter II, Batrell mentions another brother only once, Sixto Oviedo, though he provides no additional information about him.) Both fought in the First Division of the Fifth Corp of the Liberation Army, then in General Pedro Betancourt's escort squadron.

The war in Matanzas was the bloodiest and most devastating of any Cuban province. Both Spanish and rebel forces pinned success on occupying the province; thus, when Máximo Gómez and Maceo invaded in December 1895, the province effectively became the entire war; whoever won Matanzas won the war. The rebels quickly took towns and villages, but were unable to hold them indefinitely. When the Spanish retook territory, they often retaliated against the civilian population, using their own scorched-earth tactics, reconcentration, and at moments outright murder.

In Sabanilla, in fact, just weeks before Batrell enlisted, Cuban forces were forced to withdraw from the area; and according to the U.S. consul report, when the Spanish retook the region, over a two-day period they murdered a number of civilian blacks and *mulatos* in retaliation for their earlier losses.[53] The Spanish, though, pursued warfare against the civilian population more extensively through reconcentration, as we have seen, a policy that resulted in the deaths of sixty thousand civilian *mataceros,* between 24 and 34 percent of the civilian population. Adding fatalities through combat, the province lost well over one-third of its population during the war.[54]

In short, the war in Matanzas simply devastated the entire province. At the war's end and through 1899, the drop in population, the lack of livestock and farm equipment, overgrown fields, crippled infrastructure, and the absence of investment capital brought economic activity to nearly a complete halt. Elites and poor alike struggled to survive, while rebuilding the province in the wake of the war seemed unimaginable. Making matters worse, banditry—robberies, kidnapping, and extortion—became a viable means of survival for men made destitute by the war. Although 1900 and 1901 showed signs of significant economic recovery, the severe economic inequalities that had fueled the war persisted, and even intensified after the war.

The irony of the postwar reality was not lost on Batrell, who also struggled to find work that would support him and his family. In 1898, he found employment as a police officer and later as a night watchman in Bolondrón, Matanzas. As part of his job was to ensure the security of the area, he hunted bandits who preyed on the local population, and in 1905 was charged with murder after killing one. Although the charge was dropped, he was imprisoned twice that same year for "delitos de injuria a la autoridad" (offenses of abuse against the authorities).[55] The following year, the record finds him living in Havana, and as we have seen, he became an officer in the Constitutional Army during the August Revolution of 1906. Equally, if not more importantly, it was during these early years of the republic that Batrell sequestered himself in his house, as he says, and taught himself to read and write.

After the August Revolution, Batrell emerged as an even more active public figure. As a former officer in the Constitutional Army and now as a protégé of Juan Gualberto Gómez, Batrell garnered considerable recognition as a radical liberal in the Liberal Party. For example, on March 16, 1909, La Lucha reported that he presided over a meeting between black liberals and José Miguel Gómez in which a list of pressing concerns were presented to the president;[56] he worked closely with Estonez and Ivonnet, the future leaders of La Agrupación and the PIC; and although he never became an official member of either group, he continually agitated for many of the same rights and causes for which these groups were known.

It was during this period, too, that he wrote a number of political tracts advancing black civil rights and leveling criticism at officials, policies, and practices that stood in the way of black progress. In 1907, for example, he published "Manifiesto al Pueblo de Cuba y a La Raza de Color" (Manifesto for the People of Cuba and for the Race of Color); he distributed a different leaflet titled "Al Pueblo de Cuba," and in 1912 lectured in Pinar del Río on his leaflet.[57] On August 21, 1908, Batrell sent a letter to Juan Gualberto Gómez describing problems and providing solutions for a failed election in which he was a candidate, and Batrell was arrested and incarcerated in 1910 and in 1912, largely for his political activities. By 1910 he had completed his memoir,[58] and by early 1912 he was circulating individual chapters[59] and was jailed for their critical content. During this period, Batrell was also under surveillance by both the U.S. and Cuban secret services.[60]

After the massacre of 1912, Batrell virtually disappeared from public life, perhaps, as Blancamar Rosabal suggests, because of the ongoing persecution of blacks and because of the critical nature of his narrative.[61] Batrell's book seems to have disappeared just as he did. The volume was published by Seoane y Alvarez Impresores, but we know little about this publishing house—the kinds of books it published, its institutional mission and philosophy, or why it chose to publish Batrell's memoir. Furthermore, critics have been unable to find any extant reviews or any other accounts of the book's reception or impact. We do know that there are still several copies in Cuba in private hands, and one copy is housed at la Biblioteca Nacional José Martí. The copy with which I have worked, bought from a private library, passed through several hands, as the marginal notes indicate. Thus the book did enjoy some circulation within Cuba. And according to WorldCat, four copies are owned by libraries in the United States, indicating a broader, international awareness of the book's historical importance. Yet, despite these modest indicators of exposure and circulation, we still know very little of the volume's publication history; indeed, subsequent critical addresses of Batrell will need to unearth this crucial information.

Further contributing to the book's obscurity, Batrell never published a second volume as he said in the first that he would; and his life in politics seems to have come to an abrupt end. In fact, the last extant letter, dated 1922, is one that solicits financial help from Juan Gualberto Gómez.[62] After this communiqué, Batrell does not appear again in the public record.

Nevertheless, the larger cache of documents—letters, essays, manifestos, and unpublished episodes of his memoir—helps to shed considerable light on his life and the political work he hoped *Para la historia* would do. As we have seen, Batrell was incarcerated during the nationwide repression of 1912. Upon his arrest, authorities searched his house on June 12 and found "a sea of papers"—some one hundred pages of what appeared to be the second volume of his autobiography, titled "La Paz" (The Peace), another set of papers titled "Fatalidad. Para la historia" (Fate: For the Record), yet another set called "Pautas Políticas" (Political Directions) addressed to General Ernesto Asbert, numerous letters and telegrams, and a certificate of delegation to the Liberal Party assembly.[63]

In both the literal and the figurative sense, the unschooled farm boy became indeed a man of letters. The Liberation and Constitutional Army veteran had traded in his gun for a pen in the ongoing struggle for Cuban democracy and for Afro-Cuban equality. As Omar Granados points out, Batrell's transformation invokes Cuban cultural mythology concerning male leadership and national identity, a symbolic transformation in which men of letters ultimately take up arms, become men of action, and lead the nation into its glorious future. In the classic sense, intellectuals such as José Martí and Juan Gualberto Gómez conceive and promote a new vision of Cuban society, then lead the armed struggle for its realization.

Reversing the trajectory while retaining the symbolic arc, Batrell, the freedom fighter, lays down his guns, learns to read and write, then devotes his life to letters as a means of leading his country.[64] "I weighed all of the sacrifices and hardships that I endured in the war," Batrell recounts toward the end of his narrative, "and I realized that in order to be truly respected in our society, it was imperative that I learn how to read and write." Thus, his status as man of letters should accord him the authority to criticize the nation and to call on it to return to its founding ideals.

Fernando Martínez Heredia notes that a recurring set of themes and issues runs across the bulk of Batrell's writings. First and foremost, race looms central for Batrell, manifesting itself in several important ways. In his view, the black struggle for equality and citizenship is ultimately emblematic of the larger national struggle for Cuban democracy, justice, and equality. He asserts quite frequently that black freedom fighters in the War of Independence (and in the Ten Years' War) were the most patriotic, brave, and heroic, and that it was their sacrifices that made the republic possible. So too, Batrell argues on several occasions that the Afro-Cuban, as a political entity, is a product of the War of Independence and the subsequent struggles for black equality leading up to 1912.[65] Indeed, it is precisely their sacrifices that justify the contemporary Afro-Cuban claim as a political group to equality and full citizenship. For Batrell, the black struggle for inclusion should remind the republic of its highest ideals, that the point of the War of Independence was not mere independence, but the fullest realization of Cuba Libre.

As an activist, he articulates strategies for furthering this struggle, particularly the organization of black-specific social clubs to promote black causes. For example, in 1907 he argues that efforts for black mobilization should be more closely united, and thus he proposes the organization of a kind of Ateneo de Color (cultural club), a social club in which blacks would meet to discuss pressing racial issues and find solutions for them. It would "transcend" the political parties and the larger political system to advance a "decisive social battle" for the higher ideal of "*reciprocidad humana*" (human reciprocity).[66]

Furthermore, Batrell's papers criticize people, practices, and institutions that thwart the advancement of racial equality. Heredia notes that Batrell often comments on the disheartening discrepancy between the original ideals of Cuba Libre and the sobering reality of contemporary politics. In this context, Batrell derides racism and is pointed in recalling examples of racial discrimination; accordingly, he attacks whites who display prejudice, particularly liberal whites who supposedly share the original vision.[67]

Batrell's correspondence pursues the same themes. For example, a number of his letters to Juan Gualberto Gómez and other government officials decry the state of contemporary politics as an unqualified failure in comparison to the original ideal. Too often for Batrell, those in power are avowed enemies of equality and democracy, and he must continually struggle against them for the survival of these ideals. For instance, in a 1909 letter to the Secretario de Gobernación, complaining of the surveillance and harassment on the part of the Cuban secret service, Batrell writes that the agents who were unable to match his valor in the War of Independence are now monitoring his movements as if he were a threat to peace. But ironically, these agents work for a government that he helped to create (through the August Revolution) to secure his own peace and well-being.[68] In a collection of unpublished accounts of the war, he lambastes the current leaders of the country, accusing them of being worse than the despised Cuban guerrillas who fought for Spain. "Cuba . . . after so much political intrigue," he laments, "has been so trampled upon that now the guerrillas of yesteryear are worth more than the saints and fathers of the country!"[69]

Perhaps Batrell's 1907 manifesto, coauthored with Alejandro Neninger, more fully articulates the political aim of his writings. In "Manifiesto al pueblo," Batrell again couches political crisis in terms of race. He criticizes the fact that the lofty ideals of the republic have been traduced by contemporary politics, and the most obvious sign of betrayal is the political plight of the Afro-Cuban. "In the war of 1868," Batrell begins, "there were many black officers with ranks higher than many white officers and the black officers always treated their white counterparts fairly, rewarding them, like equal citizens, with the merits they deserved. This was very different from today's situation where whites treat blacks with a cruelty that rivals the odious days of slavery."[70] He insists that heroes such as Antonio Maceo, José Martí, and Guillermón Moncada died to make "a republic of Cubans and for Cubans" (echoing Martí's famous phrase), and to "establish democracy and fraternity." He proceeds to indict Cuba, whites in particular, for racial discrimination, a violation of Article 11 of the Constitution guaranteeing equality to all Cubans. Batrell and Neninger charge that white liberals particularly—War of Independence veterans no less—had betrayed blacks, using the excuse of American prejudice to garner for themselves rights and privileges that were the birthright of all. Furthermore, the manifesto lambastes white liberals for denying black veterans government jobs owed them by virtue of their service in the war. The authors note that whites, many foreign born, hold better government positions in the Rural Guard, the municipal police force, government administration, and so forth, and that blacks are routinely excluded. Batrell and Neninger also sharply criticize whites for supporting the "whitening" immigration policy that promoted immigration from Spain; finally, they take whites to task for forming all-white social clubs, the Ateneo and Unión Club in particular.

The manifesto gives little quarter to blacks either. For Batrell, Afro-Cubans have failed to live up to Maceo's example and have tarnished his legacy through their silence and unwillingness to protest. In particular, black public officials in league with whites to the detriment of black civil rights bring shame to a group that can no longer call itself a "patriotic race."

In general, in this call to redress the political crisis threatening the republic, Batrell and Neninger approach the conclusion of their manifesto imploring blacks not "to live like pariahs but to be on the political move and to push forward the progress of our epoch."[71] Such a call presages the rhetorical strategy and overarching aim of his autobiography.

Within this larger context of writing, Batrell's autobiography—his longest and most complex work—takes center stage, articulating more dramatically and more fully the major arguments found across the corpus of his life's writings. And, like his political tracts, *Para la historia* addresses a contemporary audience and contemporary politics, using his war experience as both example and dramatic contrast. Although we receive his text through the invaluable work of historians who have used it to document events and conditions in the war,[72] his text seeks to work more in figurative terms—as national allegory no less—than as historical documentation. In this sense, his text uses his experiences in the war as a means of commentary on postwar conditions. Very similar to the North American jeremiad tradition, Batrell cites the ideal, decries current political conditions that fall short of the ideal, and calls on the nation to return to the original promise of Cuba Libre.

Thus, episodes in his narrative, loosely connected through his protagonist, function as didactic tales, lessons for a contemporary audience that has forgotten the meaning of the war. In a more practical sense, Batrell divides his account into three chapters, each covering a single year: 1896, 1897, 1898. He recounts a series of personal experiences and reflections that provide a rich, detailed sense of wartime conditions and life in the Liberation Army. In a topical sense, Batrell describes the marches and daily activities of his regiment, pitched battles with Spanish forces, and conditions for civilians resulting from Weyler's reconcentration policy. He describes in detail his fellow *mambises,* the hardships they endured, the victories they won; and equally as important for him, he provides a record of the fallen.

But Batrell reshapes these events and experiences to function metaphorically by placing them within an allegorical framework in which the central struggle between good and evil animates the entire narrative. Indeed, his allegorical world is entirely Manichaean—Cuba versus Spain, liberty versus tyranny, *la patria o muerte*—in which diametric opposites collide and seek the other's destruction. In this sense, Batrell's moral landscape is populated by "damned birds of prey" such as the guerrillas of Matanzas, the villainous Governor Weyler, and the "bloodthirsty" Colonel Molina, against whom Batrell's regiment fights constantly. These "enemies of liberty" and "defenders of tyranny," as he often calls them, are the embodiment of evil. And equally as important, Cuban soldiers who waver in their devotion to the cause help to illustrate, by negative example, the level of self-sacrifice truly necessary to serve the country and thus to defeat evil. These men invariably lose their honor and die ignoble deaths. On the other hand, devoted compatriots fight with courage, and either die with honor (and so are immortalized through Batrell's tributes) or live to see the triumph of good over evil.

Yet, despite the implications of continuity that the notion of allegory overtly implies, Batrell's narrative is much more episodic than developmental. Figures do not change or grow over the course of the account;

rather, in order to make transparent its symbolic import, Batrell creates each episode so that it nearly stands alone as a rhetorical strategy. In short, each episode strains to perform as great a metaphoric effect as possible, and while these meanings are multiple and various across the text, major themes do recur, suggesting their overriding importance. At the risk of oversimplification, I suggest that Batrell focuses on five major themes or arguments: black masculinity, racial democracy, racial discrimination, black valor, and dedication to the cause of Cuba Libre.

Given the text's concern for strength and valor, it is no coincidence that it is a deeply male-identified text, and thus one preoccupied with masculinity and manhood. From the first page, Batrell reminds his readers of his youth, his small build, and his frail appearance. Almost as a refrain, he tells the reader that he was a boy of sixteen or seventeen among fully grown men; yet he is able to lead and to sacrifice for Cuba Libre in a manner that far surpasses his compatriots. He also reminds the reader of the youth of his regiment, particularly his closest friends— a youthfulness that at moments further underscores his claims to black valor and exemplary citizenship.

The conspicuous absence of women in his narrative further emphasizes Batrell's preoccupation with maleness and masculinity. Aside from the occasional appearance of an officer's wife or a female civilian, only the mother in the episode of the stolen goat (chapter I) receives enough attention to function metaphorically—this, despite the fact that historically the role of female insurrectionists (*mambisas,* if you will) is well documented. Women accompanied their husbands in the army, living with them in *ranchos* (makeshift huts) and helping to maintain the camps; they created and staffed field hospitals, and they worked in *talleres* (workshops), providing crucial support for the war effort. Hidden deep in the mountains, *talleres* produced weapons, saddles, and horseshoes; and, whenever possible, women there tended cattle and raised crops for the campaign. A significant number went into battle as well, fighting alongside their male rebel counterparts.[73] Also, by 1896 Mariana Grajales, José and Antonio Maceo's mother, had become a national icon, indeed, a "mother" to Cuba Libre because she had given birth to two of its greatest heroes, and, in Antonio's case, had given her son as a sacrifice for the cause.[74] All in all, "women's contribution to the war effort was exceptional," as Teresa

Prados-Torreira surmises, "a fact that was acknowledged by both the rebels and their enemies."[75]

Batrell would have been acutely aware of Grajales's symbolism as well as of the immediate reality of female insurrectionists. Perhaps their absence in his text suggests a deliberate attention to masculinity that cannot be confused or complicated by a substantive (and historically accurate) feminine presence. Or, more to the point (or crisis) for Batrell, masculinity and femininity are not a priori tied to anatomy, but are cultural scripts, sets of values and assignments that normative culture attempts to fix to male and female bodies in a quasi-stable manner. It is, perhaps, the difficulty of fixing these properties in any kind of permanent manner that creates a crisis over gendered identity, and therefore the desire to achieve real or stable masculinity. Batrell's preoccupation with age and his recurring comparisons to older men ultimately belie an anxiety over the process of acquiring manhood. That he also must rely on the altruism and benevolence of older white officers—at once a problem of both race and masculinity—situates him, despite his unfailing heroism, as perpetual subordinate, still the subaltern in the liminal space between boy and man, "slave" and citizen.

The episode in chapter III recounting his traumatic break with his commanding officer, Raimundo Ortega Sanguily (known as Julio Sanguily before the war), best dramatizes this driving tension. According to Batrell, Sanguily has taken advantage of both his race and his youth, denying him the official title of lieutenant aide, although he executes the duties of the position faithfully. Nevertheless, Batrell reveres the man, trusts him like a father, and dreams of always fighting by his side "as the most faithful soldier and the most affectionate son!"—until they find themselves alone in the woods. Batrell never reveals to the reader what exactly transpired, but a break between the two occurs; Batrell threatens to kill Sanguily, then returns to camp, alone and enraged. He describes the "damned return march" as an event that permanently alters him, one that compels him to lament that there are "things that crush a man's spirit and make the heart grow indifferent." Abel Sierra Madero asks if Batrell is suggesting that Sanguily is homosexual and that he made a sexual advance toward Batrell. "Although Batrell does not allude explicitly to homosexuality," Sierra comments, "he clearly intends for the episode to be interpreted in this way," particularly given his emphasis on the father–son relationship he enjoyed with Sanguily before their break.[76] If indeed a sexual advance took place, it would call into question Batrell's adolescent sense of masculinity, and destroy the model of manhood he saw in this father figure. Furthermore, for the youth, the episode dramatically illustrates the malleability of gendered identities; in effect he is feminized and objectified, made the object of male sexual desire, and, in a more immediate sense, the potential object of penetration. Perhaps it is this face-to-face encounter with masculinity's chronic instability that makes the text's preoccupation all the more intense.

Throwing this point into further relief, the specter of the feminine (or feminized male) imposes itself on the text repeatedly. Batrell's disdain for *majases* (the local pejorative for cowards) in general and Guillermo Schweyer in particular focuses on their failure to live up to their responsibilities as men. They hide, refuse to fight, then take credit for others' bravery. In this sense, they are failed men, feminized by default, and thus another peril against which all true freedom fighters must guard. Ultimately, these negative examples work to dramatize Batrell's portrait of perfected masculinity—bravery, heroism, and self-sacrifice that cannot tolerate human contradictions—indeed, a perfect man who symbolizes the hope for a perfected republic. Yet the portrait betrays its own impossibility, perhaps exposing a lingering ambivalence over the future of the country.

Regarding racial democracy, Batrell sees in Cuba Libre the promise of true equality and fraternity between races. Not only must the races recognize equal political rights, but also they must work together in the spirit of mutual aid in the creation of the new republic. Ultimately, each racial group holds the other's fate in its hands. Across all three chapters, Batrell illustrates racial democracy in action, from the white lieutenant's concern for a wounded family servant in chapter I to numerous citations of white officers who go out of their way to protect and defend black officers and enlisted soldiers against discrimination and racially motivated attacks on the part of white insurrectionists. But the fullest articulation occurs toward the end of chapter I in the passage concerning Colonel Dantin and his assistant Ciriaco. When the white officer is wounded, his black assistant risks his life to carry him to safety. While doing so, the assistant too is wounded, but more severely. So the white officer then carries the assistant to safety, where he soon dies. With self-consciously romantic language, Batrell presents this tableau as a drama of requited love and self-sacrifice, as each willingly risks his life for the other and thus for the ideal of Cuba Libre. Separated by rank and race, they are bound by a much more profound devotion to the cause—a devotion that allows them to transcend the social and political hierarchies of the old, colonial Cuba and to make real the egalitarianism that will define the new. Ultimately, for Batrell the scene illustrates "the human reciprocity that all people, nations, and civilized men fight to achieve."

For Batrell, the diametric opposite to racial democracy is racial discrimination, a theme to which he attends perhaps more consistently than any other. Whites who engage in racial discrimination attack the very foundation of the new republic; they betray Cuba Libre by placing personal prejudice above the needs of the country. Across his narrative, Batrell cites by name officers who discriminate, and he recounts the perils that befall black soldiers as a result—Martín Duen and Coyizote being the two most glaring examples of brave black officers destroyed by white racism. Perhaps the two episodes most fully illustrative of the issue are the drama over the distribution of arms by Avelino Rosa and the address of Guillermo Schweyer, both in chapter III. In the first, commander Rosa gives Batrell's all-black regiment considerably less than its fair share of a cache of arms. (According to Batrell, he does so out of jealousy for a regiment that does more fighting and is more successful than the rest in the province of Matanzas.) In the ensuing battle, Batrell's unit is unable to finish the fight and wipe out the enemy regiment because it runs out of ammunition and is forced to retreat. Thus, not only is Batrell's unit unable to deal a crushing blow to the Spanish forces, but also they lose the opportunity to take the guns and ammunition from the fallen enemy, an essential means of resupplying for the rebels. And finally, because they are forced to retreat, they give the enemy the opportunity to reorganize and to attack again the following day. Therefore, because of racial prejudice, not only is Batrell's unit put in peril, but also the larger campaign in Matanzas is severely hampered.

At the end of chapter III, Batrell returns to the example of Guillermo Schweyer to show more fully how whites too cowardly to fight took credit for the war at its end. They were able to do so because they came from privileged white families, and thus were more palatable to the privileged civilian population. Batrell here uses the example of discrimination during the war as a prelude to the postwar era and its attacks on black civil rights. For Batrell, the pattern persists, and thus continues to undermine the moral strength of the republic.

The fourth theme, black valor, simultaneously complements the theme of racial democracy and serves as the antidote to racial discrimination. Against the backdrop of racist depictions of blacks in popular culture, and pushing back against war memoirs written by white officers, this theme asserts the black *mambí* as the hero of Cuban independence. This 1912, postwar period still regarded black veterans as subordinates to their white counterparts. The prevailing wisdom suggested that they served as assistants and enlisted men who did not lead, nor did they display the courage of true heroes. In response, Batrell reminds his readers repeatedly that his is a nearly all-black regiment and that it fought more battles and suffered more losses in the most dangerous theater of war, Matanzas. His regiment attacks despite being outnumbered and engages in machete charges, riding into oncoming gunfire until the men are close enough to the enemy to cut them down. They attack forts, steal cattle from the enemy, break railway lines, and reinforce other units in need of support. Batrell's escort unit in particular garnered a reputation for bravery by being especially aggressive in seeking out the enemy and readily engaging in battle.

Perhaps the best example, one to which he returns at the end of the narrative, is the machete charge at San Ignacio, in which sixteen *mambises* charge thirty guerrillas and kill them all while suffering only one wounded comrade. That they attacked when outnumbered, engaged in hand-to-hand combat (rather than merely shooting the enemy from a distance), and won serves as a dramatic illustration of the bravery that was the envy of the Liberation Army.

Finally, while many of the preceding themes necessarily underscore the importance of devotion to Cuba Libre, Batrell further emphasizes the point through negative example. In other words, to betray one's responsibilities to Cuba Libre, in Batrell's moral universe, is to court death. One's devotion to the cause is, or should be, sacrosanct, and to betray the cause is literally to run afoul of divinely inspired justice. Batrell's most elaborate illustration of this point occurs in chapter I, in the episode of the goat. When he and his compatriots encounter a family in the countryside that has refused Weyler's reconcentration orders (and has lost its patriarch as a result), rather than helping the poor mother with a sick child, they take the family's goat—the only source of sustenance for the ailing child. Batrell blames his comrades for giving in to the ruthlessness that war often instills, rather than recognizing and supporting the family's devotion to Cuba Libre that equals their own.

Despite Batrell's arguments, his comrades take the goat and enjoy a feast, but he refuses to partake in the meal. Soon afterwards each of his compatriots either dies from a mysterious illness or is forced to surrender to the enemy. Batrell saves the most biting irony for last, for his commander, Pedro Castillo, who allowed this travesty to occur. In his final scene, we see him marching along the same road that the patriarch had taken and suffering the humiliation of surrendering to the Spanish. "Such coincidences in life," Batrell reflects, "indeed connect these events in order to make us truly believe that Providence does exist." Despite the chaos and seemingly random cruelties of war, justice and order still prevail, if we will only remain true to our principles.

Ultimately, the entire drama centers on Batrell himself, the ultimate embodiment of Cuba Libre. He never makes a mistake in judgment or commitment; his valor never falters, and he is always willing to die in service to the ideal. He is morally resolute while his comrades equivocate; he attacks the enemy without hesitation, and even defies orders from superior officers, all in service to the cause. Indeed, his life in the war is so meticulously reshaped to symbolize the hope of the republic that Batrell the author leaves no room for human foibles in Batrell the protagonist.

That he constructs a hero virtually incapable of human contradictions should come as no surprise given the high stakes involved; for not only does his hero bear the symbolic burden of the entire narrative, he must speak with prophetic authority, both to Batrell's immediate 1912 audience and to posterity. Therefore, Batrell's protagonist/narrator leaves little to chance, and actively interprets the past in the present, in order to be as explicitly didactic as possible. On numerous occasions, the narrator steps out of the narrative time frame, points to the preceding episode, and addresses the reader directly as to the real significance of the event. These moments of exaggerated diegesis serve to reveal the jeremiad at the narrative's core; they invariably stress the tension between originating hopes and contemporary reality, and often point, at least implicitly, toward the restoration of the ideal. In short, they invoke the past as a means of criticizing the present and thus of envisioning an alternative future.

For example, the vision of racial democracy cited above ends with such a diegetic flourish. Proclaiming Ciriaco's immortality, Batrell writes:

> his memory will never die, as it has not faded for me in the thirteen years that have passed since his death; nor will it die for anyone who witnessed these events in Cuba, when we saved her from the yoke of tyranny.
>
> Isn't it true, reader, that this scene inspires us to believe that humanity was perfected in such a display of democracy? Yes, you can believe it because that truly was democracy, with all of its beautiful attributes. Here was the human reciprocity that all people, nations, and civilized men fight to achieve. As a young man I lived to breathe that purified air of democracy, and so I will never be able to stand idly by and tolerate injustices that threaten the ideal of civilized humanity.

Here, Batrell violates the narrative frame in order to make three salient points: first, that his memory (and by extension his words) is the true custodian of Ciriaco's legacy; second, that the democracy to which we all should aspire was made real for that brief moment; and third, that the narrator will continue to fight for its perfection, and thus for the country's future. These points in turn underscore the jeremianic imperative of the episode. In a larger sense, Batrell asserts himself as the true custodian of national memory, and thus the authentic voice empowered to speak to the nation's identity and future. In classic jeremianic form, he invokes the past in order to critique the present and to reenvision the future.

On several other occasions, Batrell steps outside of the temporal frame in order to punctuate his more dramatic jeremiads. In chapter I, for example, he reflects on the broader implications, for the present moment, of his comrades' deaths:

> Because we were able to defeat the enemy, we honored the sacrifices made by these Cuban freedom fighters and so elevate their names that their heroism can be recognized by the entire world. But the soul is saddened when the cause of freedom is politicized the way it is today by a large number of those who didn't purify their souls in the Revolution, indeed, by those who simply left the fighting to men with honor and determination. But, they won't achieve their objective because there are always pure hearts, and the love of democracy will never die in the hearts of grateful Cubans.

By honoring the *mambises'* supreme sacrifices—through writing about them, reading about them, and ultimately through perpetuating their legacy of freedom and equality—both reader and writer are compelled to criticize the state of contemporary politics and thus to fight for a brighter, more democratic future.

Again, in the epilogue, Batrell moves from past to present in order to comment on injustice:

> I cite these events in order to make them more visible and as a reminder, because if the reader heeds their example, he will see other similar injustices in different contexts. These events prove to humans that there is a higher power. So those who feel moved by the spirit of injustice should resist the impulse. God will send them a sign to help them, even though in their hour of need they might not realize it.

Here, Batrell asserts that if the reader will interpret the contemporary scene in light of the war, and thus identify and resist injustice, God will intervene on the side of justice, as he did during the war. The reader can always be reassured of God's subtle yet consistent presence in the ongoing struggle against injustice.

In citing the American jeremiad in relation to Batrell's rhetorical strategies, I am not suggesting that Batrell is invoking the Puritan tradition per se, but simply that his pose as national prophet resonates with the North American ritual. First, Batrell's is a lamentation. In the context of 1912, and after fourteen years of assault on black civil rights, Batrell delivers a "doleful complaint" concerning the current state of race and democracy in Cuba. Beyond the dramatic diegetical moments cited above, the entire narrative follows the jeremianic format, asserting "promise, declension, and prophecy" as a "rhetoric of social prophecy and criticism."[77] Just as important, his narrative is deeply ambivalent over the implications of his prophecy; as "both threat and hope,"[78] his narrative suggests the permanent ruin of the country *and* the restoration of Cuba Libre. Or, to the extent to which the jeremiad seeks "to join social criticism with spiritual renewal,"[79] Batrell offers his text as condemnation and inspiration, and his life as witness to the nation's failure and example of its highest possibilities.

This prophetic pose becomes even more dramatic when placed in the broader context of war memoirs written and published in the same period. Although many more accounts were published after the first decade, five important memoirs did appear before Batrell's: Luis de Radillo y Rodríguez's *Autobiographía del Cubano Luis de Radillo y Rodriguez ó episodios de su vida histórico-politico-revolucionaria, desde el 24 de febrero de 1895 hasta el 1 de enero 1899* (Havana, 1899); Rodolfo Bergés's *Cuba y Santo Domingo, Apuntes de al Guerra de Cuba de mi diario en campaña 1895–96–97–98* (Havana, 1905); Bernabé Boza's *Mi diario de la guerra: Desde Baire hasta la intervención americana* (Havana, 1900–1904); Lagomasino Álvarez's *Reminiscencias patriotias* (Manzanill, 1902); and José Rogelio Castillo y Zúñiga's *Para la historia: Autobiographía del General José Rogelio Castillo y Zúñiga* (Havana, 1910). These five fall neatly into two categories, either diary or narrative autobiography. The two diaries, for the most part, record daily life in the Liberation Army camps, document marches and battles, and record official statements from government and army officials published in Cuban newspapers. In Bernabé Boza's two-volume diary, for example, the focus of the entries is on Máximo Gómez's activities. An officer working as one of Gómez's assistants, Boza had extensive access to the commander-in-chief, and so documented with great detail Gómez's life in the army. Boza reprints Gómez's letters and editorials that articulate the ideals for which the Liberation Army fought; he quotes newspapers and periodicals in order to document the tenor of debate between Cuban and Spanish officials, and he describes how soldiers carried out Gómez's orders. On occasion, Boza mentions in passing that a certain officer's assistant was black, but at no point does race become a theme; nor do discussions of Cuba Libre include addresses of race. In a sense, race for Boza is largely beside the point. He serves as witness to a national hero; his writings document in detail the birth of the nation through the decisions and actions of its greatest military leader. Yet they do not comment on the contemporary postwar context.

As for the autobiographies, they too minimize the issue of race and instead develop the middle-class white male subject in relation to his revolutionary/heroic awakening. For example, Luis de Radillo's autobiography serves as a narrative of self-reclamation in which he reasserts his revolutionary resolve in response to accusations of cowardice or pro-Spanish sympathies. As he prepares to embark on a "prestigious career as a dentist,"[80] a friend tells him that the revolution is exploding and that he should be a part of it. His friend's words awaken in him his "patriotic feelings,"[81] and so he begins his quest to join the rebel army. Indeed, his narrative begins as though he too will invoke the myth of the intellectual-cum-man of action. But he never actually makes it to the front lines. Along the way, he organizes and recruits for the Liberation Army, activities that take him across Florida, to New York City, to Mexico, and to Puerto Rico. Upon his return to Cuba, he does organize his own unit of men, but is stripped of his command. He devotes the final pages of his account to asserting the injustice of this disgrace and to reiterating his devotion to "the liberty of my country."[82]

This ultimate focus on the self, as opposed to the country, reflects many of the dramatic differences between Radillo's account and Batrell's. Radillo begins with an assertion of his class-based privilege and education, which in turn provide him access to a series of officials and dignitaries who help him along the way. Closely related, the privilege of whiteness—articulated here through class, social status, and cultural capital—remains unexamined, simply a matter of course for a man of letters attempting to serve his country. In fact, race plays an explicit role for Radillo only when he identifies racial differences in various subordinates. He states that two of his assistants in his unit are *pardos* (persons of mixed African and Spanish heritage), but never examines the implications of their color. Perhaps most dramatically, he mentions in passing that he met Juan Gualberto Gómez in his travels; and while his audience would immediately identify Gómez as *mulato,* Radillo declines to frame the leader in racial terms, in contrast to Batrell's framing of Gómez as racial exemplar. For Radillo, race runs counter to the thematic aims of his text. In a narrative that seeks to reclaim the status originally accorded Radillo via whiteness, class, and education, race is simply a part of the assumed privilege that has been threatened through the staining of his reputation. Likewise, Castillo's memoir champions the ideal of Cuban independence, but declines to broach its racial implications. As a Colombian who fights in the Ten Years' War and the final War of Independence, he constructs a hero so dedicated to the cause of liberty that he will traverse the entire Caribbean to fight Spanish oppression. Yet, as a white officer, he too makes essential both race and class, assuming as universals what Batrell would identify as race-specific privileges. In this sense, all of these memoirs by white officers either implicitly or explicitly work to support or legitimize the authors' postwar class status, and thus all of these volumes ignore or minimize the issue of race as a defining issue in the war and in the creation of the nation.

Para la historia also finds significance in the greater context of black Atlantic world autobiography of the eighteenth, nineteenth, and early twentieth centuries—a wide world indeed. Stretching from Uruguay to Canada, and accordingly diverse in theme, subject matter, and approach, black Atlantic world autobiographers nevertheless share the mark of color, and thus "a specific historical experience of plantation agriculture and African slavery."[83] Independent of self-identification, phenotypic evidence of African ancestry has, in the Americas, signified a history of exploitation and a subordinate relationship to Europeans and their descendants. Therefore, original status as person, citizen, or speaking subject is at best in question for this entire world of writers—a status to be won or achieved, but by no means a birthright. In this sense, letters for these writers serve as the sign of reason, personhood, and agency,[84] the material proof of their humanity. Often, the actual statements of their writing also lay claim to Enlightenment ideals, making overt the implicit relationship between literacy and subjectivity. Thus, figures such as Jacinto Ventura de Molina, Juan Francisco Manzano, Harriet Jacobs, or Jarena

Lee literally write themselves into history, often writing themselves—in Manzano's case, for example—into freedom. Their claims to the technology of literacy and print culture are, in effect, assertions of historicity, that as historical actors, they too shape the course of human events.

First, focusing on Cuba itself, the Afro-Cuban autobiographical tradition begins with Juan Francisco Manzano, whose *The Autobiography of a Slave* (1840) serves as the oldest (and for some, the only) slave narrative in all of Latin America. A *mulato* born circa 1797 and enslaved in the province of Matanzas, Manzano gained regional fame as the "poet-slave," writing and reciting poetry for literary gatherings in the city of Matanzas. Domingo Del Monte took an interest in the precocious young poet, and in 1836 took up a collection to buy Manzano's freedom. In 1839, Manzano completed the *Autobiography*. Although the text comes with a complex composition and publication history (too complex to detail here), the salient point that Manzano writes poems, plays, and an autobiography as assertion of personhood is enormously important for Batrell and the entire black Atlantic world autobiographical tradition. Throwing this point into further relief, Manzano's text does not challenge or condemn slavery as an institution, but rather its excessive cruelty. Within the text, Manzano does not seek his own freedom, only a more benevolent master who will respect the elevated social space for the *mulato* that Manzano tries to establish and maintain.[85] And while Manzano certainly documents slavery's physical brutality—an element essential for Del Monte's purposes—the overriding polemic does as much to reinforce the status quo as it does to overturn it. Thus, it is a position anterior to content or polemic that allows Manzano and Batrell to share the same tradition—the generative act of black writing that makes subjectivity possible.

Slightly different in this regard, the two additional Afro-Cuban autobiographies—Esteban Montejo's *Biography of a Runaway Slave* (1960) and María de los Reyes Castillo Bueno's *Reyita: The Life of a Black Cuban Woman in the Twentieth Century* (2000)—relate personal and national histories with many of the same high stakes involved, but are dictated rather than self-authored. *Biography of a Runaway Slave,* written and edited by Miguel Barnet, relates Montejo's life as a runaway slave, a *mambí* in the Liberation Army, and finally as a free citizen in the early years of the republic. And though Barnet edits the text to support the ideological positions of Fidel

Castro's new revolutionary government, Montejo nevertheless succeeds, at moments, in subverting facile teleology to assert an independent black self largely defined by his own precepts. The perpetual runaway and rebel, the solitary figure defined not in concert but in opposition to communities, Montejo invokes his status as *cimarrón* (a runaway slave), his religion, and his career as a *mambí* as evidence of his exceptionalism and thus his heroism.

Reyita, on the other hand, dictates her life's story to her daughter, a conversation with her family and her country that relates a life of dedication to noble causes. Fighting for equal rights for women, to end racial discrimination, to secure workers' rights, and to provide quality education for her children, Reyita defines herself in relation to her surrounding communities, indeed, in service to them. Perhaps as a corrective to Montejo, she rises to the level of national icon through endless sacrifices, a theme very important for Batrell. And while neither speaking subject—Reyita or Montejo—harnesses the technology of literacy themselves, nevertheless they use it and the publishing industry as their entrée into national and hemispheric history.

The content of Montejo and Reyita's narratives also informs our understanding of Batrell. Montejo, a contemporary of Batrell, narrates black Cuban life from slavery up to the 1912 massacre, thus offering additional commentary on issues of race and democracy at the beginning of the republic. As for Reyita, born in 1902, the same year as the founding of the republic, she recounts those same early years, including the 1912 massacre, which Batrell spent composing his autobiography. Enjoying a long life, she continues past the 1959 revolution, and extends to nearly the present moment a similar sense of struggle and progress that Batrell clearly held sacred.

(It is important to keep in mind that while this brief review focuses on black autobiography, Afro-Latinos and African Americans participated in eighteenth-, nineteenth-, and twentieth-century print culture in a number of capacities. Blacks wrote poetry, novels, plays, and autobiographies; they published their own newspapers and periodicals, and wrote editorials in "mainstream" or "white" newspapers across the New World. Afro-Latinos also worked as functionaries in "la ciudad letrada"—the New World bureaucracy responsible for the maintenance of the Spanish

Empire largely through writing[86]—ghostwriting letters and legal documents for politicians and bureaucrats.)

Beyond Cuba, the larger context of the Caribbean offers two texts of the period: *The History of Mary Prince, a West Indian Slave, Related by Herself* (1831) and *Wonderful Adventures of Mrs. Seacole in Many Lands* (1857). Enslaved in Bermuda, Mary Prince suffers through harsh work, meager living conditions, beatings, and sexual abuse until she accompanies the Wood family to London in 1828. There she is able to escape, to find refuge with the Anti-Slavery Society, and ultimately to dictate her narrative. Like Manzano's, Prince's narrative is used as abolitionist propaganda at a moment when abolitionist forces are pressing the issue not only in the British colonies, but across the entire Caribbean.

Dramatically different from Prince's, Mary Seacole's narrative does not so much attack slavery, but delivers the tireless globe-trotting of a black female entrepreneur. Born free in Kingston, Jamaica, in 1805 to Jamaican and Scottish parents, Seacole pursues a life of nursing and business ventures that takes her across the Caribbean and Panama, to Constantinople, and to Crimea to nurse British troops in the Crimean War. Upon her return to England, she writes *Wonderful Adventures,* published in 1857. While Seacole comments occasionally on the discrimination she encountered because of color, race does not figure as an explicit theme. Race and gender do inform the book's reception, however, and thus its effect. Here, a black female subject tours the world and celebrates her catholic experiences; a peripatetic entrepreneur, she is not bound by the domestic offices of wife and mother, nor does she feel limited to racially prescribed labor and physical spaces. In this sense, Seacole exercises the freedom that Prince can only imagine; indeed, she represents the fuller personhood to which all of the black Atlantic world autobiographers aspire.

Perhaps Seacole's example of freedom (rather than the claim to freedom) best places black Caribbean autobiography in the larger context of Caribbean and Latin American black autobiography of the period. *The Souls of Purgatory: The Spiritual Diary of a Seventeenth-Century Afro-Peruvian Mystic: Ursula de Jesús* (2004), *Jacinto Ventura de Molina y los caminos de la escritura negra en el Río de la Plata* (2008), and *An Interesting Narrative. Biography of Mahommah Gardo Baquaqua* (1854) constitute the most famous texts. *The Souls of Purgatory* presents, as the title suggests, the spiritual visions and reflections of a black nun in colonial Peru. Preoccupied with access to heaven, de Jesús's visions are often of black women—sometimes in Purgatory—and thus they compel her to reflect on if and how blacks might enter the kingdom of heaven. "During this month of March," she writes concerning such a vision, "a black woman was about to die. I went to see her and made her perform an act of contrition. She did so in earnest while shedding many tears and beating herself repeatedly on the chest. I felt consoled seeing her commend her spirit to God. Then, I saw a holy Christ and this *morena* (black woman), wrapped in a shroud, was at His feet. This meant her death was certain and that she would be saved by God's mercy."[87]

Recently recovered by William Acree Jr. and Alex Borucki, *Jacinto Ventura de Molina* is the compilation of this Afro-Uruguayan's writings. Born free in Río Grande de San Pedro in 1766, de Molina acquired an advanced education for Afro-Uruguayans at the end of the eighteenth century and embarked on a career of letters, writing prolifically on a wide range of topics. Dubbing himself the *"defensor de los pobres"*[88] (defender of the poor), de Molina uses his skills in defense and support of the black community of Montevideo. His writings include reflections on political philosophy and religion, petitions to the kings of Spain and Portugal, histories of local institutions, and autobiographical accounts of his childhood. In a very practical sense, they document features of black life in Uruguay, and, more broadly, they again assert black agency and affirm its claim to political and cultural inclusion.

For its part, *An Interesting Narrative* recounts Baquaqua's childhood in Benin, West Africa, his enslavement in Brazil, his escape from slavery in New York City, and his subsequent travels to Haiti, to upstate New York, and to Canada as he dictates his narrative, again to serve as abolitionist propaganda. All three volumes strongly suggest a black literary project across Latin America deeply invested in the defining aim we find in Batrell and the Afro-Cuban autobiographical tradition: greater personal and political freedom.

The North American black autobiographical tradition of the late eighteenth and nineteenth centuries provides yet another context in which Batrell's narrative finds resonance. A host of writers including Jeffrey Bruce, Harriet Jacobs, Frederick Douglass, William Wells Brown, Jarena Lee, and William Grimes narrate the seminal transformation from damned to saved, from slavery to freedom, from object to speaking subject. Autobiographers of spiritual and slave narratives alike constructed and asserted the black self over and against a political and cultural milieu that actively denied the possibility of black subjectivity. In a sense, for these writers the generative act of writing itself proved "uniquely self-liberating, the final, climatic act in the drama of their lifelong quests for freedom."[89] "Autobiography became a very public way," William Andrews argues, "of declaring oneself free, of redefining freedom and then assigning it to oneself in defiance of one's bonds."[90] Furthermore, many of these narratives employed the jeremiad as a means of condemning slavery and of calling the nation to repent for its sins. Most famous, perhaps, in this narrative tradition is Frederick Douglass's *Narrative of the Life of Frederick Douglass, an American Slave* (1845), in which Douglass repeatedly excoriates the Christian nation for its hypocritical embrace of slavery. Indeed, he ends the "Appendix," in which he distinguishes between "the Christianity of the land, and the Christianity of Christ,"[91] quoting Jeremiah: "Shall I not visit for these things? Saith the Lord. Shall not my soul be avenged on such a nation as this" (6:39).[92]

Douglass and the larger black jeremianic tradition also invoke, at least implicitly, a strain of messianism in which the "providential goals of history" will be realized through this kind of apocalyptic reckoning, a reckoning occasioned by God's chosen people. "A messianic people," Wilson Moses explains, "are a chosen or anointed people who will lead the rest of the world in the direction of righteousness. The messianic people traditionally see themselves as a conscience for the rest of the human race—sometimes as a suffering servant or a sacrificial lamb, sometimes as an avenging angel."[93] Blacks achieve a "special righteousness," the status of "chosen" through slavery, or more precisely through the suffering that slavery requires. And thus, as God's agents of history, they will bring about a dramatic transformation; they will not simply destroy slavery, but will erect a new, divinely inspired order.

Batrell firmly believes, too, that blacks' "moral redemption achieved through suffering" serves as catalyst for providential reckoning.[94] Indeed, this relationship between black sacrifice and national redemption charges his narrative with the broadest and deepest implications. As he asserts that "in Matanzas where only black men waged war against Spain," the black *mambí* saved Cuba "from the yoke of tyranny," he articulates the messianic implications of black heroism. To the extent to which Cuba Libre is God's plan for Cuba (and for José Martí, a vision for all of Latin America), it is Batrell's sacrifices and those of his black comrades that will bring it to fruition. Not only does Batrell carry this point forward thematically throughout the narrative, he also reiterates the overt statement on several occasions. For example, early in chapter III he cites the example of Martín Duen, and states unequivocally that black soldiers fought and died for Cuba:

> Duen's example well illustrated the kind of racial injustice that a great part of white Cuban society practiced. Martín Duen was black, and blacks made up all of the Northeast Brigade in the province of Matanzas. . . . As courageous soldiers, they withstood the vicissitudes of the war in 1897, as we all did. Indeed, for the most part, we were all black, and so each time, on the battlefield or in an ambush, that a soldier of the Liberation Army in the province of Matanzas died, it was some poor black. In the hour of sacrifice we gave our lives.

Also, in his epilogue Batrell returns to the issue of all-black regiments, and reiterates Cuba Libre's dependence on black suffering:

> I must point out that the escort that undertook these charges and others consisted of thirty men often against one hundred, and that the record of the Liberation Army shows that none of us had a rank higher than corporal or sergeant. This shows that the officer positions we deserved for the battles we waged and won were given just after the war to the increasing number of sons of distinguished families, and therefore only because of their color. They are imposters who falsify the history of the Liberation Army, especially in my own province that I know so well. They were honored and feted after the war, those very same *majases* who only gorged themselves on oxen during the war. This, while we gave life to Cuba Libre shot by shot, machete stroke by machete stroke.

Finally, fourteen years after the war's end, after learning to read and write, and after helping to foment a second rebellion, Batrell fashions a Cuban jeremiad in order to rewrite the national narrative. Armed, not simply with literacy in the literal sense, but with a compelling rhetorical strategy for social critique, Batrell does not simply suture himself into the macronarrative of Cuban independence, he fully appropriates it to make it his own. His narrative aggressively challenges the myth of racial equality, reminding the nation of racial discrimination during the war and ongoing discrimination at the moment of narration. Armed with the power of prophecy, he presents the black self and his black *mambises* as the true authors of history and presents race as the defining issue of his time.

A NOTE ON TRANSLATION
AND EDITING

IN THE FALL OF 2004, while reading background material for a yet unfinished project on Afro-Cuban literature, I had the good fortune to read Aline Helg's *Our Rightful Share* (1995) and Ada Ferrer's *Insurgent Cuba* (1999). I was fascinated by the authors' respective accounts of Ricardo Batrell and, since I was reading sources for a number of histories, I thought it would be interesting to put my hands on Batrell's narrative as well. Once I finally obtained one of the few copies of *Para la historia* in the United States, I quickly read the first few pages and was immediately enthralled by Batrell's persona, delivered in a kind of Spanish I had never encountered before. The galloping, paragraph-long sentences, the highly idiomatic, Cuban-style Spanish, the seemingly indiscriminate punctuation, the grammatical errors, and the like were real challenges, but they worked to deliver an energy and urgency that demanded my attention from the very first sentence. Here was a voice nearly leaping from the page with a story that simply had to be told: the future of the republic depended on it.

As the Introduction indicates, this volume attends to the various ways in which Batrell tells his story, and thus to the rhetoric of narration. More precisely, this translation delivers Batrell's narrative more as literature than as history, more as an exploration of language's figurative possibilities than as an attempt to record the past or to tell the literal truth. To the extent to which all translations are interpretations, this approach is my originating interpretative act, the one that informs all subsequent decisions.

In terms of voice, I tried to remain "true" to Batrell's original voice, particularly in terms of its intensity and sense of immediacy. But I did not replicate some of the features that produce such an effect. Even for native speakers of Spanish, the original text by Batrell can be difficult at certain moments. Rather complex syntax in longer sentences often makes unclear who or what is the subject of the sentence. Batrell often spells phonetically, creating words that visually can be confusing but make sense when read aloud. Among many other irregularities, he often uses Vs and Bs interchangeably, as the two consonants are pronounced identically in many Spanish accents. For example, *votar* and *botar* (the latter Batrell spells with a "v") may sound the same, but their meanings are entirely different. Also, Batrell's use of punctuation can add to the confusion. Often he begins a clause with a semicolon and "que," suggesting a relationship between the following event and the preceding one—but this is not always the case. At times, the semicolon can indicate the beginning of a completely new idea or subject.

Because Batrell was an autodidact with absolutely no formal training, these kinds of idiosyncrasies are to be expected. For the sake of clarity, though, at the level of the sentence, I substituted shorter, declarative statements for longer, more complicated constructions, hoping to replicate Batrell's energetic and forceful voice in rhythms more natural to English. I created paragraphs that help to define more sharply the topic at hand. Thus, while the totality of material is the same (I did not excise any of his material), I created more paragraphs that may occasionally separate material differently than does the original text. In two instances I rearranged material for greater clarity.

I also created dialogue from passages in which Batrell presents paraphrased conversations within a larger paragraph. This change will aid in the overall clarity of the prose.

One stylistic feature I attempted to replicate almost literally is Batrell's movement between plain and ornate language. While much of the original is written in a colloquial, informal kind of Cuban Spanish, Batrell includes passages of very flowery, overwrought language that serve to underscore episodes that he finds particularly important. This movement from the colloquial to the baroque and back is quite striking, creating a tension I endeavor to maintain in English.

I contributed a head note for each chapter, a summary of events that will make the plot of each chapter easier to follow. Finally, the text is selectively annotated, providing, among other things, an explanation of Spanish terms that remain untranslated in the narrative proper. The annotations also explain the significance of certain historical figures, locations, and events. In selecting them, I make no claim to comprehensiveness; rather, I chose what was likely least familiar to the contemporary reader yet fundamental for understanding the text.

In a broader sense, this translation attempts to render Batrell's voice and larger narrative in an English prose style accessible to contemporary readers. Yet, as my colleague Lisa Dillman points out, translations should be simultaneously familiar and alien, at once delivering a story in the reader's native tongue while pushing the reader past the known to encounter a new linguistic universe. To this end, I retained some original vocabulary and phrasing not simply because there were no convenient cognates in English but, more important, to provide sounds and rhythms fundamental to the original, reminders or echoes of that first, infinitely more colorful world of words, a world much richer than the one I am capable of reproducing.

A Black Soldier's Story

Querido Ricar

Recibí tu carta e
sa del 28, por las f
afectuosa que e
ella me dedica
doy las gracias,
sabes que yo se
pre supe quere
á mis soleda
mas á los que
tú fueron tan
tos y fueron

I.

Circumstances of Batrell's birth.—Enlists in the Liberation Army.—
First pitched battle at Puente del Río Camínar.—Cites incompetence
of commanding officers.—Retreat and discovery of abandoned Spanish
bodies.—Discovery of dying black man and first account of racial
democracy.—Second and third bloody battles at Ingenio Vellacino.—List
of ensuing battles.—Discovers a cache of arms.—Witness to heroism at
La Josefa.—First encounter with the infamous Cajizote.—Pitched battle
at the Julia de Molinert sugar plantation.—Challenge to the Spanish
commander, Molina, and the ensuing battle at Severiano de Armas.—
Three comrades taken behind enemy lines in Spanish retreat.—Accusations
of treason against Batrell's nearly all-black regiment.—Reflections on
the plight of black officers.—Difficult attack on the town of Cabezas.—
Attack on the town of Bolondrón and the loss of five comrades.—Second
account of racial democracy.—Warns camp at the Condesa sugar
plantation of the approaching enemy.—Observations on the death of
officers and former comrades becoming presentados.—An account of
the wounded.—Attack on Batrell's hometown, Sabanilla.—The crossing
of the railroad tracks near Ceiba-Mocha and the ensuing battle.—Battle
at the Monte de Oro camp.—Batrell's unit joins forces with Colón's
brigade.—Ambush of Spanish column at Vereda del Peñón.—Reflection
on execution of Commander Severino.—Attack guerrillas near the Unión
de Fernández sugar plantation.—Lose horses near a Spanish garrison
at the Europa sugar plantation.—Encounter with a family refusing
reconcentration, and subsequent death of comrades.—Steals oxen to feed
sick comrades.

I WAS BORN ON FEBRUARY 7, 1880, on the Trinidad de Oviedo sugar
plantation, near the town of Sabanilla, in the province of Matanzas. I
worked in the countryside from the age of eight until I turned fifteen years

old in 1895, the year that the uprising of Ibarra[1] exploded in response to those legendary Cubans, Antonio López Coloma[2] and Juan Gualberto Gómez.[3] They gave the cry for the redemption of our country and inspired in me, despite my youth, that sacred ideal of independence. They moved me so to go to war because I saw my race symbolized by the efforts of the great Juan Gualberto Gómez; although at the time, I couldn't participate in that glorious rebellion because I was so sick with dysentery that two doctors had declared me terminally ill. But during my recovery I prepared my horse's saddle with the equipment I would need for war. And although my heroic effort to join the fight had failed at first, I continued to wait for the invasion that, according to the newspapers, was rushing and roaring toward the West.[4]

---

1. The uprising of Ibarra: One the four locations at which the War of Independence began on February 24, 1895, celebrated as the "Grito de Baire" (the Cry of Baire). José Martí gave the orders to begin the insurrection simultaneously in four different locations: in Bayate under the command of Bartolomé Masó, in Ibarra under the command of Juan Gualberto Gómez and Antonio López Coloma, in Baire under the command of Saturnino and Mariano Lora, and in Guantánamo under the orders of Periquito Pérez, Emilio Giró, and others.

2. Antonio López Coloma: One of the commanding officers at the beginning of the War of Independence. Coloma and Juan Gualberto Gómez led the insurrection at Ibarra on February 24, 1895.

3. Juan Gualberto Gómez Ferrer (1854–1933): An Afro-Cuban journalist, black activist, and military leader. Born to enslaved blacks, yet educated in Havana and Paris, Gómez was one of the leading black activists during the period leading up to the War of Independence. He founded the Directorio Central de Sociedades de Color (Central Directorate of Societies of Color) in 1890, an umbrella organization that helped to unite black and mixed-race ("mulatto") mutual aid societies in order to advocate more forcefully for Afro-Cuban civil rights. Through his writings and his close work with José Martí in the Cuban Revolutionary Party, he helped to shape the vision of Cuba Libre, a new Cuban society based on equality and racial democracy.

4. Western invasion: In November 1895, Máximo Gómez, Antoneo Maceo, and Quintín Banderas led forces into the western provinces of Cuba: Matanzas, Havana, and Pinar del Río. Maceo led his forces to the western tip of the island and back to Matanzas. The western invasion was crucial in attacking and burning the richest sugar plantations on the island, thus raising the cost of war for the Spanish. During the Ten Years' War, the Spanish had succeeded in confining the rebellion to the poorer eastern provinces, limiting its economic impact. However, the western invasion of 1895 defied

Since the arrival of the invasion was taking longer than expected, and because I had all my hopes tied up with the cause, I tried in every way that I could to find men from my hometown who were preparing to join the heroes of the insurrection. I discovered that a group of honorable young men were trying to organize themselves in order to march toward the east, under the command of Juan Manuel Erná, who had at that time taken control of the demolished Espíndola sugar plantation, about a mile and a half from Sabanilla.

I decided to join up with Julio Echevarría; he had a good reputation, and he was going to the war with one of those determined young men. There were also several Spanish volunteers who said that they were ready to enlist in the patriotic army; so I was ordered to collect the military supplies that those men could provide for the journey toward La Provincia,[5] an area already at war. When we had gathered more than two thousand bullets and some machetes, and in the same week that we were going to march, I was informed that Juan Manuel Erná had to go to Havana to get two boxes of rifles. With those rifles we would finally be well armed and ready to begin the fight for the redemption of our homeland.

The day of our departure arrived, but our commanding officer hadn't returned; so I asked Julio Echevarría why Juan Manuel hadn't come back and if he had any letters that would explain his absence. He said that he did have some information, but unfortunately it was bad news. As it turned out, the family of our devoted patriot had discovered what he was up to, that the boxes he was after were arms with which he was going to the war; and so his family would not let him return to the sugar plantation, and made him leave the country. So we were stuck without a commanding officer. We didn't know anyone who was already a part of the insurrection and who, because of his military record, deserved

---

Spanish efforts, received widespread public support, and was successful in recruiting thousands (including Batrell) into the Liberation Army's ranks.

5. La Provincia: Circa 1880, the Spanish colonial government divided Cuba into six administrative departments in order to "adapt" and "facilitate" the election of deputies to the courts. The six new provinces were Pinar del Río, La Habana, Matanzas, Santa Clara, Puerto Príncipe, and Santiago de Cuba. "La Provincia" here refers to Pinar del Río.

consideration to be our leader. As a result, the volunteers were becoming discouraged; they believed that they had been deceived and felt that they were in danger if it were discovered that they had been stealing ammunition. In such a predicament, we were all afraid and were becoming so suspicious that I said to Julio Echevarría that we should go alone, without a commanding officer. He argued that none of us knew the direction of the war or the operations of the Liberation Army in order to travel the great distance to where the war had begun. I responded that given the situation we had to make some kind of decision, but my only comrade at the time did not agree. But, as I said before, I saw my race personified in Juan Gómez; because this great symbol of heroism supported the war, I should certainly do the same. How could I choose otherwise, because at that time I didn't know how to read or write, despite the fact that I was fifteen years old? (My mother didn't let me go the long way to town to take advantage of elementary education because she didn't have anyone with whom to entrust me safely.)

So I passed the months of 1895 in doubt, not knowing with whom I might join the revolution, but the invasion finally arrived in Matanzas, in December of that year.

1896

On February 2, 1896, I joined the glorious ranks of the Liberation Army, but only after a considerable amount of effort. The officers with whom I had spoken didn't want to enlist me because of my sickly complexion and my youth. I looked frail because of the work I had been doing since I was a young boy; it had stunted my growth and had given me that sickly look.

Finally, I enlisted in arms with two other young men and another one from the same farm where I had been working. They were sons of the farm's owner and the younger brothers of Julio Echevarría. Even after extensive planning, Julio didn't go with us because the night that his brothers and I finally left, we did not tell him. Three or four times before, I had gotten the horses and prepared to leave, and each time he had failed to show up after the family had gone to bed. So, because of his indecision, we doubted his dedication.

For three days Antonio and Pedro Echevarría, Román Vás, and I had walked alone, traveling all the way across Término Municipal de Sabanilla, to the far West of the province without running into the liberation forces. On the fourth day, we found out that one of Raimundo Ortega's (otherwise known as Sanguily) regiments was marching through the southeastern region of the aforementioned Término Municipal, and found the regiment encamped in a farm called San Pedro. There, we joined the brigade. When we arrived at the army camp it was no longer possible to make objections concerning my sickly complexion because the newspaper had already announced the new enlistees in the revolutionary forces.

After some skirmishes with the valiant Spanish troops, our real baptism of blood came at the forts of Puente del Río Camínar.[6] All the forces of the Southern Brigade, to which my then commanding officer, Commander ex-officio Brigadier Eduardo García, belonged, were gathered together to combine for the attack.

Colonel Guillermo Acevedo was at the front of the brigade when the fighting started at eight in the morning. It was the beginning of February, the same time that the Titan, Antonio Maceo,[7] was fighting in the Guamar Valley. After three hours of fighting, we were able to take the Spanish forts; but only a few soldiers from one fort surrendered, among them a corporal and a sergeant. The soldiers in the other forts didn't come

---

6. Puente del Río Camínar: A town located along the Camínar River in the province of Matanzas.

7. Antonio Maceo (1845–96): Known as the "Bronze Titan," Maceo was a military leader and hero of both of the major wars for independence. An Afro-Cuban, he began his military career on October 12, 1868, as a private in the Liberation Army during the Ten Years' War. Because of his bravery, leadership, and knowledge of military strategy, he quickly rose through the military ranks to become a general. One of the few officers to reject the Pact of Zanjón that ended the Ten Years' War, Maceo continued to raise money and to prepare for a war that would establish Cuban independence. In the fall of 1895 he led a woefully outnumbered and underequipped Liberation Army on its western invasion, successfully eluding or defeating the Spanish Army in order to reach the western tip of Pinar del Río, the westernmost province. The invasion was decisive because of Maceo's ability to burn sugarcane fields and therefore to deprive Spain and loyalist Cuban plantation owners of the monetary resources necessary to prosecute the war. Maceo was killed on his return eastward to reunite with Máximo Gómez.

out on the pretext of certain considerations for surrender. And some in one of the forts wanted to surrender as the others had, but they couldn't because they were stopped by a corporal who stood in the entrance of the fort and wouldn't allow any of his comrades to leave. When it was time for them to surrender, he exclaimed, "I said get back! The queen ordered that as long as we have one single bullet left, we will not surrender!"

If we had simply shot that "heroic" corporal, who was arrogantly walking back and forth in order to prevent any of his comrades from leaving, we would have won, not only because we would have taken control of the arms and ammunition of those forts, but we also would have avoided suffering the many casualties that we eventually took in that campaign. These problems were all due to the inexplicable timidity and ineptness of Colonel Guillermo Acevedo, who not only didn't let us shoot the corporal, our only obstacle, but endured the insults that that "brave" corporal was making in defense of his flag. He didn't even bother to read the various papers that our commanding officer gave him in the course of the operation. During this stalemate, Spanish reinforcements were able to arrive by nine in the morning; they came under the command of the Spanish Colonel Molina, who concentrated all his forces on a hill that was on our left flank. He attacked with relentless gunfire after charging with an infantry so large that in double lines it would have covered more than three city blocks.

Not only did we have to retreat and abandon our operation, but we suffered twenty-four seriously wounded men, not counting those killed by the artillery fire that punished us, raining from their advantageous positions.

During the attack, we had to set the cane fields on fire, because the smoke kept the enemy from seeing us clearly. But when they got close enough to see, they opened deadly fire. All of our wounded fell to the ground, and some were burned on one side or the other. Because of the fire we will never know with certainty the number of dead on that unfortunate day, unfortunate because of the hesitancy and "humanity" of our commanding officer! We should have proceeded as the ruthlessness of war demands. When the others stopped firing and the soldiers surrendered with the sergeant, at that point the intransigent corporal was our only obstacle. If we had shot him when he refused even to read the notes and when he was spewing insults, success would have crowned our work. With that brave soldier dead, the rest would have surrendered. We would have taken more than twenty thousand bullets and twenty new rifles before the reinforcements arrived. And then perhaps all the casualties would have been theirs, because from those same forts we would have fought off the bloodthirsty Molina. We would have destroyed a bridge worth more than fifty thousand pesos, and so we would have been able to hold up the Spanish reinforcements; Molina's movements would have been hampered in the northern section of the province of Matanzas, making it impossible for him to carry his wounded by railroad. So one lone corporal prevented the Spanish governor from receiving this great blow and possibly even more. Because if we had supplied ourselves with the ammunition that was in those forts, not only would we have been able to put up a better fight against the column of reinforcements, we would have been able to deal the blow before being attacked.[8] That would have been a great advantage in the war in that terrible province. And we could have also brought reinforcements to the great Maceo at the very moment when he was fighting; indeed, we could hear nearby the great explosions of rifles and cannons that three Spanish generals were firing on him. In that moment that Colonel Acevedo did not allow us to shoot the heroic corporal, he crippled our operation.

I wouldn't have been able to describe our success if we had shot that corporal. We would have resupplied ourselves with twenty or thirty thousand bullets, and we would have taken them to the invincible Maceo. And not only would we have delivered that treasure that in war is worth more than gold, we would have reinforced him with our numbers, eight hundred or one thousand men. Oh, those poor fighters! How memorable all of this would have been that day!

Because victory turned into a defeat, we were unable to reunite and to march toward the area where Maceo was fighting. Instead, we marched with the twenty-four wounded that we suffered toward the La Gabriela

---

8. Ammunition: Largely owing to a U.S. filibuster preventing guns and ammunition from being sold to the insurrectionists, both were scarce and highly valued. Most supplies of guns and ammunition came from military victories, either taken from Spanish forts or taken from the bodies of slain Spanish soldiers.

sugar plantation. There, we sent the wounded to the woods on the hill called San Miguel. The following day we marched toward Madruga following the direction that General Maceo had marched after his battle with Guamacaro. When we passed near the town of Cabezas, we had a skirmish with an enemy column. And when we crossed the Santa Bárbara River, we received scattered gunfire, but a squadron from General Maceo's forces came to reinforce us. Then our regiment continued to march to the town of Cabezas that was a kilometer away.

We were there a few days, relieving the cavalry for that area so that they could rest their horses. Then we remained in the area until the month of March. After two uneventful volleys with the enemy columns, we received orders to march to the headquarters of the brigade, in the mountains of Zapata. We camped near the headquarters, in Sitio de Vianda in the historic Hato de Jicarita banana plantation where, four months later, the celebrated battle took place in which one of the king's columns was wiped out. (It attacked with General Molina in the vanguard, and along with another three columns, pursued the Trujillo expedition that landed in Varadero, close to Cárdenas.)

During the three days we were camped in Zapata, we exchanged volleys with an enemy column. From there we marched in the direction of Jagüey Grande. When we went through the town of Claudio we exchanged shots with the village's forts, then went on to the sugar plantation, San Joaquín de Pedroso, where we spent the night. The next day we began a march to Murga, a swampy area and terminal point of the rail line from Sabanilla (a branch line of Jagüey Grande). We stayed there a week, and from there we went on toward Colón. When we passed through Cuevitas we broke the railroad tracks, and had skirmishes with the guerrillas[9] in the town. On that march we saw the main body of the Southern Brigade, made up of the forces of Sanguily, Dantín, Pío, Domínguez, Pío Oliva, Álvarez (El Gallego), the then Commander Sosita, and Octavio Hernández; these combined forces numbered more than two

---

9. Guerrillas: Relatively unorganized bands of Cubans who fought as auxiliary forces to the Spanish Army. Because they were Cubans fighting for the Spanish, they were especially reviled by the Cuban insurgents.

thousand men. So the Spanish were forced to retreat when such a large force attacked, led by my commanding officer.

We camped in the demolished Santa Bárbara sugar plantation, near La Isabel. And the following day we marched, attacked, and took the town of Roque, at the cost of five wounded. In the midst of the attack, Colonel Morejón, commander of Colón's Brigade, arrived with his cavalry and joined the battle. After a quarter of an hour of fighting together with Morejón's troops, Brigadier García gave the ill-advised order to retreat, leaving those who came only as reinforcements to fight alone. Later, we found out that the enemy detachment had surrendered, and, as a result of their tenacity, those reinforcements were able to take possession of the cache of arms and ammunition that should have been ours if our commanding officer had done his duty.

After the retreat, we returned to our region—the far east of the province. When we passed the Unión de Fernández sugar plantation, the Spanish commander of the detachment there sent a signal challenging Brigadier García to come a bit closer to the forts. But he didn't accept the challenge and ordered us to keep marching. Then the bellicose Spanish officer sent a train with an armored car to block our crossing of the rail line at the Isabel stop, the point at which we had to cross. And then they attacked us. When the train approached, three of our men, armed with rifles, advanced, ordered by my commanding officer. They positioned themselves facing the cane fields, aimed, and opened fire. After the first shots, the train withdrew with two or more wounded.

After crossing the rail line near the lake called La Ramona, we found the bodies of nine men killed with machetes by the Spanish forces. We learned from a civilian who lived in the area that eight were youths from the town of Cuevitas, and that they had been on their way to work after returning from changing their clothes. Moments before we arrived at that narrow pass, General Vicuña's column, which had fought with Alfredo Wood's (Inglesito) troops and had lost many from their column, took revenge on those unfortunate transient workers, none of whom were more than twenty years old. They also took it out on a sad old black man, more than sixty years old, a servant on one of the farms; the Spaniards cut him down and left him to die.

We stopped the march, commenting on the villainy of the Spanish forces. When the poor old man realized that we were Cubans, he opened his eyes and began to ask for water. Brigadier García ordered one of us to get it for him, and after he drank, the army doctors, Sigorroa and Baterrechea, treated the poor old man's nine wounds. His two hands were mangled. The left was severed at the wrist, hanging from a small cord of flesh, and the right had only two fingers left. He had five slashes on his head that slightly damaged the skin, because he had a lot of hair, and so it had blunted the force of the machete.

They treated the old man moments before one of the wounded whom we brought from Roque died, and so the Brigadier García ordered that we transport the old man in the vacant stretcher. As the order was being carried out, an armed man on horseback was spotted approaching the camp; he was a scout, a lieutenant in the Liberation Army who had a pass from his regiment in order to recover from his wounds close to his family. And as it turned out, the sad old man, cut down by the machetes, was taking medicine from the town to the lieutenant's family; he worked as a servant for the family, and had taken care of the lieutenant in his youth. The lieutenant implored Brigadier García to allow him to take the old man to his family, who would want to look after their faithful friend of more than fifty years, who had been so cruelly mutilated for his faithfulness. The lieutenant was given the dying body, mutilated by the vicious blade of Spanish domination!

After some time, we saw that old man again, recovered from his wounds. How memorable was the spirit of democracy in that young man, during those days when there were no political masks! Oh, those were glorious times!

After we took the town of Roque, my regiment returned to its regular region, the vicinity of Matanzas, Sabanilla, Madruga, and Palos. At the time, there were accusations and counteraccusations among our ranks, but one accusation emerged that was intended to erase all the glory that the regiment had achieved over and above the rest of the regiments in the brigade. This rumor, born of jealousy, resulted from the fact that we fought more battles monthly than all the rest of the regiments combined. Given the racial antagonism that already existed, even in the revolutionary camps, the fact that our commanding officer was black, commanding an all-black regiment, caused a certain uneasiness about the situation. So Brigadier García ordered us to join forces with Colonel Guillermo Acevedo. They were planning to relieve our commander of his regiment, and therefore looked for some pretext of insubordination or incapacity on his part in order to put Colonel Acevedo in command of those heroic soldiers. But Colonel Acevedo couldn't stomach the continuous battles that we engaged in, so he eventually retired without taking command of our regiment.

The Second Battle: Ingenio Vellocino

It was about twelve noon when we heard what sounded like a shotgun blast. We didn't pay any attention to it, believing that it was a shot, like so many others, that went off in the camp because a lack of military discipline failed to punish soldiers for these kinds of mistakes.

After the shot, the camp was alarmed to see members of the guard on the San Lorenzo road enter the camp, some at a gallop. We all realized that the enemy was inside the camp, and people began to shout "to the horses! to the horses!"—a clear sign that the enemy was upon us. In response, we *mambises,*[10] were more agile than acrobats as we mounted our horses. The more than two hundred unarmed men retreated, while the armed, who would have been some seventy, began to form an arc to face and fight the enemies of liberty. With the unarmed already in retreat, we saw the first enemy soldiers appearing through the three passageways between the cane fields that surrounded the Vellocino sugar mill. We opened fire on them, and they shot back as their two flanks continued to advance while their infantry covered the center of both flanks. After taking as much fire as we could, given the size of the enemy forces, we followed the order to retreat, forced back by the assault of those defending the cause of domination.

---

10. *Mambí:* A Cuban insurrectionist. Originally, Spanish soldiers fighting against insurrectionists in Santo Domingo referred to Dominican guerrillas as *mambises* or "Mamby's men" because many fought under the command of Juan Ethninus Mamby, a black Spanish officer who joined the Dominican revolution in 1846. The term was quickly generalized to include all Dominicans who fought against Spain. Later, Spanish soldiers applied the term to Cuban insurrectionists during the Ten Years' War. Originally a pejorative, Cuban soldiers adopted the term as a badge of honor.

As the fight came to the demolished Monserrate sugar plantation, the unarmed, who were three-quarters of a mile ahead of us in retreat, were surrounded by a Spanish column that had remained deployed in the hollow of the Valdivieso River that ran through the plantation. What a terrible situation! They were surrounded by a well-armed enemy column that was waiting to combine forces in order to attack. The two Spanish flanks closed their columns, and so combined, they readied for the attack. Meanwhile, some of the armed fighters came to save those who had no means of defending themselves.

When we saw the Spanish were about to attack, and saw our men surrounded, we knew that we had to break through the Spanish lines. Without even talking about how to do it, we all attacked as one man, armed and unarmed alike. We attacked from different directions, some firing, some wielding machetes trying to open a hole in the Spanish lines. But the Spanish didn't give us time to do it. They left us an open path and so some twelve of us united side by side and formed a wedge. We were able to block their horses, some of which were already tired, and others that were already dead also prevented the Spanish from advancing. At that moment the Spanish on horseback, who had had such an advantage, now had to pay attention to the enemy that was now able to defend itself with machetes. As a result, they could not pay attention to their comrades on foot. We broke through that day from three different directions. It was extraordinary what the cavalry was able to do.

It was about two in the afternoon when we left the battlefield in three separate groups, and at 5 p.m. shots were still ringing out throughout the area, as we tried to unite the different groups. We were able to reunite later after several skirmishes with those Spanish who, because of their numbers, continued to own the battlefield. At five the two Spanish columns began to withdraw; with both regiments they numbered more than one thousand well-armed men. At that same hour, five o'clock, we began to reassemble on the battlefield. We buried our dead, as there was no fighting while my regiment did so. We suffered twelve dead, among them the doctor of the regiment, Eulogio Crespo, Evaristo Crespo, Juan Santa Cruz, Joaquín Delgado, Francisco Leonard, Cándido Crespo, and others. We had five wounded from the second battle of Vellocino.

Soon afterward, we started the third battle of Vellocino in the following way. The entire Northern Brigade was camped there under the orders of Colonel Pedro E. Betancourt.[11] We received the news that the guerrillas of Sabanilla were gathering close by in the fields surrounding the San Miguel de Guardia sugar mill, taking cattle. A number of us came from each force carrying a supply of machetes, and we attacked, although without all the success that we had expected. Only two or three guerrillas were killed, and we took twelve equipped horses. We then left in three groups. All was not finished, though, that day because of the overeagerness of our commanding officer, Colonel Pedro E. Betancourt; he attacked too soon, so he didn't give the flank enough time to cut off the Spanish retreat on the road from the town. If our flank had been able to arrive before the general attacked the guerrillas, few guerrillas would have survived because the road was bordered on both sides by a line of brush that was impossible to get through on horseback. If our troops had been given enough time to cut off that road, they would have been successful. The Spanish would have been confused and disorganized because they wouldn't have had anywhere to escape on horseback. Indeed, there are times being too brave and eager can be detrimental, as it was that day with General Betancourt.

We were called by the commander of the brigade and were ordered to march united with the forces of Colonel Clemente Dantin. We were together with that democratic and heroic commander for the months of May, June, July, and August. At that time, the then colonel-in-commission, Pedro Betancourt, arrived in the month of June in the province of Matanzas. Later he was my commanding officer, and the commander of the province afterward.

During those maneuvers with Colonel Dantin, we traveled across the entire province "batiendo el cobre,"[12] as we said, in the war. We had

---

11. Pedro E. Betancourt: Major general in the Liberation Army, and later governor of Matanzas. As a decorated war hero, he was chosen as a leader of the delegation representing the Cuban Constitutional Convention in the discussions with President McKinley concerning the Platt Amendment. He was also elected senator in the first legislature of Cuba. A town in central Matanzas is named after him.
12. Batiendo el cobre: "Doing what we do best."

battles with all of the brigades, as well as with the militia of the Spanish Army.

We, in the Northwest Brigade fought battles in the following places: Magdalena, Laguna-larga, Vija, Labatá, San Ignacio, Gavilán, Sangroni, and Viajaca. Those in the Southeast Brigade fought in Margarita, Los Cocos, Galión, Los Chivos, Jicarita, Oito, El Siervo, Manjuarí, Sabana Grande, El Cuco, Casaley, Jagüecito, Europa, Potrero Lucas, and Jesús María Mesa.

We also fought in Los Jardines, Jabaco, La Yuca, Ingenio Asturias, Unión de Fernández, San Joaquín de Ibáñez, Socorro, Claudio, Manga-Larga, Sarabanda, Prendes, and we returned to los Jardines, Jabaco, La Yuca, and finally San Antonio de Estalella. There we received notice, in June, that General Lacret needed both forces in Camarioca, in order to carry out an attack on Trujillo. We started to march immediately, crossed the rail lines close to Bolondrón, and in two forced marches arrived at Camarioca. When we got there, Miqueline and Regino Alfonso's forces (auxiliary forces escorting General Lacret) were put in charge of the operation, and were already under continuous fire from the enemy columns. They had been fighting from the morning until our arrival at four in the afternoon, just after the Spanish forces had retreated. We camped without feeling the fatigue from the day of fighting, and we shouted "Viva Cuba!" because we found five wagons of ammunition and more than five hundred new Mausers[13] and other kinds of rifles. We joked with each other that the Spanish bullets don't kill many of us because we had so many of theirs to shoot with.

We camped there for four hours, during which time we ate, then divided a treasure more coveted than a patriotic soldier: ammunition, more in fact than each cavalry rider could carry into battle. Each soldier was made responsible for one box of one thousand rounds. No one was allowed to complain that his horse was too tired to carry the ammunition, because to say so would be to contradict the superior officer. So when the horse couldn't carry the load, the soldier had to.

---

13. Mauser rifle: Designed by Peter Paul Mauser, the bolt-action .276-inch caliber rifle was standard issue for the Spanish Army during Cuba's second war for independence. Considered the best military rifle of its time—particularly for its rapid fire, velocity, and range—Cuban soldiers valued it highly when taken from Spanish troops.

At eight o'clock that night we began to march again, close to Playa de Camarioca, where we passed two enemy columns on the road. We climbed the hill of the Perlas sugar plantation, going toward the railroad crossing of Limonar, near Sumidero. When the vanguard got to the top of the hill called Diamante, it opened fire on the well-defended rear guard of the enemy column. The then Lieutenant Colonel Regino Alfonso and his troops held back the advance of the enemy while the vanguard and main body of our forces saved their ammunition. We waited on the hill that we had just climbed in order to be able to fight if the enemy came in a combined force.

As it turned out, this is exactly what they did. Unfortunately, we had just packed the ammunition away at the railroad crossing of the destroyed town of Sumidero. One kilometer away from there, we found ourselves cut off by a train. At that moment General Lacret ordered our bugler to sound the charge, and so we charged. It hasn't faded from my memory the way that the cavalry attacked with such spirit, looking like a long rippling ribbon extending across the open plain. With our new guns we charged toward the train, shooting with great confidence. We looked like the swell of the sea when it wants to destroy some obstacle in its path. So we advanced on that train, shooting like a Gatling gun, so to speak. That bold force that tried to intercept us had to retreat with the train boiler broken.

We continued to march, and camped about a mile and half from the battle site, at twelve noon. We did all of this after having marched from eight o'clock the previous night. The place where we camped was a coffee plantation, La Josefa, close to Limonar. We were not there an hour and a half when someone opened fire on the guards. In that moment the horses for the general's escorts were all unsaddled so that the soldiers could bathe them in the coffee plantation reservoir near the camp headquarters. When the general heard the shots, and he saw that all of his soldiers' horses were unsaddled, and that so many of the guns were still piled up on the ground, the first thing that he asked was, "How many men are there in the guard on the road?"

The officer of the day responded, "Twelve, General."

"Whose forces are they?"

"Sanguily's, General," replied the officer.

While he was asking these questions, the escorts saddled their horses and men loaded the guns onto the mules, and still the enemy soldiers hadn't been able to dislodge the guards from their positions, even though two enemy columns were attacking. At this point everyone was ready; in fact, one or more lines of troops were already in place, waiting for the enemy. Because there was so much gunfire, we knew that they had a large number of troops; so the general asked, "Which officer commands the guard?"

Someone answered that it was not an officer, but a sergeant. To this the general responded, "He who calls that lieutenant 'Sergeant,' from this day forward will be reprimanded by me. I order that that brave soldier retreat in order to allow the rest of the force to enjoy the fight. He shouldn't be the only one to display his patriotism."

As the guard retreated, all of the forces entered the battle. In order to appreciate fully the intensity of the battle between the two sides of equal arms and ammunition, one had to have been in the war and to have seen its effects. At one in the afternoon we opened fire, and it was past two when the thunderclaps of gunfire were still vibrating, deafening the entire area! Oh, to behold ourselves with hearts so swollen with satisfaction as ours were that day!

We saw the Spanish soldiers fall in their vain attempts to pass their two columns through the only opening between the two farms. Seeing that it was impossible to get through, with bodies scattered everywhere, they spread out to find the weak points in our formation in order to break through at different places. They succeeded, and so they were able to advance.

In response, we began to retreat because we didn't want to use up all of our ammunition in one day. During the retreat, we had to pass near the Petrona sugar plantation, where the ex-commander of a Cuban force was now the head of the Spanish guerrillas, the celebrated Cajizote. We didn't want to fight him because we didn't want to use up our ammunition on the guerrillas, fearing we would be short of ammunition to fight the Spanish forces. And he led us to believe that we were still comrades, that it was like the old days when he was still in the Liberation Army. But he was wrong, and we opened deadly fire so intense that he didn't believe that we were Cuban; his guerrillas were so amazed by the intensity of our fire that they thought we were Spanish.

After our first volley, they yelled to us, "Spain! Spain!" without firing, paralyzed by astonishment; but when they gave their cry, "Spain," without firing, they received an even more intense round of shots, and then we attacked them with machetes. They ran like someone being chased by the devil to the plantation and to the protection of the fort.

We then marched to the hill call Liaño, where we camped at seven in the evening. We had been marching continuously for almost twenty-four hours, except for the one hour that we had on the La Josefa coffee plantation. At one o'clock on the same night, we began to march again, in order to accompany General Lacret, who was going to the mountain called Zapata.

Colonel Dantin's forces and ours remained in the area of the Trinidad de Oviedo sugar plantation, with five wounded that we took from the forces at Josefa. It was impossible for them to march any farther. Nor could the horses of those two forces continue; they had already gone five days without resting and almost that long without having their saddles taken off. So we camped on the piece of land known as Guacatá, because it had a good pasture for the horses; the wounded were taken to the mountains of the Reforma sugar plantation; they went directly to the camp for their protection in the case of an alarm.

At daybreak, Alfredo Wood's (Inglesito) forces joined us. He didn't have a single cartridge for his soldiers, so we provided them that rich delicacy of war, enough at least for a "feast" of Cuba Libre.

At one in the afternoon of the same day, our first day there, one of the Spanish columns that we had fought the day before at Josefa passed close to our camp on its march to Bolondrón. But as it passed the Julia de Molinert sugar plantation, one of the brave soldiers of our forces, Sabino Hernández, shot at the column to provoke the soldiers into pursuing him. As a result, they chased Hernández, firing. The entire camp got on horses, and made a rainbow of shots. When the three forces came face-to-face, there were more brave soldiers of the province there on that date than ever before. Our column retreated; it was somewhat weakened as it marched to the mountains where the wounded had been taken. So, in order to prevent the Spanish from attacking the wounded, our regiment retreated in another direction so that the Spanish would follow us. But when we saw that they were not following us, we aborted the retreat in order not to weaken the cavalry more than it already had been.

During the night of that same day we had to stay with the wounded at camp headquarters, in Zapata. When the column retreated, we returned to the camp and then we found out from the sentries that the bugler's report that came from the column wasn't to cover our flank but the bugler had sounded a retreat for lack of ammunition. It was already late and the column was going to enter the town of Bolondrón that was close by.

Dantin, Sanguily, and Inglesito never had a better opportunity than the one that had escaped them to wipe out Colonel Maroto's column. He was one of the most tenacious fighters in battle, although a humanitarian with the defenseless. He was an exception in that era, in that the other columns did not show any mercy to any Cuban, even if he weren't a part of the revolution. The explanation for not attacking Maroto was that the column didn't have Cuban guerrillas. They were cavalry, but entirely Spanish.

The predicament of the soldiers was so bad that upon the arrival at Bolondrón, as soon as they were given ammunition, one of the soldiers, more of a descendant of Pelayo[14] than the rest, shot himself and took his own life. We received that information during the war, and just after the war, when I was employed by the Bolondrón police, I was able to check this fact against those they gave during the war in that town.

Let's return to that day of the frustrating battle at Guacatá. We kept marching through the night with the wounded toward Zapata. The wounded were from La Josefa, the Lieutenant Colonel Regino Alfonso, Captain Río, and Sergeant Matamoros of Dantin's forces, and General Lacret's aide (also known as Inglesito). The wounded were on stretchers because of their grave state, completely incapable of mounting their horses. Dionisio Martínez and Domingo Hernández were from Sanguily's

---

14. Pelayo (?–737 AD): Leader of the Spanish insurrection against the Moors at Covadonga in 722. The victory established Asturias as the first independent Spanish kingdom and Pelayo as its first king. The victory also began the Spanish reconquest of the Iberian Peninsula. Therefore, the phrase "descendant of Pelayo" simply refers to Spanish heritage.

force and our own; they were wounded in the foot, but able to ride their horses.

We had only one wounded soldier from the battle of Guacatá: Brígido Cardenal. He was known as Simplicio, and was wounded through the thigh of the right leg, but he didn't need a stretcher.

At seven at night, we started to march, with stretchers, from the mountains of Reforma. We crossed railroad lines near the Atrevido de Pierda sugar plantation and arrived at a farm called Severiano de Armas (in Zapata) at 11 p.m., and spent the night there. Meanwhile, a commission went with the wounded to the field hospital, Hato de Jicarita.

When we arrived at Severiano de Armas, General Lacret ordered a challenge to be sent to Molina—a Spanish officer and a brazen criminal; this happened during the last days of June. By July 4, Molina was already in command of three Spanish columns, all of which arrived on the road to our camp. Before they got to Hato de Jicarita, he tried to countermarch in order to avoid fighting us, but as soon as General Lacret found out, he ordered Juan E. Abreu (now a lieutenant because of his heroic resistance fighting in the guard at Josefa) and his twenty men to lure those three enemy columns to the camp, or to the headquarters that was at the entrance of the historic Jicarita banana plantation.

At nine in the morning, twenty of us began firing at the columns, and by ten the columns had already charged. General Lacret sat in a rocking chair reading a newspaper until bullets from the Spanish fire tore it in two, right in his hands; his soldiers had to urge him to move from that spot. At that point the battle began in earnest, as regiments from all of the forces of the province that had arrived to get fresh ammunition from headquarters took part in that memorable battle. The total force was made up of Dantin, Ortega, Sosita, and El Inglesito's troops; Pío Domínguez had all of his forces there too, and factions of others arrived, under General Lacret's command.

From ten in the morning until three thirty in the afternoon, it was as if only one continuous shot could be heard on either side. Those shots were like deafening claps of thunder in the month of May, muffling the entire area! The two contending forces were well armed, and the battle was extremely hard fought. Each side heroically defended its position with such bravery that is impossible to describe.

The Spanish columns were under Molina's command. One was the "Del Rey," the elite of the king's forces, in the vanguard; "María Cristina" was at the center, and "Aldea" was in the rear guard. The Del Rey lost so many men that after the battle it couldn't operate anymore; they were down to only thirty men who were stationed in the Félix de Piedra sugar plantation. The other two columns had to be reinforced in order to go on another campaign. By three o'clock their columns had already run out of ammunition when they began to retreat without having succeeded in taking the door of Hato, our position. But they didn't retreat before throwing their dead into a well sixty or seventy yards deep. They had thrown a mule on top of the bodies so that we wouldn't be able to tell how many losses they had suffered. And worse than this, three houses close by (houses used to make starch) were full of bodies, and were later set on fire. Even though they burned the houses, they still couldn't conceal the number of dead, because although the human body is combustible, the intestines are especially difficult to burn. So there were still piles of bodies that didn't burn in the houses, revealing the high number of casualties.

After treating our few wounded, our unarmed soldiers camped in a secure area, while part of Dantin's and Sanguily's forces left to catch up with the retreating Spanish columns. We caught up with them as they were leaving the extremely mountainous area of the old Jesús María Mesa sugar plantation. There, we fired on them because the cowards who made up the rear guard were trying to escape, shooting while they ran away.

It was already getting dark, so we left them close to the town of Bolondrón. They had left there that morning boasting of their Spanish heritage and of their enthusiasm for adventurous expeditions, believing it was going to be the same as their previous mission. In that expedition, known as Collazo, they had seized almost all of the military supplies they now had. But this fight was very different in that they left, as the great General Máximo Gómez[15] said, running like a dog with its tail between its legs.

---

15. Máximo Gómez Báez (1836–1905): The general in chief of the Liberation Army during the War of Independence. Born in the Dominican Republic, Gómez immigrated

There were two striking aspects of that battle. The first was that we weren't yet accustomed to using machetes. If our forces had gotten used to using them in time, perhaps not a single enemy soldier from the three columns would have escaped.

One example of our inexperience is the way in which the fighting proceeded near Hato Jicarita. Colonel Dantin and Sanguily turned back in order to fight the rear guard of the Spanish columns that was inside a banana plantation where the Spanish had retreated in order to treat their wounded. Dantin and Sanguily attacked them unexpectedly with machetes. The Spanish were there because they thought that it was safer for the wounded, and it was a strategic location for the two commanding officers. They opened fire from the banana plantation that was just a short distance away. The location gave them cover so that they could escape with the help of the rear guard, who were expert fighters. But when we fired on them, that bees' hive awoke. One lone company that had taken care of the wounded began to respond to our volleys. And those same wounded, about one hundred of them, used their weapons instinctively for self-protection, more than out of bravery. Thus the shooting from the wounded and the company treating them alerted the other soldiers; so more Spanish forces came.

If the rear guard had attacked with machetes, not only would we have ended the battle with those wounded and that company treating them, the other Spanish troops would have also fallen before our ranks as we shouted "Viva Cuba Libre!" This was our signal to our troops coming to reinforce us to stop firing—to avoid hitting us—and to charge with machetes as we were doing. Then only the prisoners would have been saved and perhaps the celebrated Molina would have fallen.

The other aspect or mistake in that battle was on the retreat when we caught up with the Spanish in the afternoon. Knowing the way the Spanish Army fought, and knowing that they always took the offensive

to Cuba just prior to the Ten Years' War (1868–78). With the outbreak of war, he joined the revolutionary forces and quickly rose through the ranks to become general. He subsequently fought in La Guerra Chiquita (1878–80). After the deaths of José Martí and Antonio Maceo, early in the War of Independence, Gómez came to symbolize the cause of Cuban independence.

with us after suffering a defeat, it was crazy to think that they wouldn't mount a new attack by their rear guard and fight back. But the fact that they didn't attack was a sign that they didn't have any ammunition. And so it was possible for us to make a charge with our machetes. But, as I said, we weren't used to the famous machete charges. We failed because the Spanish retreat was too fast that day, so fast that they carried three of our soldiers on stretchers along with their wounded without even realizing it. And two of those revolutionary soldiers carried their cartridge belts of ammunition on their waists underneath their shirts. How unfortunate it would have been for those soldiers if those terrified lions of Castilla had realized who the soldiers were. They would have satiated their appetites for human flesh and their thirst for blood on those defenseless soldiers.

Those three liberators were surprised in the house of their respective families living in that area. They were going to their houses in order to change clothes, and they were sure that the houses were safe. They paid attention to the battle, as they could still hear it, but it was not likely that the columns would hang about to rummage through the houses.

However, there were a lot of the fallen, and the Spanish didn't want them to be an obstacle for the forces that were still free to fight. Therefore, in their retreat, the Spanish cavalry was gathering up all the men who were in the houses of the noncombatants.

Those three confident liberators had to pass for *pacíficos*[16] in order not to be victims of the sweep. When we opened fire the second time, in the new attack that we launched on the Spanish, there was a lot of confusion in their lines. And we were so eager to take the town at any cost that our soldiers nearly let go of the stretchers of the severely wounded that they were supposed to be carrying, in order to take the last section of the woods that remained before the plain of Bolondrón.

When those three comrades arrived at our lines, they told us that the Spanish columns were short of ammunition. The shortage was so severe that when the Spanish soldiers heard us firing on the rear guard, they advised their commanding officers who ordered the column that was going toward the rear guard to open fire. The officers said that that column

16. *Pacífico:* A civilian; an unarmed Cuban who is not a member of the Liberation Army.

was the only one with ammunition, so they had to cut the march short. But by the time our three comrades had escaped from the hands of those demons and had told us all of this, it was already getting dark. Who knows what would have happened if we had known this at three in the afternoon when we started our retreat? No one would have been able to describe what would have happened to Molina. I can only say that whatever he would have tried to do, we would have sent him to eternity for the good of Cuba and of mankind.

Dantin's and Sanguily's forces continued to fight together after the glorious battle of Jicarita, famous in the annals of the War of Independence. However, some were preparing an accusation of treason against Sanguily for lack of discipline, just because the entire regiment, except for ten or twelve, was black, including the commanding officer. Dantin was against this unpatriotic and antidemocratic plot, and therefore continued to fight with us and to support us. In this way, he was able to undermine the plot until General Lacret ordered the transfer of our regiment from the Southern Brigade to the Northern Brigade, under the orders of then Colonel Pedro E. Betancourt.

Some were plotting against our regiment because we fought and defeated more Spanish troops all across the province of Matanzas, and therefore took greater risks. The fact that we fought so valiantly should have been cause for admiration and affection from the rest of the commanding officers, but it was a source of hatred, particularly because our commanding officer and his soldiers were black. The prejudice was so great that the other black officers who didn't have a supporter free of prejudice, like Dantin, were ruined by racial prejudice, and others were killed. Among those ruined were Cajizote, Simeón Sánchez, Ceballo, El Tuerto Mato, Severino Ricardo (cousin of Matagás), etc. They were all accused of plotting. They tied up the first officer, Cajizote, but he didn't suffer the others' fate. He was able to escape, and had to abandon the revolutionary cause, surrendering to the enemy, because he didn't know how to defend himself. If he had gone up the chain of command, he could have avoided staining his reputation. He should have gone to General Maceo's headquarters, or to the government of the revolution, and told what happened. Then, perhaps, he wouldn't have had to ruin his brilliant record, and he wouldn't have given encouragement to those who wanted to get rid of the black officers who were performing brilliantly.

As I mentioned earlier, after the glorious battle of Jicarita, Dantin's and Sanguily's forces continued to march together. At that time, the commanding officer of the brigade, Brigadier Eduardo García, called on them to capture the town of Cabezas. For that operation they were consolidating all of the forces in the village of Vija. Ours were the last to arrive, and when we got close to the headquarters when the captain, known as Sucumbento, told us not to come into the camp because they had prepared a noose with which they were going to hang Sanguily. We ignored his order, and with guns loaded continued on to the headquarters of Brigadier García. When we got there, we found Colonel Pedro García (the brother of the Brigadier), the Lieutenant Colonel Francisco Guedes, Colonel Guillermo Acevedo, and Pío Domínguez at the brigade headquarters. As soon as we gathered in the headquarters, we were ordered to camp near the town of Cabezas. It was about four in the afternoon; although we were ordered to do so, we didn't get out of formations because we didn't want to leave our commander, Sanguily. But by seven at night we left and went to the nearby town.

The location designated to each officer having been decided, I couldn't understand why our forces were to charge the entrance that was judged impossible for an all-out attack, through the area called Esperanza Domínguez. It was a place where the two best forts that defended the town stood. So it was impossible to spread out like guerrillas in order to avoid the deadly fire. Furthermore, north of the road, there were some hills, ten meters high, covered with trees that blocked our approach. So there we had no other choice than, suicide-like, to attack the fort. But Providence is more powerful than humans; and when it doesn't want something bad to happen, it doesn't happen. When we came to the front of the fort where we were about to be victims, a Spanish soldier yelled to us, "Halt!" and we shot him dead. He was a corpse before he even had the chance to fire. Meanwhile, the soldiers inside opened fire on us in order to repel our attack. We lay down on our stomachs, crawling, and we were about to fall into a ditch that served as a moat for the fort. The Spanish were shooting directly at the road we were crossing as we approached the bridge that went to the fort. But we were protected by the ditch and the darkness of the night. So when the other fort liberators were taking their strategic shots in order to attack the weak forts (weak because they were thought easier to enter), we were already inside the town, yelling "Viva Cuba Libre!" surrounded by enemy fire. It was then that the others realized that we had succeeded in our attack more quickly, despite the fact that we had attacked the more heavily fortified position.

Leaving Cabezas, we marched with Colonel Dantin and camped the following day in view of the town of Bermeja. I believe that it was the month of August. Later, we went to Jagüey Grande, which was in the area of Europa between Claudio and Navajas. The Spanish column arrived moments after we succeeded in breaking the railroad lines in four different places, each a mile and a half apart. This did great damage to the Spanish governor, because not only did we cut his troops off from Claudio, Navaja, and Jagüey, but the Spanish had to redeploy many troops in order to repair the lines. And they wanted to do it quickly because in addition to breaking their rail lines we had taken the boxcars, pulling them by oxen to the woods of Manjuarí. From there we countermarched, passing through Jabaco, Jardines, and Yuca, where we had a battle after we had rested the horses.

After several skirmishes in that area, we returned to Zapata in order to relieve the cavalry there; from there we began a march to take the town of Bolondrón.[17] We attacked it with three regiments of cavalry: Dantin's, Sanguily's, and el Inglesito's troops. Until that day, no one had seen any town defended with such heroism as that one, given its relative size. We yelled "Long live Quintín Bandera,"[18] in order to terrify their

---

17. Bolondrón: A town in the province of Matanzas approximately twenty miles south of the city of Matanzas.

18. Quintín Bandera: One of the few Afro-Cuban generals in all three wars for Cuban independence. He joined the Cuban Army as a private in 1868 at the opening of the Ten Years' War. Like Antonio Maceo, he rose quickly through the ranks to become a general of a division. Like Maceo too, he rejected the Pact of Zanjón and continued to fight after its signing. He also led forces in La Guerra Chiquita (1879–80), and he led forces during the western invasion in the final war for Cuban independence. Although

troops as we charged as infantry, but we didn't scare them very much. They opened fire on us and we assumed that it wasn't only with double-action rifles; it was as if there were a Gatling gun in each one of those strongholds. But we didn't let this slow us down, as we destroyed their best commercial establishment called El Gallo; nor was it an obstacle in destroying most of the houses in the neighborhood of Lladó, a rectangular area connecting the forts. There, we lost five brave soldiers; one of them was killed simply because he was too brave. The situation was such that two men had fallen in the living room of a burning house, and "the necessities of war" required us to leave them there. We resigned ourselves to this reality, like so many others in war, when patriotism is deaf to human pain, deaf in order to enable us to continue to serve our country and to injure the common enemy of liberty. But a sergeant of our regiment, Simeón Cárdenas, boldly entered the house in an attempt to rescue those two comrades. It was impossible, and his efforts were in vain. The burning house was so bright from the light of the flames that it lit up the area as if it were day. And when the heroic Simeón fell, pieces of burning wood fell on those patriotic heroes who were already dead from the bullets of the tyrants. We witnessed that incredible event, but it didn't amaze us: we were used to seeing such things in war. Nevertheless, we felt for those three great men, who moments before gave cries of "Viva!" for the liberty of their dear Cuba (although later that liberty was stained by peacetime politics).

We remained there at the house, unable to prevent their deaths. Not only was it impossible to help them, but we also exposed ourselves foolishly to the descendants of Pelayo who were cutting down the liberation forces, picking us off as if they were taking target practice.

Because we were able to defeat the enemy, we honored the sacrifices made by these Cuban freedom fighters and so elevate their names that their heroism can be recognized by the entire world. But the soul is saddened when the cause of freedom is politicized the way it is today by a large number of those who didn't purify their souls in the Revolution,

his forces did not penetrate as far west as Maceo's army, he fought in order to distract the Spanish, allowing Maceo and Gómez's forces greater range of movement during the invasion.

indeed, by those who simply left the fighting to men with honor and determination. But, they won't achieve their objective because there are always pure hearts, and the love of democracy will never die in the hearts of grateful Cubans.

That night in Bolondrón, I witnessed one of the great events of the war, although in peacetime its significance has been ignored. Colonel Dantin was shot in the leg, so his assistant, Ciriaco, a large, very strong black man, carried him on his shoulders from the center of the town until they got to the opening of the fort that faced the Armonía sugar plantation. As they were crossing the barbed wire there, the heroic Ciriaco was shot and wounded more severely than his commanding officer, whom he was trying to save. When that courageous Cuban fell in that supreme effort to rescue his commander, Colonel Dantin threw his devoted and heroic savior on his shoulders. The wound that Dantin had received was in the leg, through the calf; so, as he carried the taller and larger man, the wound bled even more profusely. And when he arrived where we had left the horses, he had almost bled to death.

It was four in the morning when we started to reunite to mount our horses, and by five o'clock we were already marching as the light of day broke. At seven we stopped to dig a grave for the self-sacrificing Ciriaco, whose wound was mortal, so severe that after he was shot his spirit didn't last three hours more in the world of the living. But his memory will never die, as it has not faded for me in the thirteen years that have passed since his death; nor will it die for anyone who witnessed these events in Cuba, when we saved her from the yoke of tyranny.

The wounded officer was being carried by the soldier, when the soldier too was wounded. Then, with a supernatural resolve, the wounded officer threw the soldier on his shoulders because the soldier's wound was even more severe, so serious, as I said, that he didn't live three hours longer. Isn't it true, reader, that this scene inspires us to believe that humanity was perfected in such a display of democracy? Yes, you can believe it because that truly was democracy, with all of its beautiful attributes. Here was the human reciprocity that all people, nations, and civilized men fight to achieve. As a young man I lived to breathe that purified air of democracy, and so I will never be able to stand idly by and tolerate injustices that threaten the ideal of civilized humanity.

Before taking the town of Bolondrón we had had a fight with enemy forces on the Condesa sugar plantation. That day the advanced guard hadn't been posted because it was sufficient to have a sentry on top of the plantation house. The surrounding area was flat, so the sentry was able to see the enemy at a distance. That afternoon, when we camped, they caught a lot of horses in the fields of La Antonia that had never been saddled; so we had to break them. The next morning I rode one of those wild horses that none of the other soldiers had the nerve to mount. I left, going in the direction of Limonar, with the intention of taming that wild animal that only looked like a horse. When I was just a mile and a half from the camp, I saw a large enemy force; so I tried to slow the horse to make it easier to guide him. The Spanish were already close, and I noticed that they were down in the guinea grass that grew two meters high in the area. All of them came very well armed and spoiling for a fight. And because of the shininess of the arms I could tell that it was not a Cuban regiment, but Spanish. Then I tried to whip the horse, but at first it didn't obey because it wasn't used to the reins. But Providence wanted him to obey, and eventually we went bolting, you could say, back to the camp. When I arrived, those who were in the camp still didn't know that the enemy was so close, because the sentry who was on the sugar mill had fallen asleep. We wouldn't have been alerted if I hadn't paid attention to the signs I saw out on my ride. When I got there, I sounded the alarm, alerting the camp that we had the enemy nearly on top of us. It was then that they realized that the sentry was asleep. Everyone scrambled for their horses, most of which were still without saddles. Sanguily and some others who hadn't unsaddled their horses mounted them as soon as I sounded the alarm and went to identify the enemy.

The gunfire had already begun. Only we fully understood the situation and so we, the Cuban *mambises,* were lighter than cats. In less than ten seconds I had changed the saddle from the wild horse to mine that I had untied. Already the shots were falling inside of the sugar plantation house, whistling by our heads. The battle was intense and lasted a quarter of an hour, during which we had one death, Manuel Betancourt, and several wounded, among them Victoriano Montes de Oca and Bonifacio Oviedo. It helped us in that unexpected fight that another regiment had arrived during the night and had camped close to us for the first time,

Commander Andrés Tavío's force. He liked the way we fought so much that his regiment marched with us for a few months after that fight.

His regiment had only twenty-five men, what was left of the squadron from Clotilde García's brigade. García was the heroic officer in the San José de las Ramos brigade who had died a short time before. We were together a few days, with the Northeast Brigade. During that time, we had several fights with enemy forces.

Concerning the Condesa sugar plantation fight, the regiment thanked me for the happy conclusion of that battle. If I hadn't tried to ride that wild horse—and given that the lookout was asleep—almost the entire regiment would have died. Because the area was flat and clear so that the lookout could see a long way, they were confident that they wouldn't be surprised by the enemy. We had unsaddled the horses, assuming that there would be enough time to react at the shout of alarm from the sentry. It was just a coincidence that the enemy arrived when a soldier named Andrés Brindis was on duty. He was a bit of a dimwit, and didn't understand that during his watch he was protecting the lives of everyone in the entire camp, not to mention his own.

We were now marching with the Northeast Brigade. The wounded were sent to a safe place, and a few days later we had a battle with the Spanish Colonel Moncada's columns. Moncada took into his vanguard almost all of the former insurrectionists who were in the brave Octavio Hernández's force. He had died not long before, near the town of Madruga, where he was born.

It was a bad habit at the beginning of the War of Independence that when an officer died all of his former troops, both Spanish and Cuban, however brave, surrendered (or became *presentados*)[19] to honor his heroism. The result was that old comrades sometimes went into the vanguard of a Spanish column. This made encounters dangerous because they could see that we weren't always fully equipped with ammunition to fight the battles. For this reason, they almost always attacked with intensity from the first moment to see if we had the ammunition to fight back.

---

19. *Presentado:* A Cuban soldier forced to surrender to the Spanish Army and to ask for clemency. For many Cubans, to surrender meant a great loss of military honor and a betrayal of the revolution.

As a result of that battle with Moncada, we suffered three wounded. Two were from Dantin's force, with which we had united. Of those who died, one died just after the end of the battle. And the other one wounded from our force was Juan Sardiñas y Villa, the then captain, added to our regiment from Brigadier Francisco Pérez's forces. Pérez was the commanding officer of the Colón Brigade during 1895 and part of '96, until Colonel Morejón, "the Lion of the Tropics," assumed his command.

We went to the mountains of Zapata with the wounded from both forces. They were later moved for their treatment to the mountains of Galión. Misfortune had joined the two captains, Victoriano Montes de Oca and Juan Sardiñas y Villa, with our forces. Two of the wounded were these two, both only recently wounded. Montes de Oca was more seriously wounded than the other captain, because in Condesa he was shot twice, once on the battlefield and once as he was retreating. The first shot went all the way through his chest, and the second went through his leg; this other captain, Sardiñas, only had one bullet wound in the leg, a shot that went through without damaging the bone.

Consider the coincidences of the war! Who knows if Captain Sardiñas's wound was inflicted by one of the bullets from the Spanish vanguard? It might have been shot by *presentados* who in their insurrectionist beginnings were brave soldiers who fought with their commanding officer Octavio Hernández. What else could they do now but fight under the command of the intrepid Spanish colonel, Moncada?

After the fight with Moncada's column at Vija, we attacked and took my hometown of Sabanilla for the second time, and it was the last attack for the night. We took the town without firing one shot on the forts, and we searched the entire town without sounding the alarm. But, as almost all of us were sons from there, with the exception of Dantin's forces, we didn't want to come and go in silence, so we shot off our guns. As soon as we did, the Spanish answered as they usually did, for the simple reason that throughout the war they had more ammunition. It was like the fight of the poor against the rich; while the poor do not spend because they don't have anything, the rich have an abundance of resources to waste.

As a result of disturbing that wasps' nest, we suffered one wounded from our force who died a few hours later. He was a son of the town, Francisco Diviñó. It was such a tragic irony! This man was shot in the same house in which he lived before leaving for the war and after traveling all over the town that night.

A few days after the taking of Sabanilla, Dantin's force went to Zapata to rest the horses. We remained united with the then Colonel Pedro E. Betancourt and his forces in order to take the town of Nueva Paz, an operation that we carried out gladly. All of this took place during the first days of September.

Camp Monte de Oro

When we crossed the railroad tracks at the bay between Empalme and Ceiba-Mocha, we fought with Pavía's column, which attacked us at the strongest part of our force, right at the point where we were crossing the tracks. The fighting began at about five in the afternoon during a torrential downpour. The rear guard, under the orders of Lieutenant Colonel Rafael Águila, was unable to cross; the vanguard was under the orders of Lieutenant Colonel Raimundo Ortega (Sanguily); and part of the main concentration of forces was with the commanding officer of headquarters for the brigade, Commander Eduardo Rosell. We crossed the rail lines in this relentless downpour, fighting until it got dark. We then camped a mile and a half from the point where we crossed. During the night, a division of the rear guard arrived along with Sanguily. Although we, the vanguard who were in his force, had crossed the tracks, he was left in the back talking with Águila, so he arrived much later. At dawn, the camp moved to the hills of Monte de Oro. One member of the guard, Commander Rosell, became commander of the force when, I believe, then Colonel Pedro E. Betancourt was wounded. He received the wound in the battle of Magdalena, fighting with Rabadan. He was shot in the back just as he tried to advance his flank against the cavalry of the Civil Guard[20] that was accompanying that force. I repeat, I believe that the commander of the brigade, Colonel Betancourt, was recovering from that wound; that's why Commander Rosell became the commander of the force.

---

20. Civil Guard: The Spanish government "security force." Its main function was to act as a police force on behalf of the Spanish, at times conflicting with provincial or municipal authorities. Because the Civil Guard often engaged in extralegal forms of intimidation and brutality, it was reviled by most Cubans.

But back to the camp at Monte de Oro. It was 9 a.m. when we heard shots on the road that Águila's forces were covering. We mounted our horses and within our camp we formed a defensive line in order to protect Águila's forces during their retreat. Because terrain in that area was very rough, made up of ravines and holes in the ground, we didn't see Águila's forces as they crossed near us, retreating through one of those narrow ravines. The Spaniards' shots went by us from a distance of just two city blocks. When we were able to see the first Spanish soldiers, they were already close despite it being a clear morning. They were crossing a nearby stream that was in front of our line of fire, so close it was possible to use a 38-caliber revolver. They were Pavía's troops, with the guerrillas from Matanzas in the vanguard. We opened fire on them, but after fierce resistance, we had to retreat because we ran out of ammunition.

We went in the direction that all of the forces were going, under the orders of Commander Rosell, to the camp of the Havana infantry regiment. That regiment was found close by, and that force almost always had ammunition; so they could cover our retreat. Before arriving at their camp, two more columns attacked our flanks: Guadalajara and España. What a situation, without ammunition and attacked by three columns! Words can't describe the courage that we displayed! They didn't attack us because in situations like that the quality of our forces prevailed, so much so that it concealed our lack of ammunition. Although we had used up our ammunition, we advanced two by two toward the Spanish. Taking fire and firing back only sporadically, we proved our resolve to the enemy. This was our opportunity to devour their fiercest fighters.

As we were going up a hill to gain the protection of the infantry, our efforts were hampered when second lieutenant, Ángel Piedra, was wounded. He lost so much blood that he fainted and fell off his horse, with the guerrillas so close there was no time to pick him up. José Matilde, the attaché for Sanguily, was shot from his horse and we weren't able to pick him up either. The brave Remigio Oviedo, only some twenty years old, was riding a horse that tired, just as his comrade Sabino Hernández's horse did. So together they went through that hail of gunfire, fighting and shooting on foot, before getting to the mountain where Remigio would meet an ignominious death. He didn't want to follow his comrade any further and thought that he could take protection behind the trunk of a silk-cotton tree, a thick tree that grows in that savanna. He didn't listen to the pleas of his comrade, Sabino, to keep moving. And there he became the victim of the evil blades of the Matanzas guerrillas, Pavía's vanguard. So there were three killed in Sanguily's forces, although in the first moments we thought we had lost seven because when we got to the infantry's position, upon review, we missed seven of Sanguily's men, and two of Águila's men.

At 1 p.m. we camped at the old La Viuda sugar plantation, close to Canasí. The camp looked and felt like a house in mourning when a close family member has died. Those seven comrades, whom we missed, had left a deep impression on all of our hearts. Our force ran out of ammunition for those dear comrades, and that was the only reason that those pariahs were able to attack. Furthermore, we couldn't charge the Spanish with machetes for three reasons: first, their forces were three times as large as ours; second, they were well armed and well positioned; and finally, the ground was rough and very difficult to navigate, as I said before.

At five in the afternoon, four of our dead arrived in the camp: Lieutenant Manuel Quintero, Sabino Hernández, Candelario Alfonso, and Domingo Hernández. It was confirmed that the three dead were picked up by Pavía's column, which returned to Ceiba-Mocha, where our wounded were buried along with the two dead from Águila's forces.

In the afternoon, or as it was getting dark, we moved the camp from La Viuda to Cuatro-Pasos, a nearby location where we stayed the night. At dawn, reveille was sounded, and we got into our formations. As the sun began to shine brightly, it occurred to me to look to the tops of the nearby hills of Cuatro-Pasos. Just a half-kilometer away I saw a large group of Spanish infantry crowning the hill. I called out the alarm so that we would spread out like guerrillas, because if we opened fire in our tight formation, the incoming fire would have been devastating.

As soon as the force spread out, and saw the situation, we knew that we were going to serve as the targets for those enemies of liberty. We hadn't spread out completely when they opened fire with an intense round of shots. Those of us who had ammunition responded, while the rest continued to march in the direction of the nearby little town of Pan de Matanzas. The Spanish column saw that we couldn't open fire properly, and pursued us to the same hill, Pan. There we met up with twenty-five men under the command of Vicente Jorge. They had ammunition with which they protected our rear guard with continuous volleys. Their strategy was to go higher up the hill and to charge along the road that went to the town of Corral-Nuevo.

We marched on and crossed the railroad tracks between Matanzas and Ceiba-Mocha. While a column of the rear guard doubled back to Corral-Nuevo, as I said before, our vanguard took fire while crossing the tracks. Despite the fire, we were able to camp by about 2 p.m. in Quincena, a place not five miles away from the city. Although we didn't have any ammunition, not only did we cross the tracks at Weyler, near the city of Matanzas, we camped for the night as usual at the farm called Quincena. There were no woods there that would prevent the Spanish from seeing us. Indeed, it was a place where the trains went back and forth between Havana and Matanzas; so they could see us perfectly. At nightfall we moved the camp to San Francisco de Paula, a little burned-out town that was our usual camp.

The next day, the heroic Colonel Pedro E. Betancourt became the commander of the brigade. We spent three or four days skirmishing daily, sometimes without ammunition, only receiving fire without being able to respond to the tyrants' shots. In that month we were under Sanguily's command, and we would later be transferred to the command of General Juan F. Ruz.

At that time, General Ruz arrived at the camp of the Northeast Brigade when General José Lacret Morlot, commander of the province, was there. The two generals camped and completed plans for something that had been brewing for a long time: the transfer of our forces to the Northern Brigade. We didn't then want to be a part of the Southern Brigade. So we obtained the orders to become escorts for General Ruz to the Colón Brigade, as I already have described.

Being in Colón's brigade proved deadly for our cavalry! We lost many men because of the stony terrain in that area and because the pasture in that area was different from what our horses were used to eating.

Before our anticipated return to our normal area, we fought with several Spanish brigades. One of those battles was the celebrated Vereda del Peñón fight, in the Prendes Mountains; and I say celebrated because it is memorable in the history of Cuba Libre. It was there that the general in commission, Carlos Agüero, was a victim of betrayal when he tried, in 1886, to collect funds for the war.

And days before we arrived, escorting General Juan Ruz, Colonel Eustaquio Morejón had been killed because of his extraordinary heroism. Morejón became the commander of the Colón Brigade, after Brigadier Francisco Pérez was relieved of his command. The heroic Morejón was black, and I called him "The Lion of the Tropics" because, like a lion, he had come to reinforce us when we attacked the town of Roque months before.

There at Vereda del Peñón, we planned to ambush Colonel Ambert's column; he had a regular camp there in Calimete. We killed a lot of his men; then later we fought with Colonel Almendaris's column, which was made up of convicts and the very worst of vile Cubans who defended the government of Spain in Cuba. That day we went at dawn to the place where that column of despicable soldiers was camped, according to the information that we had received. They were getting into formation in order to begin looking for us, and just as Colonel Almendaris was raising a cup of coffee to his lips, one of our shots broke it in his hands. Because we were pretty close, behind a stone wall that formed the *batey*[21] in which they were encamped, we could watch with glee as those outlaws floundered in their own blood. Their wounded fell, and the others were so confused that they could barely reorganize themselves. But they were able to get over the shock and to regroup, nevertheless, because we had no more than twenty men. If we had had our entire force, the attack would have been devastating for them because we took them by surprise. We were able to do so because they had been emboldened by Colonel Morejón's death, moving about as if there were no enemy.

The Spanish guards for the area had left before our march began without realizing that the new Cuban force for that area wasn't as large

---

21. *Batey:* A square or yard usually formed by slave quarters (*barracones*) placed in a square formation. The yard area served as a location to congregate and was used for different forms of recreation and celebration (dancing, playing music, etc.), as well as a place to grow vegetables and to safeguard livestock.

as Colonel Morejón's regiment. But we were the same in quality. Indeed, we could compete with the best of the liberating forces. The Spanish didn't follow us to the ambush that we had prepared for them with the main part of our force, in order to punish them in their own area. They had to retreat to their headquarters in Jagüey Grande, with the wounded that we inflicted on them. Several days passed without news of the enemy, until we found out one morning that the guerrillas of the Santa Rita de Baró sugar plantation were looking for some oxen. We went in search of them, but those guerrillas were very experienced in that area. So, when they heard the trampling of our horses, they positioned themselves for an ambush. When we arrived, they opened fire unexpectedly; it was just by chance that they didn't kill any of us. And I say by chance because the trail that we were following was so narrow that we couldn't spread out to defend ourselves. And then they blocked us into several hollows where some of our riders fell along with their horses. In fact, my dear comrade, Leocadio Montalvo (known as Tito), fell in one of those hollows and was on the verge of being trampled by the stampeding cavalry, while so many of those outlaws were just ten meters away shooting at us; nevertheless, we escaped that ambush unharmed.

The following day the execution of Commander Severino, cousin of José Matagás, took place. That execution caused quite a stir in the area of Colón because three officers—two white and one black—had been facing a Wartime Tribunal.[22] For several days the first two were accused of recent infractions so serious that it looked as if they were guilty. The black officer, Severino, was sure that he would be exonerated because there were no witnesses to support the charges that, in reality, were unfounded. If the crimes of which he had been accused were true, no one would have protested the execution. But they claimed that his wounded cousin, José Matagás (wounded in the invasion in 1895), had given him a watch that he was to have delivered as a gift to General Máximo Gómez,

---

22. Wartime Tribunal: Replicating the Spanish model of military tribunals, the Liberation Army imposed military discipline through Wartime Tribunals, or Courts Martial. Consisting of a panel of officers, these councils heard accusations against soldiers and the defense against accusations. They judged the merits of the case and decided innocence or guilt. If a soldier were found guilty, the council also ordered the punishment.

on his arrival in the region of Colón. He was also given five hundred centenes,[23] which he was to have put toward arms and ammunition to fight the Spanish. But a few hours after Matagás was wounded, he died without having been able to write a statement that would have provided incontrovertible proof to exonerate Commander Severino of all accusations of thievery.

A full year after Matagás's death, what proof could the tribunal have to order this execution? We thought that the black commander would be acquitted, but it turned out differently. The two white commanders were acquitted. They were Alfredo Escudero, my good friend in the war and in peace, and Carreras, who had been in the Civil Guard and had had the glory of killing a Spanish general, Vicuña, in one of Morejón's charges. When Carreras, who knew Vicuña, got to the Spanish camp, he shot him in the stomach with his 44-caliber revolver. The wound eventually killed him, although the Spanish account said that he died of yellow fever.

All of us hoped that Commander Severino would be acquitted as well. General Ruz's force, made up of some four hundred cavalry and two hundred infantry men, was ordered to stop its march in observance of the trial and possible execution. It was dawn and we were on the road that goes to the mountains of Prendes, between the pastures of Jabaco and Las Algarrobas. We were to go into a pasture on the side of the road to rest, and there we were ordered to form the headquarters for the cavalry. We saw, passing by, four squadrons of infantry with the commander, Severino. When we saw this, we realized that Augustín Cervantes's wishes were going to be carried out. He was the commander of General Ruz's general staff. It was earlier rumored that the execution was really a personal vendetta on Cervantes's part because Commander Severino had been the best dressed of the officers and that Cervantes had ordered him a change of clothes, made from a coarse fabric, the same as his. He had also ordered a pair of boots for Severino that were the same kind as his. He was able to get these clothes with ease because he was in the region of his hometown, where the war had been waging since before the western invasion. Severino refused the change of clothes because of the way

---

23. Centén: Spanish gold coin worth twenty-five pesetas or one hundred reales.

that Cervantes had requested it. Some said that this refusal was the cause of the tribunal's decision and the execution.

In light of those rumors, I notified Commander Pedro José del Castillo of our force in order to mutiny in protest of the execution. We felt that there was no justification for the conviction, and our force was willing to try anything that could be done to avoid that execution. But our commander replied that we were going to jeopardize the force if we protested, because it was well known that others wanted to accuse us of insubordination. They were looking for a pretext to get rid of the force of which they were so jealous. Severino was the only black commander of a force in the province because most of the others had died. Nevertheless, there was still envy and an antidemocratic spirit in the revolutionary camps that robbed courageous soldiers of their glory. Severino gave up his life, and with rare exception, the death of the poor commander was felt by all.

We decided not to protest for the reasons our esteemed commanding officer gave. He was highly respected during the war, but hated in peacetime because he didn't recognize or reciprocate all of the efforts we made under his command.

The execution was carried out, though I still don't believe that it was justified. I was moved as I watched that man, so full of life and glory, as they took his commander's star from him in order to execute him! That which Spanish bullets had respected in thousands of hard-fought battles, Cuban bullets did not. He was smoking a cigar as the four infantrymen, standing in front of him, waited for the cornet to blast, signaling them to take their mortal shots. Meanwhile, Colonel Cervantes gathered our corps and tried to explain the reason for Commander Severino's execution, but his explanation was unintelligible. I at least didn't understand the reasons he gave for Severino's execution. At the end of his address, the bugler blew the signal to fire. At the same moment, Severino shouted "Viva Cuba Libre!" as the shots knocked that valiant leader into the dust.

The entire camp was ordered to march by the body, but I left the line and went to the nearby banana plantation and waited for the entire regiment to finish its procession. Colonel Cervantes saw what I did; so, when the last soldiers had filed by, he came toward me and ordered me to go by where the body lay. When I refused, he drew his machete, threatening me. I grabbed my rifle, and he left me alone to go where I pleased, but threatened to punish me later when we arrived at the camp.

When we got to the camp, he wanted to carry out his threat, but he needed the permission of my commanding officer. When he asked for it, my commanding officer asked him why he wanted it, then denied him permission. From that day on, in order to avoid further conflict (and given that we marched as the vanguard), I was assigned the duty of scout.

Because of the nature of the warfare, the scout had to go out a considerable distance ahead of the force. After two days on this particular maneuver, we passed behind the Unión de Fernández sugar plantation, close to the town of Cuevitas. As I passed by a door to a stone wall, I saw two guerrillas playing a game on the other side. They were unaware of me, despite the fact that they were the sentries for a force just a city block away. When they realized that I was there, we were so close that only a small wall separated us. It was a terrible situation, for them and for me. I was separated from my regiment, and to have the enemy so close! They ran, surprised, shouting the alarm, "Who goes there?!" And with the response "Cuba!" I shot my rifle at those two renegade Cubans who were in the service of the Spanish government. Immediately afterward, our vanguard approached and also opened fire. The other guerrillas responded from behind a pile of firewood that the *pacíficos* had cut for the sugar plantation that was about to begin the harvest. Shots were flying by, and I had run out of ammunition. Just then I saw that General Ruz's troops were in a position to help our auxiliary, but instead of helping them, they left in an ill-advised retreat, chasing the guerrillas who had just scattered. So I went to look for ammunition among the general's escort and ran into a Filipino from the escort who was carrying more than sixty bullets in his equipment bag. I took them from him, but not before having some words with Colonel Cervantes, who didn't want to leave a soldier of the escort without ammunition. But I argued that the ammunition was for shooting the enemy, not for running away. Just as he was asserting his colonel's rank, my commanding officer, Castillo, arrived and took my side, ordering the Filipino to leave the ammunition. And I took it.

By then the guerrillas had already entered the sugar plantation that was close by. Just then, there was an alarm in the headquarters, warning that a force was coming from the east, and that it appeared to be the Spanish cavalry. So we left, but it turned out to be the force of Colonel Enrique Junco, who came as our reinforcement because he heard nearby shooting. When the rest of my regiment came from the camp in response to the shots, they found the two guerrillas whom I had surprised and shot lying near that same door. We took their shotguns, boots, Browne belts,[24] and the rest of their equipment. But we lost all of it trying to catch up with the general staff and the rest of the forces that were retreating unnecessarily.

My commanding officer and Cervantes had an argument about the bullets that I had taken from the Filipino. Cervantes wanted me to return them when we camped, which I refused to do, and my commanding officer supported me. They had already had two run-ins, and Colonel Cervantes was still angry about having to fight in that area. We had already spent approximately a month in those mountains and in that rocky terrain. It was a little less than impossible for the cavalry, so none of us liked being stationed there because the horseshoes fell off of our horses, and we didn't have the means to reshoe them; we had a lot of sick troops too. So the commander, Pedro J. de Castillo, and I resolved to march in the direction of our zone and to carry all of the sick with us. There were four of them: Norberto Domenech, known as Modesto Domés, Quirino Delgado, José Mirabal, and Evaristo Sardiñas, as well as an additional pair of solders who accompanied us.

We met a farmer in a pasture called Jabaco, close to Jagüey Grande. He had resisted reconcentration[25] by that criminal Weyler,[26] and still lived

---

24. Browne belt: Equipment belt used by both Spanish and Cuban soldiers.

25. Reconcentration: The policy of Governor Valeriano Weyler, beginning in 1896, to remove Cuban farmers and peasants from the countryside and to "reconcentrate" them within cities and large towns. The policy also placed the entire island under martial law. The purpose of the policy was to deprive insurrectionists of food, material support, and information that noncombatants often tried to supply. More than three hundred thousand civilians were relocated under the policy. Because of scarce food and inadequate sanitary conditions, *concentrados* died of starvation and disease at an alarming rate.

26. Valeriano Weyler (1838–1930): Appointed the governor of Cuba in 1896, expressly to crush the rebellion, Weyler was given carte blanche in his use of military

there. We found some chickens and made soup for the sick with seven of them. And in the morning the sick soldiers said that they felt more vigor for the march. From there, we began to march to our western region. We crossed the railroad tracks close to the town of Claudio and Jagüey Grande. We then camped at three in the morning at the entrance of the woods of Manjuarí, very close to the demolished Europa sugar plantation. Assuming that the area was secure, we released the horses that had been saddled for the march. When the sun rose, we were still sleeping, and when we finally woke up we realized that our horses were running in the direction of the railroad. Then we saw a Spanish flag over the houses of the old Europa plantation. What a predicament that was! We had to go stealthily in search of our horses because we didn't know if the area that we had crossed approximately a month ago was now fortified by the Spanish, or if there was a Spanish camp there. If the area had been fortified, it would have been less dangerous to go in pursuit of the horses. But if the opposite were true—if the Spanish flag signaled an encamped force—it would be much more dangerous for the company. Not knowing the situation, we hesitated, but complaints or doubts won't solve problems. So I made up my mind to look for our horses close to the area where the Spanish flag flew. Already the sun was so high that every moment that passed it became more and more dangerous to go looking for the horses. We had some luck in that after our last pass through the area accompanying the general, Juan Ruz, there were some new forts that they had erected where the flag had been seen. I had some luck too in that even when they saw me, they didn't shoot. How costly that mission would have been for us if they had opened fire!

It was well known that the soldiers in the fortified garrisons didn't fight unless they were attacked. So we were successful in retrieving the horses, and we retreated from the area having received a great lesson for future marches: we no longer released our horses.

---

force and tactics. His main policy was one of reconcentration, in an attempt to control the countryside and to cut supplies to the insurgents. Because the policy largely targeted the civilian population, Weyler was reviled by the Cuban rebels, who regarded him as the symbol of Spanish tyranny.

From there, we began to march through the woods of the Manjuarí swamp in the direction of the Hato de Jicarata, where we spent the night. And a curious thing happened there. We ran into all of the *mambises* of the other forces; they were in that plantation with fevers, perhaps because of the bad smell that the rotten bananas gave off. We left the sick there while Castillo and I went looking for meat for a good meal. We caught some guinea hens, and ran into a family that had moved closer to the liberation forces before having to obey the reconcentration orders of that criminal Weyler.

The family made us a lunch of those four guinea hens and in the afternoon, at 5 p.m., we began to march again. And at eight in the evening we arrived at the Zapata Mountains in the region called Oito. A family lived there in that isolated place; they too had resisted the reconcentration orders of the Spanish columns, a real danger for everyone in the family.

On the day of our arrival, the hands of those hardened guerrillas had brought that house great sorrow, in that those criminals had taken out their anger on the poor father of that family. That morning he had gone in search of medicine for his young child who was sick, and although it was almost night, he had not returned, proof that the damned birds of prey had satiated their brutal intentions on the defenseless father. Such a sad picture was presented to my eyes. I had never seen a creature of that age—two or three years old—so thin and in such a sad state. It shocked me so that Commander Pedro J. del Castillo and I almost fought because he wanted mercilessly to take one of the goats that provided the sad child its only source of sustenance. He argued that the three sick men whom we were carrying also needed food. He didn't agree with my argument that the food that the sick had received during those last two days before our arrival would sustain them two days more, until we reached our region of Las Lomas, especially since they were already improving. They hadn't had continuous fevers since we took them from the mountains of Prendes.

Not only did Castillo insist on taking the goat, but all of the soldiers agreed with him, and didn't want to leave the only resource that the mother had to sustain the life of that skinny creature, who, in her arms, appeared more like a cadaver than a living being.

The family was united with their poor father because he chose to be in the insurrectionist zone before it went to the Spanish. Because he hadn't returned at such a late hour, we all believed that he had been the victim of the cowardly blades of those miserable guerrillas. That should have been enough to move my comrades to have compassion and to leave without taking the goat. We discussed the mother, who was drenched in tears, that wife of the patriarch who wouldn't be seen again. And the story of her misfortune made us sympathize with her because all her grief came from her support for our cause: the emancipation of the country. She found some consolation in my efforts, although my intervention was not enough to keep my comrades, with hearts of stone, from taking her invaluable goat. When we left with the goat tied to the tail of one of the horses, the poor mother fell down on her knees, put her child on the ground, raised her arms to the heavens, and prayed for mercy. Despite all the time that has passed, I still remember that moment with great sadness. The only thing that I could say to her was, "Ma'am, you have my promise that I will not eat any of that animal, and I deeply regret that my comrades have not listened to me." And I followed my heartless comrades at a distance. When they saw me approaching, they broke out in laughter, even the sick ones, along with Castillo.

We camped in Alianza Cuco in Juan Pedro Baró's sugar plantation, Conchita. There, they killed the goat, and there was blood everywhere. The main one preparing the goat was prefect Alférez Julián Gómez, of Dantin's force. They used salt and sour oranges so that the stew emitted an aroma that would have made others with less willpower eat it and forget their promises. But I had said to that poor mother, who was victimized not only by the war but also by the excesses of cruelty that war unleashes, that I would not eat that seasoned animal, and I didn't have the heart to do so. All of them made fun of me, saying that I had the "scruples of a nun," but they couldn't mock me enough to make me participate in what I regarded as a crime against humanity.

We left Alianza Cuco at six in the afternoon in a march to attack Villanueva's line at the demolished La Lima sugar mill; we hoped to arrive at our area of Las Lomas by the early morning. But that march was a disappointment because in our entire journey we didn't see any liberation forces. So it appeared that since our absence, made by the Brigade of Colón, the Spanish had pacified our region.

By 2 a.m. one of the sick soldiers, Modesto Domenech, couldn't go any farther and wanted us to leave him in the house of a Cuban civilian whom we had met before and who was an acquaintance of his. Without being overly judgmental, I took note that Domenech had been one of those who savored with great pleasure the famous stew of the aforementioned goat, and who, before the dispossession of that poor woman, had withstood, with his broken health, a march of more than twenty-eight miles. But after eating from that animal, without any feelings of guilt, and after walking only eight or nine miles, he declared himself exhausted.

We left him at the house, and after ten days Castillo and I returned and were told that he had died. The story of his state during his grave illness and agony horrified us (he was one of those who had ridiculed me most when I didn't want to eat the goat). The family told us that his body was constantly covered by filthy worms, and that despite their efforts to keep him free of them, all were futile. Each day they cleaned him meticulously, but the next day he rose weakened by the same worms. Just imagine, reader, such a terrifying death!

The other three sick soldiers, Quirino Delgado, Evaristo Sardiñas, and José Mirabal, were also punished for their transgressions, so severely in fact that within six months they abandoned the honorable camp of the insurrection where they had fought for the liberty of their country. They had to surrender to the enemy because from the day of the celebrated banquet of the goat they had very bad luck. They thought that sure death awaited them in the Liberation. After two months we found out that the Spanish had killed one of them, José Mirabal, as if he hadn't surrendered. Before Quirino Delgado was able to surrender, the same insect began to grow in his knee, and he was killed by the same worms that had covered the body of his comrade, Modesto Domenech. Evaristo Sardiñas, the guide who led us from the mountains of Prendes, was macheted to death by the Spanish in their retreat.

Cayetano Vareda, another soldier who came on that mission, surrendered in the town of Palos when his life was in great danger because of an argument we had before the arrival of the main force. During that argument, he was so enraged that he was about to attack me; so I shot at him, and missed splitting open his skull by just a millimeter. The shot parted his hair from the front right to his ear on the same side.

Pedro José Castillo was the commanding officer of the group that took the goat. Until then he had been the second commander of the force. After eight months he lost his second command, and we didn't find out why until after the war. He never liked the Montaña de Zapata, and I don't know what was the reason that he ordered us to go there. He contracted smallpox wandering around the area with only three men. There was not a Spanish force operating on that mountain because the liberation forces had taken it.

I said earlier that Castillo was seriously wounded after many eventful journeys through those places where, months before, my comrades had eaten the goat. He was shot in the right hand, and the wound worsened, so much so that he had to surrender in the same town where that sad family had been, this according to that grief-stricken mother who had lost her husband that memorable day.

Perhaps this was the ultimate lesson. It was Castillo, the commanding officer of the company that had robbed that poor mother and devoted wife of her only source of sustenance for her son, who was now on the same road as that father was on in search of medicine. It was Castillo who took the goat, and so he abandoned the glorious ideal of the emancipation of the motherland. Later, he was on that same road, going to be stained by the sad stigma the penitent of that era bore: *Presentado.*

Such coincidences in life indeed connect these events in order to make us truly believe that Providence does exist. Because only in this way can we find a cause for the sad fate that my comrades had in pursuit of the ideal of the motherland. Although we didn't act in the same way in regard to the defenseless, nevertheless they loved, as best they could, the cause of the redemption of the soil on which we were all born.

Now let us return to the expedition. One could believe, because of my description of one of the episodes, that I had left the troop, but this is not my intention. We arrived at the mountains of Viajacas–Sierra that sits in the vicinity of Madruga, Pipián, and Palos at the beginning of December of the same year, 1896; there we remained until the 22nd of the same month. Then we received news that others in our force had arrived at the mountains of Purgatorio, close to the town of Ceiba-Mocha. The unit was made up almost entirely of soldiers who had come down with fevers and for many days had not eaten meat. We got the news in the middle of the day, on the 22nd. Then we left during the night of that same day in order to look for oxen in the surrounding enemy areas near the forts in the vicinity of Palos, near the Josefita sugar plantation. That night we were able to take four oxen while taking fire from the forts. Bringing food, we returned at dawn to welcome our recently arrived comrades. There was overwhelming joy at our return; the sickest were those who most wanted to eat those beautiful animals that we had brought to them like manna. We stayed in the camp until the afternoon and saw that everyone had a fever. Also, all of our horses were tired and didn't have horseshoes; our regiment was truly a disaster. How different it was from when we were escorting General Ruz. Then, we were the best riders in the province, so superior in fact that in one week we covered the entire province, hitting the Spanish militia in all the brigades. The excellent condition of our cavalry helped us to achieve all of these successes.

Seeing the sad state that the force was in now, and given the responses from the tired people in the expedition, Castillo and I went to look for new oxen that afternoon. We ventured into the same areas where the night before we had taken the four animals. On our new mission, it didn't take us long to find two more oxen, after going all around the forts of the town. We moved them, putting them in a safe place, and later we went on to the Josefita sugar plantation with the hope of capturing even more. But this was impossible because it was our second trip and all of the oxen had been put in the *batey,* surrounded by the houses of the plantation. The whole area was protected by six forts, and what's more, a lookout on the plantation house could see the entire area easily. The moon was shining its full light as it does in the months of December and January. The Christmas Eve moon on the 23rd and 24th would have revealed our presence. In view of the danger, it was absolutely impossible to take oxen from there. So we decided to abandon our mission there, although the decision made us feel for the soldiers of the guard unit. Castillo asked if I wanted to fire on the forts just to bother them. So we began to shoot randomly, and they responded with fire so intense it was as if they were trying to drive back a much larger force. This went on for a quarter of an hour, after which we heard a train whistle in the vicinity of Palos, less than two kilometers from the plantation.

After these crazy events, Castillo wanted to have a cup of coffee that we had ordered to be made on the farm San Gabriel, close to the area of Palos. The Spanish allowed the owners to remain at the San Gabriel farm because they thought that it would be impossible for them to be useful to the insurrectionists; because, during the day, in that area, the Spanish could see everything that went on. When we arrived to have coffee, Castillo entered the shed of the farmhouse, but I didn't follow him. Because it had an iron fence, we were able to enter or leave only one at a time. While he was trying to persuade me to enter, and while holding the cup of coffee in his hand, I could hear a loud group quickly approaching from two different sides. I pricked up my ears, and I could hear someone say, "Quickly to the left flank." I realized that it was the Spanish cavalry, and I alerted him: "Castillo, soldiers!" At this, he dropped the cup even though he had not finished the coffee he had wanted so badly, and left the shed in a hurry. If the two of us had been inside together, as he wanted, in the ensuing rush to leave one by one, we would have been killed, because as soon as we left the house, the Spanish closed off both flanks, and shouted, "Halt! Who goes there?!" They responded "Spain! Spain!" in order to recognize one another. With the stillness of the night that helps to project the voice, I could hear them ask the family the reason for the noise that they had heard—our leaving. The family replied that the noise was the horses. Because they couldn't be used, they were loose and always running away at the slightest noise: "When they heard Maroto's brave cavalry, those poor animals were frightened. Look closely to make sure that the *mambises* didn't take them all when they heard you coming," they added. They were convinced, those "lions" (in Castilla). Indeed, they didn't want to look too hard for us; every time we had enough ammunition, despite how much they fought, they had to retreat, because our valor made the battle too intense for them. This is why I don't honor as "lions" (in Cuba) that army, an army that once all of Europe respected.

After hearing the response that the family gave to Maroto's soldiers, Castillo and I went quickly to look for the two oxen we had hidden a short distance away. We brought them back with us to the camp at Purgatorio, bringing fresh food to our comrades. It was the 24th of December, Christmas Eve, the day that Christian humanity celebrates with meals and merrymaking. I can say to you, reader, that on such a day our comrades were overjoyed to see us again with two oxen. Although the day before we had brought back four, it was because of that success that they thought we wouldn't bring back any the next day. Normally, after an initial success, the area is watched more closely, increasing the likelihood of an ambush. But we were lucky that night that the Spanish didn't believe that we had the nerve to return. Our luck served us well, although we were at greater risk of being caught by the claws of Colonel Maroto's cavalry.

We stayed in the Purgatorio camp for several days, allowing the cavalry to recover until the then colonel, Pedro E. Betancourt, arrived. He was commander of the Northern Brigade to which we were earlier ordered to escort General Juan Fernández Ruz.

buena conduci

Yo supongo que
ya estarás en liber-
tad porque el Fiscal
de esta Audiencia
dijo que habra escri..
al Juez de Alacra..
que es un buen hom-
bre y muy justo ..
.. que te pusiero..
en libertad pro..
General hasta que
se celebre el juicio
oral en la Audiencia
y como en esa ca..

II.

*Batrell's regiment takes the town of San Nicolás by surprise.—
Batrell serves under the commander Pedro Betancourt.—Pays a
fortune to have horse shod.—Attack on Spanish column.—Gets
separated from his unit and wanders into enemy lines.—Massacre
of mambises at Oito.—Severely injures his leg and left by unit
dangerously close to a Spanish camp.—Witnesses Spanish murder
of a civilian.—Encounter with the treacherous presentado Roque.—
With leg healing, retreats to Viajaca.—Steals Commander Domingo's
horse, and reflects on General Rosa's reputation as a cannibal.—
Relates two events at Cana Blanca: almost being captured by the
Spanish and the narrow escape of a dear friend, Leocadio.—Serves
as lookout for the camp and narrowly escapes a Spanish ambush.—
Contracts a fever at Loma Blanca and endures a difficult march
while sick.—Retrieves a cache of arms.—Arms distributed unequally
to regiment according to race.—Attack by Spanish at the Regalito
sugar mill.—Batrell tends to his sick brother.—Made lieutenant
aide.—More reflections on the presentado Cajizote.—Fire on the
Spanish cavalry.—Batrell's unit fires on Molina's column.—The
reading of Paco's letters.—Molina returns with greater forces.—The
attempt to cross the footpath from Camarones.—Batrell protects his
unconscious brother.—Retrieve arms from Camínar.—Fierce battle
with Molina on the hill of Pan.—The betrayal by Cayetano.—March
to unite with Clemente Gómez's unit.—Spanish forces attack Gómez's
and Sanguily's respective units.—Combined Cuban units stage an
ambush, and a pitched battle ensues.—Reflections on the nature of
warfare in Matanzas.—Various skirmishes with the Spanish.—
Wounded mambises defend themselves against overwhelming
numbers.—The death of Lieutenant Colonel Escobar.*

1897

IN THOSE FIRST MONTHS OF THE YEAR, Colonel Pedro E. Betancourt's regiment, our force, marched with Colonel Cuervo, commander of the Southeastern Brigade of the province of Havana, and his brigade. During that period, we attacked the towns of Nueva Paz[1] and San Nicolás,[2] and we took them both without incident. We had thought that only San Nicolás was protected by a fort, but after getting inside the town we discovered that there was a Spanish column camped there. They didn't seem to notice our presence at first, until we were already in the streets walking up on those exhausted soldiers resting in the sheds next to the houses. We were right on top of them, taking them for *pacíficos* and *reconcentrados,* and they, in turn, took us for loyalists because the night was so dark and rainy. I say that they thought we were loyalists because of the way that they finally realized who we were. One of our soldiers walked under one of the many hammocks that were hanging in the sheds, and when he disturbed the soldier sleeping in the hammock, the soldier said, "Be more careful because I'm Sergeant Muñoz."

When he said that, we realized that all whom we had come across were enemy soldiers, not *pacíficos* as we originally thought. At that moment we broke the silence with a cry of "Viva Cuba Libre!" and then the crash of gunfire began; up until that point its hoarse and terrible voice hadn't been heard. We were able to enter the town with great stealth and operate in their region because Cuervo's regiment had many soldiers who were from there and who knew where the forts were. Therefore, they served as our guides. Also, the darkness of night helped us, and the rain made the lookouts take shelter, although their officers didn't know this.

It's impossible to describe their exclamations when the column saw the enemy inside their town, and right in their camp. They ran into the streets, and you could say that their scattered shots dried the fine and

---

1. Nueva Paz: A town near the Havana/Matanzas border, approximately twenty-two miles south by southwest of the city of Matanzas.
2. San Nicolás: A town near the Havana/Matanzas border, approximately twenty-five miles southwest of the city of Matanzas.

persistent rain that was falling, mixing with their shouts of "Viva España!" and "Viva el Colonel Maroto!" To which we shouted back, "Viva Cuba Libre!" and "Viva!" to our various commanders, without interrupting the *danzón*[3] rhythm of gunfire that deafened the entire area.

We took the town on foot as infantry, then left at three in the morning, returning to where we had left the horses. We camped in the hills of Guanamón in the area known as Hato de la Manteca,[4] about three leagues from San Nicolás. It was our normal procedure to wait there in the early hours of the morning for the Spanish column to follow. Our regiment stayed in a secured position and guarded our trail that the enemy was going to follow. And they did indeed follow us, coming along the trail at nine in the morning, but they were content just to kill one of our scouts who, because of fatigue and the bad night, had fallen asleep under a tree a short distance from the camp. We found this out later from the other scout who had gone out with him.

After more than an hour had passed without the arrival of the enemy, new reconnaissance was ordered. The scouts brought back news that they had only seen a trail of blood where the first lookout had been killed, and the other soldier had gone off toward the vicinity of Las Vegas, leaving our comrade for dead. The Spanish column was afraid of running into us after making our unfortunate comrade their victim. Indeed, it would have been something terrible to behold if they had followed our path to the center of our camp at Hato de la Manteca.

From there, our regiment separated from Colonel Cuervo's forces. (Cuervo surrendered a few months later, turning to the protection of that damned governor Weyler, the executioner of Cubans.)

We marched under the command of the brigade colonel, Pedro E. Betancourt. We made our first camp in Zapata, between Tinajita and the colony of Cuco of the central Conchita.[5] We stayed there several days,

---

3. *Danzón:* A slow, rhythmic music and dance style popular in Cuba in the nineteenth and early twentieth centuries.

4. Hato de la Manteca: An area about nine miles from San Nicolás. The "Hato" no longer exists.

5. Cochita: On the Zapata Peninsula in the province of Matanzas.

and when our horses had finished grazing in the pastures there, we moved on to Cuco in an area called Alianza;[6] we stayed there three days. I remember that because my horse didn't have any horseshoes; it could barely walk through the rocks of the mountains of Zapata. So I asked a prefect who had four horseshoes, from Colonel Álvarez's supplies, to shoe my horse with them. He looked at me with astonishment, as if I had asked him to touch the sky with his hand. So then I showed him a handful of centenes, as many as I could hold in one hand, and I said, "If you shoe my horse, I will give you all of these."

He wanted to refuse, but the brilliance of the shining gold before his greedy eyes made him hesitate, and then I knew that he would do what I asked. Later, I came back making the same offer, and I could tell from the anxiousness that he showed so clearly that he had already made up his mind. At that moment I made my offer again, saying, "This is proof of my resolve," as I took off my hat and threw the gold coins into it.

"Which is your horse?" he asked me, and I showed him my horse; and so he went to his work. After he finished, for curiosity's sake, we counted the gold coins, and there were twenty. Fifty would have been all the same to me. In those days, money was of little use to someone like me who was in the army, always on the move, without any fixed place, and without so much as the hope of sending into the towns for whatever we didn't have in our camps.

The day after I paid 106 pesos to have my horse shoed, we moved the camp to another place on the same mountain, Galeón.[7] We camped in Oito between Galeón and Sabana Grande. That day I was on guard duty, guarding the road that went from the camp toward Sabana Grande.

The Battle of Oito

It must have been eight in the morning on one of the days in February when it was ordered, as we had come to expect, that pairs of scouts go out in different directions in order to gather information about the enemy. One pair was ordered to go along the road that went from the camp toward Hato de Jicarita, until the two came to the main road of Bolondrón

---

6. El Cuco in Alianza: A region located in the province of Santa Clara.

7. Galeón: A camp on one of the mountains in Zapata.

where there was an old store, El Galeón. Once there, they both went to sleep, at some distance apart, under the shade of some trees. They hadn't learned the lesson from the episode when the Spanish killed one of our scouts near Guanamón. And so the vanguard of Colonel Pavía's column surprised them where they were resting. How unfortunate for our forces, because we always lost more soldiers in our battles with Pavía's column than in our battles with any other column.

Because the trees were a good distance apart where they surprised our careless scouts, they could kill only one of them. When the other scout heard the noise that the soldiers were making as they made their surprise attack, he jumped on his horse and rode quickly back to camp with the Spanish following close behind. But they didn't shoot at him because they wanted to kill him with their bayonets. They arrived at the same time as our fugitive guard. This was the situation when twelve of our guards came to realize that they had Pavía's vanguard and our careless scout all inside the camp. He was riding hard, as you'd expect, and none of them were slowing down as they approached the camp. We opened fire on the Spanish as they flew toward the camp where not two hours earlier everyone had unsaddled their horses, assured that the scouts would provide security and would bring back news of the enemy before they appeared. But as the scout and the enemy entered the camp at the same time, it was difficult to saddle some of the horses while other soldiers were firing on those guerrillas from Matanzas who always served as Pavía's vanguard.

That day we were reinforced by Bolondrón's forces, made up of local peasants who knew every nook and cranny of the area. So they could appreciate the position that we were in as we realized how difficult it would be to maneuver our horses in that terrain without the support of the infantry. Reader, you can imagine our situation with a Spanish column inside our camp and in terrain difficult to navigate because of so many rocks! There were many holes in the ground, some so deep that they could swallow a horse that was unfortunate enough to fall into one.

We were accompanied by additional troops, guards who came from a different direction than the enemy. They were the following: Liberoto Acosta, corporal, Sergeant Candelario Alfonso, and several other corporals. But they had to serve as guards like foot soldiers because our forces had been depleted by the trip to Colón, during which only those of us with good horses continued to fight. We had twelve men in this situation, unable to occupy their proper place in the ranks because we had to fulfill all the required duties of the camp. I cite the names of those soldiers to the best of my memory: Pedro Lamar, Casimiro, Cayetano Valera Flores, Domingo Hernández, my brother Bernabé. And there were three more who helped, but I don't remember their names.

When the fighting in the camp was at its most intense, I said that we should follow the other soldiers in retreat, but the others, perhaps because of their greater maturity and experience, didn't agree. They feared that without knowing exactly where the worst part of the battle was, we would run into it, face-to-face as it were. But someone like me, not yet seventeen years old, is prone to making mistakes. Was I going to abandon the camp as if the sky were falling? I followed my brother toward the camp, but I couldn't hear what he was telling me. After I caught up with him, I avoided the fighting by going along the edge of the woods that went toward the west. Three or four others, who were hanging back, followed me until they got to the border of the woods; they didn't follow any further because it was the route that the unarmed were taking to retreat to the camp. Their survival instinct told them to stay around there, given that without knowing the positions of the opposing forces, there was the real possibility that they could get caught in the crossfire. The camp probably had ropes ten inches long and three inches thick out in the open to mark its boundaries.

The two groups of fighters were positioned in different parts of the cane fields, as I remained standing in the camp without knowing which cane field the Cuban forces were in. The shots whizzed by me from both forces, while I stood there anxiously wanting to take part in the *danzón* of Cuba Libre. The shots flying by confused me because the cane leaves made it difficult to distinguish our troops from the Spanish. After a few seconds of indecision, I finally had the bad luck to choose the cane field where Pavía's evil soldiers were hiding. Just as I stepped through the first cane stalks, the bloodthirsty guerrillas prepared to open fire. The guerrillas and I ran into each other at the foot of a jagüey tree, a leafy tree that grows in the area. I could then identify those I had tried to avoid when I was choosing where to enter the cane field. When they saw me they shouted "Viva España!"

And they tried to kill me with their machetes, so I turned to run. At that moment, I thought that they had knocked me down with their "magnificent" horses. I didn't fire my rifle, as I had intended, because I thought that I was dead after getting hit by the horses. But when I realized that they hadn't knocked me down, and as we fought man to man, I had the hope that I would survive. I opened fire because the horses continued to advance on me. Then, after that first shot I heard, "Shoot him, Juan Manuel! He killed Santos Vegas's horse!"

I shot again and knocked Juan Manuel off his horse with a shot through his left leg, although at that moment I didn't know where I'd hit him. (We would eventually be seeing these same Bolodrón soldiers switch to our side during the blockade of 1898.) When the evil Juan Manuel fell, they shouted, "Shoot! You can't kill him with a machete!"

By then I had reached my lines that had pulled back from the position they had been holding when I mistakenly entered that hostile area. When the guerrillas started to shoot at me, Lieutenant Juan E. Abreu—we called each other "cousin," because of our mutual regard—saw my situation and joined me, opening fire on them. Then the guerrillas stopped their horses and waited for the infantry of their damned column, the most deadly force for us.

When the infantry got there, there was a great slaughter because the infantry came to the entrance of the mountains where my comrades in the guard were retreating, those who had followed me but had hung back a bit, and so didn't make the same disastrous decision that nearly got me killed that day. We were the last to arrive at that wretched pass where we had to enter single file in two rows, making ourselves targets for the Spanish. Our group was Brigadier Betancourt, Juan E. Abreu, and Sanguily. They were the only ones to survive, and they're still alive to write about it. Others, including commanders and officers, died there. When we got there the slaughter was horrible. Because of insufficient ammunition, our troops weren't able to fight back against the deadly Spanish fire and so they couldn't get through the pass.

Our group was almost all from Inglesito's forces. Inglesito had been killed a few days earlier, in an attack on the guerrillas from San Nicolás.

I believe that that attack was the reason that we took the town, which wasn't even in our province; nevertheless, they took from us a jewel—Inglesito—that was invaluable in the war.

This group, to which I just referred, charged on the Spanish column that was deployed in the form of a horseshoe. And at a distance of less than a city block, the Spanish killed a horrifying number of us, nearly everyone; and no one killed had a rank lower than corporal. Unfortunately, I was the last to go through that pass, and so I could see the ground covered with bodies. We suffered eighteen dead. Among them was our commander, Lieutenant Colonel Eduardo Rosell, commander of the general staff, to which Captain Fernando Diago had already been proposed for promotion. Diago's horse was wounded with three gunshots for his heroism in the battle, and Claudio Poyendo was killed, a brave youth only eighteen years old; he fell carrying his Winchester close to his commanding officer. It was a memorable day too in that afterwards Captain Fernando Diago was promoted to Commander Rosell's post because of Diago's exceptional valor, an example for the entire force. Cuba would be happy if many of its white sons were like Colonel Diago.

Although the Spanish killed our commander, Colonel Eduardo Rosell, his conduct showed that he was from a distinguished family. Because of the uniform that he was wearing, they thought that he was Brigadier Pedro E. Betancourt. When they arrived at the opening where the ground was covered with the dead, those outlaws' shouts reverberated throughout the area with the cries of "Viva España!" and "Viva María Cristina!"[8] Afterward, they took over our camp, and took two of our oxen. We had to leave all of the dead right there where they had fallen.

The ironies of war! All who were killed that day were the ones who took most of the booty in the taking of San Nicolás. Commander Rosell, as commander of the general staff, not only took important papers, he

---

8. María Cristina: The rallying cry of loyalty to the Spanish regime in Cuba. María Cristina was the wife of Fernando VII of Spain. When Fernando died in September 1833, his daughter, Isabel, inherited the crown. But Fernando's brother, Carlos, insisted that he was the rightful successor, therefore precipitating a war of succession, the first "Carlista" War. Thus "Viva María Cristina" originally signaled loyalty to direct succession from Fernando VII. Here it also champions the army division named after the queen.

also took five hundred coins from the war contribution. Captain Zalazar, who also died, was the medical officer of Rafael Águila's squadron.

What was left of Inglesito's force objected to their new commander's style of command; he wasn't a man of action when compared to Inglesito's fighting style, may he rest in peace. On that date, the group didn't accept José Antonio Laza as their commander, and marched on with Inglesito's older brother, Coliseo, to the Río de Auras area where he would be killed a few days later. This fraction of a squadron was wiped out as well. Such was the character of the War of Independence; a brave commander of a small force would fall, and then the force would disintegrate if the soldiers didn't feel that their new commander was as brave as the one whom they'd just lost.

There in Oito, Lieutenant Perfecto Acosta fell; he was also part of Inglesito's forces. But he didn't die in battle; in fact, he was one of the ones who made a desperate machete charge into the Spanish lines at that hopeless pass. He was already acting like a commander of a regiment that he didn't even belong to. This heroic lieutenant, a black officer, died later, close to the Spanish lines. But they couldn't kill him that day because fighting beside him was his brother Salutiano, a soldier of lower rank, but equally as brave. Salutiano jumped off his horse and threw Acosta on his shoulder and, almost beneath the horses' hooves of those bloodthirsty guerrillas from Matanzas, reinforced by the guerrillas of Bolondrón, the two made their way to the woods a short distance away. A few days later the lieutenant died from his wounds. The brother buried him and marched off to resume his position as sergeant, the rank he had before this battle. He wasn't awarded a higher rank even though he showed the same heroism as his brother who died in that holocaust for the liberation of his country. But for very rare exceptions, there did exist during the war this antagonism and antidemocratic spirit.

The rest of the wounded, of which there were few, remained under the command of the prefect at Alianza, who was in the line at that unfortunate pass. (It was there that three months before my heartless comrades had eaten the goat.)

The Spanish left our camp at four in the afternoon, after taking all of the money from the dead. Then, just an hour later, a commissioned group went out to bury the dead whom the Spanish had left. That battle was unfortunate for us because we had never had so many killed due to the forces from the forts of Camínar in Antonia. The first time that the commission went out to bury our dead, they couldn't do it because the Spanish column that was still camped there would shoot at them. But finally they were able to bury them close by. Also, the unit was frightened by the unsubstantiated rumor, despite what I said to the contrary, that Sanguily had been killed. I told them that I saw him get to the woods safely when they killed the horse next to me, but my comrades continued to insist otherwise. Because Sanguily was such a good commander in the war (although in peace his reputation has been sullied), Castillo and Abreu went to see if the rumor were true. Castillo, the second in command, and Abreu, the lieutenant, were crying like little boys who had just lost their father. They were all together and so couldn't see, as I did, what happened next.

I was the last to enter that cursed pass because I didn't get off of my horse. Captain Toribio, of Águila's forces, got there as did Lieutenant Alfredo Gonzales, better known as el Gago, from the same force. They saw that it was impossible to get through the pass, so they jumped off of their horses and went toward the woods, although they were close to the pass.

The temerity to stay on my horse allowed me to see the scene more clearly than many of those brave ones that day. I could even see where they shot Commander Rosell, who was at the side of the pass with his machete unsheathed, fighting fiercely at the opening. At that moment they shot him in the left side of the chest.

Our only good luck that day, after so much misfortune, was that our commander, Brigadier Betancourt, didn't see Commander Rosell fall, because if he had, only the facts can describe what would have happened. Those of us who knew of the general's exceptional bravery, especially in a fight like this, knew that he would do anything to avenge his friend's death, because those two loved each other so much; they even looked like brothers. But when General Betancourt got to the pass, he couldn't see Rosell because moments before, nearly surrounded by the Spanish column, Betancourt's horse fell into one of the many holes in Zapata. And when he got off of his big horse in that deep hole the horse hit him in the head, in the eye that then became swollen. While the general was getting his horse out of the hole, Abreu, Sanguily, and I were at his side shooting so that those ruthless guerrillas couldn't get to him. And at that moment an orderly was shot and fell across the general's chest so that Colonel Diago couldn't see him. Because of the orderly, we all waited to see if the general had been killed by the gunfire.

Before the scouts returned from the battle, Sanguily arrived on foot at the new camp, Los Cocos, in Tinajita. After them, Captains Toribio and Alfredo (el Gago) arrived also without horses, as I had thought they would. Others arrived who had also lost their horses because of the intensity of the fighting in that massacre in the pass called "The Cemetery."

That afternoon, after everyone reunited, we began the march back to our zone after the burial party returned from burying our comrades who had fallen so heroically in that fateful battle. The small infantry in our area, under the command of Loreto Escobar, was soon reinforced. Once reinforced, the general ordered that Colonel Sanguily, my commander at the time, be the unit's chief commander, and that Escobar be its second in command. Meanwhile, a very brave cavalry unit, of which Rafael Águila was put in charge, was operating in the area. We made up the infantry that was called the Infantry Regiment of Mantanzas. None of us had good horses. Even though I had paid twenty gold coins to have my horse shoed in the days before Oito, the horse wasn't very good. As it turned out, the horseshoes only made the retreat easier the day after I had had the horse shoed. But if I had had the horse shoed a day earlier, God only knows how it would have turned out when I mistakenly ran into those vile guerrillas! But before the horse was shoed, it was impossible to walk through those rocks, although I used my spurs harshly. So, because my horse wasn't of very high quality, I stayed in the infantry, as everyone in my situation did.

We Continue as an Infantry Unit in the Month of March

The first time that the Spanish infantry attacked us, it was in the same place where our company had been formed under the command of Escobar. This was in the area known as Viajaca, a mountain ridge between Madruga and Nueva Paz. I would be the *práctico*[9] who would eventually

---

9. *Práctico:* An enlisted soldier who, because of his familiarity with the region, is designated as the temporary guide for the regiment.

save the force, although I didn't know the area well; I hadn't seen the area since the days Castillo and I came there from Prendes on a mission.

It turned out that when the shooting started the unit fell back in confusion for lack of a *práctico,* although there were some who knew more about the area than I. Indeed, the more experienced ones had the moral responsibility for finding a way to escape, but no one wanted to take that responsibility. So I took the lead. And because we were taking fire from the Spanish and didn't have enough ammunition to shoot back, the other soldiers wanted to run. When I didn't run, they knocked me down in their haste to retreat. The unit had between three hundred and four hundred men. As we were going down a steep incline, I was thrown down hard, and the company trampled over me. My leg got caught in one of the crags in the rocks and was dislocated from the force of the blows that I received.

At nightfall we began to march to the mountain of Zapata. This was our first march as infantry, our first march of real self-sacrifice and one for which we had no experience. This was especially difficult for me because since the age of seven I had always traveled by horse, until I joined the Liberation Army, and even then I always had a horse because I was in the cavalry. So in this first march on foot, I really didn't appreciate this kind of sacrifice. And to make things worse, my leg was wounded and hurt so much that it was almost impossible to walk.

That march was one of the most painfully cruel marches of the entire war, because I had to walk on a badly injured leg for the four leagues from Viajaca to the woods of La Margarita or Los Cocos (Zapata). We left for Viajaca at 5:30 in the afternoon, with me in the sad condition that I've already described. It was impossible for me to keep up with the healthy soldiers; so the soldiers arrived at Margarita at daybreak, and I, who came with the rest of the wounded, arrived in the full light of day. In fact, I was just arriving when they were getting in formation to begin the next march toward the nearby woods of Pedroso. I was completely covered in dirt because sometimes I had to crawl on the ground just to get there. What a sad beginning in the infantry! All of my comrades and my brother, Bernabé, criticized me for not having warned them about my condition and how slowly I was moving. I just responded that I was bearing the pain as best I could.

I was able to continue on the march because Bernabé, who was in the cavalry, joined our infantry. He also reprimanded me for my self-pity and insisted that I take his horse; I did and rode the two kilometers from Margarita to the woods of Pedroso. We set up camp there, while Sanguily made a separate camp with his wife and her assistant so that she could rest peacefully; I stayed with them. There, my dear friend Leocadio Montalvo Pérez (Tito) took care of me. During this time, our regiment had to retreat, because on the sixth day we were camped there, the unit fought with Aguilera's column. After the battle, our forces marched to the woods of Camarioca, close to the town of Cárdenas.[10]

During the month of May, it was impossible for me to walk, though Spanish troops, under Colonel Pavía's command, were all around. His troops were marauding through those woods because they had their headquarters in Bermeja—a neighboring town—and so they were marching around through the area. They were so close that every day they shot at our camp, and they shot some of the defenseless civilians who were living in those woods. There were several African families in those woods; they didn't want to be reconcentrated in the Spanish zones, and preferred to die there. Indeed, more than two hundred civilians died, hunted down as if they were wild animals. Every day, the Spanish column would come to our area just to show five or six bodies, people whom the Spanish cowardly murdered, claiming that they were insurrectionists from the town. What the Spanish didn't know was that they were just unfortunate old people who didn't want to die of hunger in those sad reconcentration camps. They preferred to live in the woods surrounded by the banana-tree plantations, and did so until their lives were cruelly uprooted by the bloodthirsty and evil Spanish. This happened every day.

There was one particular peasant family that refused reconcentration; they stayed very close to the area where we were camped, and so I was in a good place to hear their conversations as they talked in their camp. One day a Spanish column arrived there. In order to intimidate this family they shot at them; then they took them prisoner after killing

10. Cárdenas: A port town in the province of Matanzas, approximately twenty-five miles east of the city of Matanzas.

one man they said was an insurrectionist. They killed him with a machete as he sat on a stool, sick from a fever.

While this was going on, there was another tragedy perpetrated by those damned Matanzas guerrillas, this just as Pedro María and his assistant, Pablo Espinosa, were retreating with a sergeant in Colonel Álvarez's forces. The sergeant's name was Roque. I was with my devoted comrade and friend Leocadio Montalvo; he didn't want to retreat with the others because I still couldn't walk, even though we insisted that he retreat. We presumed that that family, out of fear of being victimized, and knowing we were there, would turn us in to the Spanish. I said to Leocadio that he should retreat with the others, just as they had insisted. But my devoted comrade refused to do so. In fact, I even threatened to surrender in order to force him to leave with the others. I had to make such a threat because he was so extremely devoted and loyal. But still, he simply refused to leave.

The Spanish asked that family that they had just taken prisoner if there were more insurrectionists or other families in the area. And despite the threats of death the Spanish soldiers made, the family didn't inform on us. Finally, the Spanish were satisfied with the family's misfortune, and the family said nothing of our camp nearby; and so I was saved from certain death.

The Spanish soldiers retreated with the imprisoned family, just after the family had seen one of their loved ones killed right before their eyes. They hadn't committed any other crime than not having gone to the reconcentration area; and yes, they had stayed in the insurrectionist zone. When we no longer heard the sound of conversation from the column, Leocadio left in the direction of our camp, to see if our regiment had retreated successfully. He returned with the stool that that sad old man had been sitting on when the Spanish killed him; it was covered with blood that was still warm. I sat on the stool so that he could treat my wounded leg. After ten days, and with a kind of crutch, I was able to walk, but I couldn't put any weight on my leg.

While coming back to our camp, Leocadio had an argument with Roque—one of Álvarez's sergeants—whom we ran into in those woods. While they were arguing, I limped up to them on my crutch and took my friend's side. But Roque didn't want to listen to our arguments; he called me a little boy, and said that I wasn't part of the discussion. Seeing that I couldn't stand up well without my crutches, he acted like he was going to attack me. I had my 38-caliber revolver with me, my only weapon, and fired twice at that mistaken man. Perhaps because he was so large, and I was only seventeen years old, he didn't want to believe that I was capable of anything like shooting at him in defense of my good friend.

After I shot at him, he ran away into the woods. We thought that he would return later or go to Álvarez's regiment, but he did neither. In fact, he went to Bermeja and surrendered to the Spanish. It was certain that they would make him a prisoner or kill him as an insurrectionist from Sanguily's forces.

The day after the disappearance of that wicked man, Sanguily arrived at our camp bringing medicine, and by the following day I was better. The day that Sanguily arrived, the Spanish didn't come. Despite the guarantee that Pavía would take me prisoner, he wanted to allow a day before coming back to the camp. Perhaps he was confident in the information that the coward, Roque, had given him.

Roque didn't have the nerve to respond to my aggression in defense of my devoted friend; so he wanted to take revenge by giving me over to the most bloodthirsty Spanish column that was marauding through the area. And they wanted to be able to present my dead body the same day that I argued with that fugitive.

Our soldiers didn't come the next day to attend to me because I had improved so much. It was the hand of Providence, because if I hadn't improved, Roque, who had just surrendered, would have satisfied his lust for revenge on me. Indeed, after three days, he returned at nine in the morning to get me!

But by then I could retreat from the camp, although with sharp pains in my leg. Sanguily, Pedro José del Castillo María, his assistant, Pablo Espinosa, and my good friend Leocadio all were able to retreat much faster than I because my wounds hadn't completely healed. I was able to march until I got to a ceiba tree that had been full of leaves sometime before, but had fallen down and was now decaying. It was a roadblock for me; so I lay down on the ground next to the tree, and covered myself with dirt; and as it turned out, that saved me.

If I hadn't hidden next to the tree, those evil Spanish would have caught me. Their only exploits during those months were with the family that refused to be reconcentrated, and with the sick who couldn't keep up with their regiment. Now they were crossing right over the spot where I was lying, and they said to the *práctico,* Roque, "Didn't you say that one of them couldn't walk. How was he able to get away?"

After the questions they kicked him and hurled more insults at him. I could hear everything perfectly from my hiding place.

At that moment a torrent of rain was unleashed on them, as those miserable outlaws deserved. When the rain started, those murdering guerrillas left with their vengeful *presentado* for the woods. The bugler began to play because the downpour was so heavy that it got as dark as nightfall in those woods.

When those guerrillas reunited, they walked along a path very close to where I was still lying on the ground, so I could hear perfectly the apologies of the *presentado,* as he reassured them that they would find me and kill me, given that I couldn't walk. It was true that I couldn't walk well, but as chance would have it, after I shot at that traitor, I could already put weight on my injured leg, and it continued to improve from that day on.

Roque apologized to the Spanish, while the head of the column slapped him and blamed him for their getting soaked and failing to find me. Indeed, the sudden downpour was very helpful because they couldn't search for me any longer. They certainly couldn't carry out their plan to kill a *mambí* fighter, this, according to what the *presentado* had told them, and given what they were saying to him: "Didn't you say that he was Sanguily's *práctico*? And didn't you say he couldn't walk? Why haven't we found him, you liar?"

In their retreat they took Roque's wife and her three daughters, and they killed two or three Africans who had been living close to us. Those poor Africans! They who didn't want to die of hunger, and so preferred to take their slim chances, without glory and without being remembered.

When the column retreated, it made it difficult for us to reunite because each one of us retreated in a different direction in order to avoid their shooting at the entire group. Given the situation, in the retreat you could see the different groups of guerrillas along the slope and among the trees.

But finally, we all reunited, and we passed the following day in the woods close by. And that night we began to march to Viajaca, the aforementioned ridge.

From there, Ortega went to the forces that were in Camarioca. Those of us who were in Pedroso stayed alone. In the month of June, Castillo came looking for Pedro María and his assistant Pablo Espinosa.

The day that Castillo arrived at Viajaca, Domingo also arrived; he was a commander in the Liberation Army, though a Spaniard. He was head of the Liberation forces of the province of Havana. And as one would want it to be at that time, several officers accepted positions of authority: José Cuervo, known in the war as Pepe Cuervo, as commander of the Southeast Brigade, and Massó Parra in the province of Santa Clara. These two men were Cubans with ranks that deserved admiration and respect, so much so that they should have had hearts overflowing with devotion to the land that had nurtured them. However, they gave up their positions with shame.

I had my doubts about Domingo even though he was a commander in the Liberation Army; he still seemed to have the aura of the peninsula about him. So while he was talking during the retreat, I took advantage of the darkness of the night and stole his horse, his rifle, and his 44-caliber revolver. The celebrated General Avelino Rosa was camped very close to us. In the morning, when Commander Domingo went to saddle his horse, he couldn't find it. That man roared like a lion in those woods. After he tired himself out trying to find his horse, and given that it belonged to General Alejandro Rodríguez, commander of the province of Havana, finally Domingo was directed to General Rosa's camp. Rosa offered to execute whoever had stolen the horse, so I didn't want to move it from where I had hidden it. But Castillo saw an opportunity to get to Pedro María on that same horse. In order to get the horse out of where I had hidden it, it was necessary to hoist it up by rope, because it was impossible for the horse to get out on its own. No one could explain how I had gotten the animal in there in the first place, and afterward I couldn't explain it either, because in the darkness of that night I still don't know how I was able to enter that part of the mountain ridge. But after a great effort we were able to get the horse out.

When Castillo and Captain Gabriel Hernández of our regiment retreated, Leocadio Montalvo, my devoted comrade, and I stayed together. He protected me in that period because I still couldn't march with the regiment.

From Viajara, Leocadio and I marched to the ridge called Caña Blanca, very close to Viajaca. We had to make this march because Rosa was insisting that he wanted to know who had taken Commander Domingo's horse. Rosa had earlier had the prefect, Pedro Valera, executed for a small infraction. So we marched to get away from the Colombian assassin. Even though he was a general in the Liberation Army, it seemed as though his purpose in the war was to kill Cuban liberation fighters. It was as if he wasn't really human; he was an adventurer who had traveled to all the American republics wherever he could fight in their wars. He loved war so much that he said that he had eaten human flesh. But when he saw that some of us didn't believe him, he tried to prove it. In one of the battles that took place at La Loma del Grillo, in an area known as Llano de García, the Spanish had left some of their dead and wounded on the battlefield. Rosa cut off some muscle from one of the dead soldiers in order to make a steak, and when he brought the flesh to the fire to roast it, Lieutenant Colonel Sosita grabbed it saying, "General, don't do that!"

To which that monster Rosa responded, "No, my boy, these Spaniards are good to eat, I have eaten them in South America. Their little fingers are delicious to suck because they are so juicy."

But in no way was Sosita going to let him eat human flesh. Indeed, he helped us by teaching us to eat horse meat. In the province of Matanzas, before he arrived, we didn't do that because no one had thought of it.

But let's get back to the subject, Caña Blanca, where we stayed until our regiment returned from Camarioca. There, we met three more comrades coming from Zapata: Julián Gómez, his brother Emiliano Gómez, and Julián's assistant. Two more of our forces from the fatal battle at Oito met there at Caña Blanca as well: Pedro Lamar and Casimiro. They stayed there with us because they chose not to march with the infantry, given that their horses were of little use at that time.

There were so many enemy columns in the area and so few of our regiments to fight them then!

We had many difficulties during our stay there, waiting for our regiment that was resting in Camarioca. I'll recount two such events. One day we were waiting for some of the *pacíficos* of Palos to return from foraging for food. We were talking with some of the women close to the road, when we heard an enemy column approaching through a glen very close to us. We didn't have time to escape so we jumped behind a nearby stone wall, leaving the women with a charred stick that we had been carrying. The first soldiers in the enemy advance guard saw us jump, but they couldn't be sure that we were insurrectionists, because the two whom they were able to see (both sons of Chinese immigrants) hadn't cut their hair for several months and they weren't wearing hats. So their long hair made them looked like women.

We flattened ourselves out in a straight line behind the wall because we couldn't do anything else to try to save ourselves. The only other thing there to hide us was a *romerillo* "French" tree, a type of bush, barely as tall as a grown man. From our hiding place, we could hear the questions that the soldiers asked the women: "Who were those people who just left?"

The women replied, "Just us. We were on the other side of the wall because we had to relieve ourselves."

Then the soldier asked, "Why do you have that smoldering stick?"

"In order to smoke," the women replied, "and if we have fire, the *mambises* leave us alone."

The soldiers then said, "You all look like *mambises* to me," pushing them ahead in order to take them to their commander, camped a mile or so from where we were hiding.

While the soldiers were talking with these reserved and loyal women, I held on to my dear friend Tito's shirt, which he all but ripped trying to get away from me. He wanted to try to slip away while they were talking because he thought the women would betray us, but I grabbed him tightly; if he had moved one bit, all would have been lost because they were on horseback and we were on foot. So, without the woods in which to escape, we would surely have been victims of those murderers' machetes. When they left for their camp, we left on the trail to our camp that was nearby. From there, we could make out the Spanish camp. They didn't know that the enemy was right under their noses, and Providence kept us from being their victims. In those few days those events clearly showed that in certain situations like that, you need as much bravery as in battle.

The other event was Rafael Águila's cavalry approach and attack on Palos's guerrillas. We left our camp and saw our forces make their charge. When we returned to our camp, we saw several strange footprints that I said were from the *pacíficos* fleeing the shots flying at the guerrillas who were running with them to hide in the woods. It was those guerrillas who were going to take our camp; so I thought it was a good idea to move. But my comrades didn't want to leave because we had ten traps in the area in which we were catching five or six animals daily. On the second day, I saw the suspicious tracks again, after hearing the noise of two battles, one with the Havana infantry and the other with the Havana cavalry. We thought that it wouldn't be dangerous near our camp that day because we assumed that the enemy columns that normally were close by would be marching toward the noise of the battles. But this wasn't the case. We were sold out by the *pacíficos,* the owners of those footprints that had made me so suspicious. And there was another reason to think that we were safe—at one in the afternoon it began to rain. So we found shelter in a cave and fell asleep there.

I was dreaming about our country's enemies, when at about four in the afternoon, I woke up and called my compatriots. They woke up as I left the cave and stood outside on top of an outcropping that made a roof for our cave. After five minutes, I heard Spanish voices haranguing the cavalry to close their flanks into a horseshoe formation in order for the infantry to go into the aforementioned woods.

I called my friend Leocadio to come out immediately to see that I wasn't still dreaming, as they had thought at first. Despite hearing the trampling of horses' hooves, he wanted to go out to a grove of trees that we used for a lookout spot in order to see if what we heard might have been the movement of our troops. We weren't separated by more than two meters when I saw a pair of guerrillas a short distance away looking at us. They didn't fire at us because they didn't want to hit the other flank. Because the infantry was just a short distance away in a small wooded area, the guerrillas waited for them to approach. Well, there was only a large square of woods separating us and it was very easy to walk through it because there were only small trees there. I didn't have time to tell my friend because those two miserable guerrillas were already so close. So I had to hide myself by lying down and crawling through the underbrush. Julián Gómez, Emiliano (his brother), and the assistant all followed me. But it was impossible to get away because the Spanish infantry was just ten steps away, coming through the little woods. I stopped under one of the trees that was full of leaves, and although it was the middle of the day and the sun was shining bright, it kept things dark.

Julián and Emiliano came with me; and before I hid myself, Julián's assistant ran for the woods around the demolished Brito sugar mill. It was safer there than in our little thicket of trees. Julián and Emiliano wanted to run there too, but I grabbed them because I heard Spanish officers' voices ordering the flanks of the cavalry to go around to the woods near our camp. When I grabbed the two brothers, they stopped trying to run because I showed them with a silent gesture that the enemy was directly ahead of us. And because the infantry was already too close, there was nothing else that we could do. So we all stayed there underneath that tree, our hiding place of salvation that day.

Five minutes didn't go by before Leocadio heard shots and the voices saying, "Give yourself up! Give yourself up!"

The cavalry shouted this at my friend, who thought I had followed him. During the confusion, we made our quick escape from that little grove to Brito.

When they shot at Leocadio, one of the bullets grazed Julián's assistant's head. He thought that it wouldn't be dangerous to run the short distance across the savanna to get to Brito. So, believing that they had shot at him, he ran from his hiding place and ran into a soldier of the cavalry who was just about to hit Leocadio.

That day was one of the most memorable days of the war. That poor assistant, whom they hadn't seen, was hit by a bullet meant for Leocadio, who had already been taken prisoner. So, running through the savanna without the cover of the woods, and on foot, with the soldiers of the cavalry closing in, I was sure that Leocadio had been taken prisoner or killed. But Providence saved him from that impossible situation. It made the assistant run in the belief that they had shot at him, but the shot had passed very close by Leocadio and so changed his life. The assistant fell over the soldier who was almost on top of Leocadio. Not only did this surprise the soldier, he stopped attacking Leocadio and turned to the assistant. And so the assistant interrupted the soldier while he was trying to tie up Leocadio. So Leocadio was able to escape by crawling away on his belly. If he had been standing, the other soldiers, the ones who weren't next to him trying to tie him up, would have seen him. But they weren't far from where I was, so I shouted, "Don't kill me. I will give you the one you're looking for. There's one who is Sanguily's *práctico*."

The soldiers all replied in unison that they would spare his life if I gave myself up to be taken prisoner (or possibly killed). But they asked where I was hiding, because they didn't know exactly where I was. I only said, "There are three more over there," but I didn't tell them exactly where my comrades were, and because the soldiers were getting wet from the drizzle without having completed their mission, they were getting very nervous. Meanwhile, because of the alarm of the shouting at Leocadio, the flanks thought that an entire force had come, so they withdrew from the area. And, as the soldiers were asking the assistant questions, it continued to rain. Because they couldn't find out from their prisoner where the other three were, their commander ordered them to form a march with the one unfortunate prisoner. But because he hadn't seen where we were hiding, he couldn't tell the Spanish. And so, in this way he saved us. We were so close—one meter away—to the flanks that we could see every detail of the feet and shoes of the infantry soldiers perfectly. In that tense situation, one guerrilla named Camacho wanted to inspect the "suspicious" *zarza* bush where we were hiding—that blessed *zarza*, our only salvation! But when that soldier was beginning to cut the foliage with his machete, one of the officers stopped him, telling him to fall into line as he had been ordered; and so he left the "suspicious" *zarza* uncut.

At that instant the sky cleared up. The first strike by that miserable guerrilla on the *zarza* that was our shelter made the branches and leaves move and almost hit us on the head. But God caused the Spanish officer to discipline Camacho, and so he wasn't able to hit the grass a second time. If he had continued to clear away the foliage, we would have been victims of the malevolent swords of the enemies of liberty. But the Spanish officer who reprimanded Camacho stopped him telling him to resume the march as he was ordered and to leave that "suspicious" *zarza* alone.

And he went on ridiculing him, saying, "You're not Spanish and you've never been to Madrid, so don't use a Spanish word like *'sospechosa.'*"[11] He was so mad that he almost hit him with his sword.

As it began to get dark, we finally left to look for another, more secure place for camp. We didn't find one, and the day after having been saved by a miracle, we were victims of our own foolishness for staying in that area. We went back to the same cave, but when we arrived, there was another problem in that none of my comrades wanted to go in for fear of an ambush. They had good reason for their fears; the cave was dangerous because we had to go all the way in to get to the spot where we had hidden our equipment. (We hid it to avoid losing it as we had before in a similar situation.) But because doubt and fear do not solve any problems, I had no other choice but to throw myself into it and to go in. We just couldn't leave without the equipment. I entered gropingly with my eyes shut because if it was an ambush, I wanted to be killed by surprise. I got to the spot safely, after so much fear, and took the equipment while my two comrades stood outside at a distance. Just in case they heard me cry out, they would be far enough away to save themselves. When I came out again, everyone admired me for having gone in. I gave them their equipment and we marched toward Viajaca.

The celebrated Avelino Rosa was no longer there, the one who had made us stop in that terrible grove of trees called Gavilán. This almost cost us our lives. During that march to Viajaca we walked with no one saying a word because I wasn't sure if Leocadio's luck had run out, although I had reason to believe that he hadn't been killed. I didn't know if he had been wounded by the shots from the cavalry or if he had escaped when they seized the other soldier. So I was very worried, although I thought that if he wasn't seriously wounded, he would go to Viajaca, just as we were going.

At around eleven o'clock that night we arrived at the woods just short of Viajaca, at a sugar mill, Valera Acosta, owned by a patriot by the name of Teresa Rueda. We told her what had happened to Juan Cabanga,

---

11. *Sospechosa:* Suspicious. At the time, a word more often used in peninsular rather than Caribbean Spanish.

75

a prefect in our regiment, who was in those woods with the sick and the invalids.

I didn't stay there to find out what had happened to my comrade Leocadio because an enemy column was camped close to the mill. Therefore, it would be impossible to walk through the area in daylight. The Spanish had already retreated late in the day, and so in the morning they would be able to use the assistant as a *práctico* and so cover the area meticulously. For all of these reasons I didn't stay.

The captain prefect, Juan Cabanga, had a pair of mounted scouts. I told him that he had a moral debt to honor all the dead, including Leocadio. It was his duty to tell the commander what had happened to the fallen in each case.

So, as soon as we informed him, he ordered his two scouts to saddle their horses and to go back to where all of these events took place and to find out what had happened to Leocadio.

The scouts completed their reconnaissance mission, but the only thing that they could find out was that the prisoner the Spanish took had been macheted to death during the night in the same camp; indeed, the body could be seen the following day. And as far as Leocadio was concerned, no more was known because they didn't see a trail of blood. The pair had returned to the camp at eleven in the morning, and by three in the afternoon our dear Leocadio appeared before us! Never before had I seen a human being so completely covered with thorns. It took me two days to get them out.

The next day I took lookout duty because we heard enemy fire close by. When I was watching the area from which we all thought the Spanish were coming, they came from the opposite direction, approaching me from the rear. If I hadn't had a natural crevice in the rocks to hide in, and if I hadn't been young and small enough to get into it, I would have been killed. I was on an elevated lookout spot, about twenty meters high. The rocks were high like walls, so there was no way for me to get over them, and the Spanish were behind me so I couldn't retreat.

My only protection was to get into that crevice that formed there naturally in those rocks. So I got a rock to cover the hole that I was hiding in, and the soldiers passed over me without realizing that they were walking over someone who would do them harm a month later. And so it appeared in those days that I was protected by the hand of the Divine Creator, and I would pass the test of war.

They went back after taking several families prisoner. And my comrades, who were still back at the camp, thought that I had been taken prisoner because they saw the Spanish column approaching, cutting me off from the camp; they didn't know that by chance I had found a place to hide.

When my comrades saw me coming back to the camp, they were amazed; they couldn't see how I had survived. When I explained to them how I avoided the enemy, they made me take them to the crevice so that they could see how I was able to save myself.

We stayed there at the sugar mill until the month of June when Camarioca's forces arrived. Then Leocadio and I joined that regiment.

From there, we went through the woods of Guanamón de Armentero to Viajaca. The day that our forces arrived at Viajaca and I saw my comrades once again was a very emotional time for my brother and my other close friends who thought that I was dead. They had been told what had happened at the little grove of El Gavilán where Julián Gómez's assistant was taken prisoner, but without all of the details, and it had been reported that I'd been killed.

At Guanamón, we were camped near the Providencia sugar mill, in the area of Güines. After fifteen days, an adviser from General Avelino Rosas arrived. After his arrival, we marched toward the Grillo hill, and from there we went to Loma Blanca, in the province of Havana. We went there in search of armaments because a Spanish expedition was in the area. That march was so difficult and memorable because fourteen men died of exhaustion! And during the march I became sick with a fever.

In Loma Blanca we met up with the infantry of the Havana regiment. They were under the command of Lieutenant Colonel Miyeres. We camped with this force for two days in order to rest, and we went looking for the arms and munitions that were nearby. On the third day there, the Spanish column of Guadalajara showed itself and we fought them for half an hour.

That day I thought I was going to be taken prisoner because I retreated in the first moments of the battle without knowing exactly where I was going. For two days running, I had had a fever so severe that I couldn't see. But my vision cleared up at the beginning of the retreat, after having received a face full of enormous scratches from some thorned trees. My entire chest was soaked with blood from the wounds on my face from the thorns. Finally, in this desperate state, I arrived at the Guanabo River. There, we waited for nightfall in order to march to the place where the arms and munitions were stored. Because we were at the edge of the sea, we walked in the water en route to the arms. Indeed, those who were healthy enough could walk in the water up to their knees in order to alleviate the fatigue of walking through sand. But I couldn't wade through the water; the waves kept knocking me over due to my delicate condition. So I had to walk in the sandy areas away from the waves, and the pain was unbearable. If the healthy had to walk in the water in order to avoid becoming overly fatigued, how difficult was it for me, already suffering from a fever? So, because of the fever and because it was at night, I got separated from the regiment; I just couldn't keep up with the pace of the forced march.

There were four or five other sick soldiers like me in the group. And I could see that some of them would surely die if they were left behind. Given this situation, and taking into consideration that we could see the lighthouse at El Morro in Havana, I made a concerted effort to keep up, and not to be left behind. I took a branch from a tree on the beach known as Uva Caleta and made a crutch to support my leg. This was the way that I tried to keep up with the rest of the force. I caught up with them at nine in the morning. When I arrived, they were resting beneath some mango trees, and of all of them I was the only one who hadn't eaten.

After a few minutes of my arrival—after I reported on the condition of the sick whom we had left on the beach—we reassumed the two-kilometer march to where the stash of arms was hidden.

Once we were there, Lieutenant Colonel Miyeres, the guard, and the expert for the supplies went inside the hiding place, and we began taking boxes of bullets of different calibers. And there were boxes of Remingtons too. How greedy we were to get them! And as we took them, our spirits were lifted; I confess that it is true that from that moment on, I felt inspired to confront the vicissitudes of war. We all wanted the Spanish to come. And as it turned out, we didn't have to wait long. We still hadn't finished distributing the load (I say load because there were seventeen thousand rounds and fifty guns divided among 250 men in the infantry), when shots were heard from the advanced troops who were just a kilometer away. When we heard the shots, we quickly finished dividing up the arms. We stayed in the same area, a small clearing in the woods that looked like a bullfighting ring or a baseball diamond. There, we all spread out, and kneeling on one knee, we waited for the enemies of liberty whom the shots had announced.

We waited there for more than an hour, deployed in lines ready to open fire. When the Spanish didn't arrive, a reconnaissance scout was ordered to go find out why. Our advanced guard who had retreated back to us, had engaged the enemy, but the Spanish hadn't arrived at our position. And we waited for them in three firing lines, well prepared to give them a feast of bullets that was sure to leave them quite satisfied. We hadn't eaten that day; nor had we eaten the day before because of our fight for liberty. So we were so hungry as we waited for them; we waited for our only possible meal: them.

The scouts returned with bad news for some, that the Spanish had retreated in the direction of Jaruco. I must confess that I was one of those who was really upset that those *cipayos*[12] hadn't arrived. Because, if they had, then maybe I would have gotten my payment, not only for the scratches on the face that I received the day before, but also for the terrible march that almost cost me my life (as it did for the other sick ones, whom I assumed would die. They fell in the sand with no hope, and surely they died there because there wasn't any food in the area).

But those Spanish were lucky that they didn't arrive there, because for each of our men that day, there was a box of one thousand bullets. Mohammed himself would have shaken with fear that day.

We collected our arms and went to camp close by. We divided the equipment we took; then our forces left in the afternoon to return to our area. Each soldier received more than two hundred rounds, an enormous

---

12. *Cipayo:* Sepoy. Literally, a native of India serving in a European army, usually the British Army. Normally, in this context, *cipayo* would serve as a pejorative for Cubans who fought for the Spanish, but in this particular case it functions as a general slur against Spanish forces.

weight. The same day, we passed by Jaruco. It was a dangerous area for such a small infantry force, but because we had so many rounds, perhaps we were a bit cocky.

In the first days of August, we arrived in our region and camped on the Plain of García (Loma del Grillo). It had been liberated the day before in a bloody battle with Colonel Raúl Arango y Sosita's forces, and it was now desolate like a graveyard. Sosita was on the same mission as we were, to resupply with arms and ammunition.

There, on the ground, we found lots of hats and other pieces of equipment from the Spanish soldiers. Some of the hats and equipment we found thrown up onto a ridge ten meters up—such was the punishing fire from the liberators. We camped there, and in the afternoon began a march toward Purgatorio. We arrived at our camp there at seven at night, weakened by fatigue. Just then, the celebrated General Avelino Rosa, then commander of the Mantanzas forces, ordered that we pick up the seventeen thousand rounds that we were carrying. After we piled them up, some were taken and we were left only three thousand rounds; he took fourteen thousand rounds from us to give to Sosita's forces. He did this only because every soldier in our regiment, from the last soldier to our commanding officer, was black, and Sosita was white, as were a great many of his soldiers.

The men in our unit almost cried because of this abuse from a superior officer. But as a severe punishment by Providence, those bullets that cost us so much (indeed, we lost fourteen men to fatigue in that march) were never used, not by Sosita nor for Cuba. What an injustice that that ammunition had been taken from us! With an antidemocratic spirit, Rosa took arms from us in order to give them to a force that hadn't proved itself, while we were an experienced veteran force of the highest quality.

Indeed, there was no other reason that could explain why he unjustly took the munitions from us, except for his racial prejudice. It would have been patriotic justice to have left us all of those armaments. Because it is well known that for a veteran force like ours there is no greater restorative medicine in war than to arrive in your region with a supply of ammunition. It elevates the spirit with the anticipation of punishing the enemy and making them respect us. In this way, Rosa's betrayal weakened us.

After three days, Sosita went to the woods of Zapata with that ammunition, claiming that they were in for a big battle. He made his camp in the woods of Pedroso, in the same place where three months earlier I had been injured and unable to march. There, they surprised Pavía's column, and killed more than twenty men, including Commander Francisco Guedes. They took almost all of the Spanish munitions.

We stayed in Purgatorio for two days, and then marched to Camarioca to see if we could rest in that region that had so many wild animals to eat. After we crossed the railroad tracks to Matanzas running through Guanábana, we stopped to resupply ourselves with meat, then continued our march. Later, a soldier in Clemente Gómez's infantry lost his rifle. At the time, Gómez's forces were coming from Purgatorio to unite with our regiment. We lit some *guano*[13] on the ground in order to look for the rifle. After we found it, the guerrillas from Matanzas began to shoot at us. They were camped near the place where we were hunting for food, but we didn't know that they were there. And surely they wouldn't have known that we were there either if we hadn't made that fire to look for the rifle. As soon as they shot at us, we went toward where we thought that they were camped, and returned their fire. That gunfight lasted an hour; then we marched and camped on the other side of the Canímar River, after wading through water up to our necks, at three in the morning.

We stopped at the sugar mill called Regalito, close to Canímar, and waited there safely for the enemy until early in the morning. Right when we got there we started to prepare a meal so that we would already be eating at daybreak, because we assumed that if we didn't run into the Spanish at night, we would see them by eight in the morning. And just as we thought, at 8:30 our guards and the Civil Guards exchanged shots. We all joined in the battle that went on for just a short time, but was successful nonetheless. We killed four men and five horses, and in their retreat they left two healthy horses along with all their equipment and clothes.

From there, we left with two more men from the cavalry in order to unite with ten or twelve more of Clemente Gómez's men; they served

---

13. *Guano:* Palm tree leaves usually used for thatching roofs.

as our scouts. We camped in Cuevas de Cuajaní, the same place where the regiment stayed for two months while I was sick, and where they had taken me for dead, given the information that the incoming soldiers had given them.

We were there for close to fifteen days with a great many sick soldiers, sick from that terrible march in search of those munitions. The last day there, we had a battle with Molina's column. Our retreat was difficult because we had so many sick soldiers who couldn't walk. My brother Bernabé was among the sick. While we were camped there, I had to attend to all of his needs, and during the retreat I had to carry all of his equipment. And so the retreat through those crags and across that stony ground was more difficult for me than for him. Indeed, I had to fight for him the way a lion fights to protect his cub. So this was what the retreat was like for me that day.

It was already afternoon when we started the march. I had a small argument with Sanguily because he didn't want me to stay with my brother in the area designated for the sick. But he couldn't get me to leave because I told him that no one had the authority to make me leave my brother alone in his condition or with someone else to take care of him. Given his delicate state, I wanted to stay with him because it was quite possible that he could have a turn for the worst. So Sanguily had to leave me.

Because of the great sacrifice Sanguily saw me making during the march to Loma Blanca, he named me his lieutenant aide, although at the time I didn't receive the official title because I was only seventeen years old. But while I was in the infantry in the Matanzas regiment I functioned in that capacity. It was my job to communicate orders during battle. Because I was so young, Sanguily took advantage of my age in not giving me the official title; this made me very angry at him. With considerably less enthusiasm, he wanted to give me the title, only to keep me from leaving his force. Not only did he need me in battle, I was the *práctico* in difficult marches, made worse by that criminal Weyler's invasion.

Let's return to the day that I stayed to care for my brother. When Sanguily saw that I wouldn't change my mind, he had no other choice but to leave me to care for my brother. We retreated to the woods near the Canímar River to see if he would improve there. There were fourteen other sick soldiers who couldn't march at all, some because of fever and others because of crippling fatigue. Many times in fact, up to two days would go by without food for these soldiers. The breakfast that we could find, just to have something in our stomachs, was red-roasted *mamey,*[14] or boiled avocado, and *curujey* water. The *curujey* is a weedlike plant that grows on the great trees there and keeps the dew and the rain on the leaves of the trees. We would stick a small hole in the leaf with a piece of wood and a small amount of water would pour out; although it was a bit muddy with dregs in it, it helped to quench our thirst.

And so a great weight weighed on those debilitated soldiers. They were all black men and all normally full of an indomitable vigor beyond description.

But the sick men who remained in Canímar all died, except for my brother, who survived because of my care. The morbid history of the Canímar River didn't defeat me, because every afternoon I crossed the river to find food for my poor brother. It was difficult because the river was high owing to the constant rain. So I had to go a half a mile or so to another spot that was shallower; I would hold on to *guayaba*[15] branches to steady myself, and wade across the river. On the other side, I would cut some cane stalks and throw them one by one across the river. I lost some in the river, but a few landed on the other side and during the night I made a kind of cane syrup. And I roasted two or three yams in the morning and served them for breakfast.

It was the responsibility of the other people taking care of the sick to do the same, but they didn't because they were afraid to go into the dangerously high water. So in the morning those poor sick soldiers had nothing for breakfast. And worse than that, if someone asked for water because they were unable to get up to look for it, his cruel nurse, if he was sleeping, woke up cursing him. He would say something like: "Why don't you just go ahead and die and stop bothering me!"

This is why some didn't bother to ask for water that they needed to

---

14. Mamey: A fruit-bearing tree native to the Americas.
15. Guayaba: The plant producing the guava fruit. Because of the strength and flexibility of the guayaba branch, it was traditionally used to whip horses.

quench their thirst. Seeing this, I was glad that I had stayed with my brother, who was the sickest but the only one to survive.

My brother benefited from the fact that I had eight pesos with which I bought a strip of meat every day from the prefect, Julio Rodríguez, who saved it in one of his bags. So, in addition to the cane stalks I just mentioned, we also had some meat for breakfast. But with no sense of pity, he stopped supplying me with meat when he saw that I had run out of money. But, given my brother's situation, I said that even without money, he would not go without meat! So, I got my rifle and without saying a word, carried it loaded to where Rodríguez had put the bag of meat, and I took the rest of it. When he asked me why I took it, I told him it was for my brother who needed to eat. We argued until it looked as though we were going to shoot each other; he had a revolver, and, as I said, I had my rifle. But he reconsidered the situation and let me take the meat. Given the scarcity of food, that little bit of meat should have been given gladly to the sick, out of human kindness. What a cruel comrade!

My brother improved quickly and from there we left for the hill of Mogote, climbing through the woods of Doméch (Arroyo la Vieja). He was able to walk, but he still hadn't regained his full strength. In this march we had to carry Colonel Cepero, whom we met near there. Several months before, he had received a wound that rendered one leg useless; he was wounded in a battle with the guerrillas of Limonar, where Cajizote was located.

As it turned out, Cajizote had had to abandon the glorious liberation cause. The white Cubans wanted to kill him, so he had no other choice but to surrender even though he was already a commander in the Liberation Army. In order to save himself he went to a town occupied by the Spanish. Cajizote had had the honor of having been distinguished by General Maceo in the invasion of the West. Indeed, this man was so anti-Spanish that before the war he never lived in compliance with Spanish rule. His patriotism made Cubans jealous, and so he was forced to give up his ideal of loyalty to his country. Those envious Cubans didn't dare to attack him openly; so, during one of his trips through the province of Havana he was demoted. This was the ultimate betrayal. There had been a great rivalry after the taking of the town of San Antonio de Río Blanco. There, Cajizote and his unit performed more heroically than the regiment of Havana that was three times as large. This filled the cup of bitterness for his enemies in the Liberation Army, and so they deceived him by citing him at General Aguirre's headquarters. So, when he arrived at the headquarters, already at the same rank as Aguirre, they promoted Aguirre above him and disarmed him. And later, all of his forces were divided and put in the regiment of Havana. So they eclipsed that black star, but they couldn't make him disappear, because what plans man makes, God can destroy. After three days of being held prisoner, he escaped from the guards and went to the protection of the Spanish lines.

We arrived at Mogote with Cepero on a stretcher, and were there a few days after giving him to the prefect. We were there less than ten days when our forces arrived and we joined them, my brother, Sixto Oviedo, and three others, and we all marched to the hill called Loma del Pan. We had rested a few days there, then one afternoon, when the force had gone out looking for food, Sanguily and I went to Clemente Gómez's camp that was on the side of the hill toward Corral Nuevo. We got there during a heavy rain, and we weren't there ten minutes before we saw a cavalry comprised of the Civil Guard and guerrillas. They came in order to cut off the retreat of our regiment that was all spread out in the valley foraging for food.

When I saw the situation, I wanted to open fire so that our troops would see that they were in great danger and so would be able to hide in the undergrowth that grew in that valley. But at first Sanguily and Gómez wouldn't let me shoot. The Spanish were just below us on the hill (we had nine men in our group), no more than five or six meters lower down, and we could hear a Spanish officer say, "Strike and cut them off on the hill and they are ours!"

I couldn't wait any longer and opened fire, and when I shot everyone else fired too. They were so close that we were able to do a lot of damage with just low-caliber revolvers, killing five horses and several men. We had caught them in a narrow pass where the path becomes a kind of canal with high ridges on both sides. So it was impossible for them to turn their horses around. They left us the horses, their equipment, and two shotguns. And they dispersed immediately because we opened fire on the central part of their forces.

So, in the face of our deadly fire, their vanguard retreated as quickly as it could. We left the trap that was formed naturally by the two ridges of rocks and crags, as the Spanish rear guard and the bulk of their force had to withdraw, after firing a few times at us in order to escape. Leaving that cemetery, they turned around toward the east to look for some of their soldiers who had scattered about a half a league away. The thick undergrowth prevented them from reuniting. We opened fire on those targets and estimated the damage our shots inflicted on them. Later we stopped to collect the booty of war that they had abandoned in their retreat.

Our soldiers were as thankful for the horses as for the rifles, because the horses served as a source of meat for those who couldn't go out to forage for food. And even though there were just a few of us, this scuffle could be considered combat, because we ended up with more booty than in other fights in which more of our forces participated.

From Pan we marched the next day to the nearby ridge, Palenque. We did this because at four or five in the afternoon the Spanish cavalry acted as though it were planning to attack us as we foraged for food, to avenge our infamous ambush. From Palenque we then went to the ridge called Ponce Centella and Picadura facing Canasí. We arrived at four in the morning and we camped in a place known as Cubilinganga.

The Battle of Cubilinganga:
The Mountains of Ponce, of Picadura, in the Jaruro Steps

When the sun came up, we saw an enemy cavalry force on the hill of La Botina. We climbed the ridge and at that higher elevation we began to prepare a meal; we wanted to save time in case the sighting of the enemy would mean a day of war. While our assistants prepared the food, Sanguily and I observed the movements of the Spanish cavalry down below. When the assistants finished, we ordered them to bring our meal to the spot where we were watching the enemy. As we finished eating, I heard a cough at the foot of the ridge. Because of the echo of voices I could tell they were Spanish. It took a great effort on my part to see who coughed. You see, the ridge was about eight meters or more above the Spanish location, and covered with trees; so it was difficult to see all the way to the base of the ridge. Nevertheless, I was able to see a formidable column of infantry. I suspected that they were the criminal Molina's forces. Indeed, I was right; they were his troops! The day before, they had brought a *presentado* to the town of Aguacate, making him serve as a *práctico* for those damned Spanish. They were sure that they had imprisoned an insurrectionist commander, and held him prostrate in the hut of a family that had refused Weyler's reconcentration. The family went deep into the woods, because one member of the family had gone to join the Liberation Army; his name was José la Campa, a merchant in my town. He had gone to the war, and after becoming an officer, the Spanish surprised him bathing in a river and hacked him to death with their machetes.

All the members of that family were sick, as were the commander and three or four more liberators, all of them officers. I said to Sanguily, "Let's open fire on those soldiers climbing the hill toward us, but don't know we're here."

Sanguily didn't think that this was a good idea, pointing out that we were short on ammunition. But I argued that there was no better place from which to surprise them than where we were. The climb was very difficult; often the soldiers had to sling their guns over their shoulders in order to grab hold of rocks with both hands, and they couldn't let go. After I pointed this out, Sanguily agreed with me and we decided to attack. He gave me orders that I was to communicate to the rest of the troops. So, according to Sanguily's orders, Captain Félix Díaz, of Clemente Gómez's force, was to come to the front of our unit.

As soon as the order was given, we formed a line along the edge of the ridge and we opened fire on the Spanish infantry that was coming toward us, trying to take the hill.

When those soldiers heard the first shots, and as the first two or so we hit fell back down on the rest, they saw that they had very few options. The first option was to jump down the hill even though they were high up and the hill was rocky. The other option was to expose themselves to get shot, swatted down like mosquitoes. Some tried to retreat in all the confusion down that rough slope, but when they let go of their grip they fell. Some of the ones who had already climbed higher on the slope were unable to retreat. They tried in a vain to advance on us, but they all fell due to our deadly shots.

Among them was a soldier named Paco, who had seventeen letters in his backpack, and appeared to be from a good family. According to the letters, one of his uncles was the Commander of Court in Spain. The mother wrote to him telling him to take care of himself because the war was beginning to change, in that there had been diplomatic exchanges between the United States of America and the government of the "mother country." These letters, at that particular moment, helped us to avoid adding to the great number of *presentados* that was such an affliction of the war, one cruel as no other.

We read those letters every day that it didn't rain because they lifted our deflated spirits. And more, the mother told her son to take care of himself because, according to her brother, the war was not going to last another year because of the strained diplomatic relations between the Americans and the Spanish government.

We felt a sense of vindication and justification because of the letters, and so we gave Paco an honorable grave, given the circumstances of war and the difficult terrain where we were. So we found a good place among those rocks, and dug him a deep grave.

We continued to camp in the same place because our victory had been so overwhelming that even the criminal Molina's life was in danger. We had wounded his horse in his retreat as he tried to avoid our fire. And it also helped our cause that they had left the edge of the ridge, the one from which they fell, making it look like the volcano Vesuvius spewing out lava. They had also fallen from their own bullets; when Sanguily and I jumped down on Paco's body in order to get the ammunition that he was carrying, we let out a shout of joy when we saw the abundant booty: three hundred rifle rounds. That heroic Paco, who had tried to charge at us, fell just two strides from the top of the ridge where we were positioned. Those three hundred rounds were for us the same as a hungry person finding a thousand pesos. If we hadn't found the three hundred rounds on Paco, we would have had to watch the column's retreat with the distaste of not being able to fire on them as they ran. But as soon as that valiant defender of Spanish injustice fell, I took the ammunition and distributed it among our troops who had rifles, some thirty men in our force and that of Clemente Gómez who had come on Sanguily's orders.

And so, with the ammunition it was a massacre for that mass of a thousand infantrymen trying to flee.

As they retreated, I saw a horse and his rider fall. The soldiers rose up and made a tight formation. We assumed that those soldiers were hiding something important for them, because then they carried the heavy load of the rider and the horse.

If we had had the help of the cavalry positioned nearby, we would have been more powerful that day, and it would have been bloodier for the Spanish generals and especially for the celebrated Molina. (Before Weyler came, Martínez Campos[16] limited the bloodiest of fighting because he wanted a civilized war.)

Because we didn't have our cavalry, they were able to recover from the initial confusion and to reorganize in their lines. Then the horse was shot, and it turned out to be the bloodthirsty Molina's horse. We concentrated our shots on the group that was carrying that miserable commander and his horse; we were trying to kill as many as we could.

Just then, the cavalry's column that had managed to get out of range of our shots jumped into a stream that they thought they could cross. Fifteen or twenty horses got stuck there and the cavalry left them. After the retreat, our infantry took the saddles off the horses and killed them, and so they had meat for two or three days.

Although those soldiers had gotten beyond our range of fire, we could see them machete to death that *presentado*. He had brought those soldiers to kill those poor sick people in that patriotic family—that same family that by coincidence our forces had come to protect. Later that afternoon, when our regiment went out looking for food, we found the *presentado*'s body.

We stayed in the same camp because we had only two wounded soldiers, Sergeant Caridad Prendes, who was only slightly wounded with a scratch on the shoulder, and Captain Félix Díaz, whose rifle blew up with the first loading of Paco's bullets, which I had given him when I was handing out ammunition in the middle of the battle. Díaz only sustained burns on his face and kept fighting, with the dead soldier's rifle this time. Really, Díaz was pained more by losing his rifle than by the burns he received.

---

16. Martínez Campos: Appointed Captain General of Cuba in 1876, during the Ten Years' War. In February 1878, he offered the rebels amnesty, autonomy, and civil liberties.

We stayed there, and this was very brave because we didn't have enough ammunition for another battle the next day. The decision to stay was questionable, knowing how vengeful Molina was. Given the tremendous defeat he had just suffered, he would come the next day with all of Spain, if that had been possible. So I thought that we should have marched that afternoon. But the commander wanted to be compassionate toward some of the soldiers who, because of infections in their feet, could not walk through the rocky ridges; so we stayed. And the next day at ten in the morning, as I had thought, eight Spanish columns arrived made up of three regiments.

They attacked us from the north, south, east, and west. Very few times have I seen so many Spanish soldiers together in that war!

But that day luck was with us. Our camp at Cubilinganga was in a mountain range called Escalera de Jaruco, which extends from the center of the province of Havana to a little more than a league from the province of Matanzas. And the area could only be crossed by disciplined troops like the Spanish. They had to march as a large force to ensure their own defense.

Although this was the case, the roads they took were a good distance from each other. The smaller group of Spanish troops took an approach that was a league longer in order to cross from the north to the south, and vice versa. But going that way, there was only a footpath from Camarones going to Aguacate. That tough terrain was our only salvation. Without it, that dirty Molina would have gotten his revenge, but he always got punished, as his vindictiveness deserved.

After running into our guard, the Spanish column and our guards exchanged shots. The column entered the area by the ascent of Ponce Centella to the west of our camp, to attack us at our rear guard. They came the same way they had come the day before, but this time it was safer for them.

When our guard exchanged fire with the column, two or three columns were entering the woods from the south, which was flat and turned out to be at our back.

We began a necessary retreat toward the east, toward the same location where we had divided before arriving at the camp. Luckily, we were able to save those who, if not for our arrival, would have been victims;

they would have been handed over as disgraced *presentados* whom Molina would have taken to those awful black birds of prey who raped and slaughtered defenseless human beings.

Since we were marching in the woods, they couldn't open fire on us because the thickness of the forest prevented them from seeing us. The only danger was the narrow footpath from Camarones, where we assumed there would be Spanish troops positioned to prevent our crossing.

We approached the path cautiously, and because we didn't hear any noise we began to cross it on our retreat. The first to cross were Sanguiliy, Félix Díaz, commander of Clemente Gómez's troops, Captain Manuel Quintero, commander of our first company, and Juan F. Abreu, commander of the second company. So all of the highest-ranking officers left first; this was highly improper. The understanding during the war was that in a situation like this, facing so many enemy troops, the commander was the one to stay in order to ensure the luck of his company. But on this day I don't know why they did the opposite. I was the one ordered to stay behind to hurry our troops along. When some sixty troops had crossed the path behind the officers, a Spanish soldier appeared in an ambush very close to where I was crossing. He shouted the alarm to alert the *práctico* of Iglesias's column. I heard that voice say, "Iglesias!! Which way do we go so that they don't escape?!"

I was held up helping the soldiers cross the path quickly when I heard that voice so close by. I lifted my head to look toward the area the voice had come from, and I saw the soldier who was just a short distance away. Only ten paces separated us. I had my rifle loaded and I shot at him at the same moment he shot at me. I could have followed in the same direction that the others had gone to cross the path, but I didn't because there were still two hundred or more soldiers who hadn't crossed yet. In fact, when they heard the shots from the road they turned back. I understood that I had to live up to the faith that the soldiers had in me, possibly at the sacrifice of my life; so I went back with them and took my chances with my comrades who couldn't cross.

It was truly a miracle of destiny that we were saved that day. When we turned back, we had to fight two columns of infantry that were attacking from the rear. So we got off the path and tumbled down a slope to a place where they were very unlikely to think we would be. We dragged ourselves into the cane stalks, trying to escape into the little mountain range close to the middle of the savanna. We were close to a Spanish camp, so close that we could see the soldiers' faces clearly and hear everything they were saying. The column that came into the woods on the path arrived from Camarones, and the ambush party informed them that almost all of the insurrectionists had fled in the face of their gunfire. And so they were able to hide their carelessness in letting us escape. But if they had been alert, none of us would have gotten away. They believed us to have escaped their trap, and so they went to prepare their lunch where the other column was, the one that was so close. We spent that day like sardines in a can, one on top of the other from one in the afternoon until it got dark. And although they marched away at five in the afternoon, we were afraid that they would stage an ambush in the woods; so we didn't want to leave before it got dark. When it was dark we came out of our hiding place in those blessed hills.

Because none of us had any experience in that area we had to link ourselves together in a human chain, so that we wouldn't lose anyone. Sergeant Bernardo Elisea wanted us to try to find the camp before daybreak. But that was impossible because it was too dark. By three in the morning we simply had to sit down and wait for dawn in order to know where we were and how far away the camp was.

When the sun finally came up, we saw that we were back at the unfortunate Paco's grave. The Spanish had thought that it was one of our graves and had sacked it. But when they saw that the body was one of their dead, they left it disinterred. Barbarians!

So, under the circumstances, we oriented ourselves and found that we were almost at the camp. We passed the day there because it was impossible to start another march given the bad condition we were in, without having eaten the day before. We left there at 5 p.m. to go to the hill called Pan where we assumed our officers would be. But at that hour a torrential downpour began that made some of us pass out on the march.

The highest-ranking soldier with us was Lieutenant Ferndando Naranjo, who was the commander for the day.

At seven in the morning the following day, we arrived at Pan de Matanzas, our destination. A kilometer from Pan, my brother also passed out, but it was too dangerous to stop there. If the enemy had appeared just then, we both would have been in danger because I stopped following the troops in order to stay with my brother. I tried to carry him but he was larger than I, and his *jolongo*[17] rifle and my rifle were too much to carry; so I decided to leave the guns, and carried him first. With great difficulty we arrived at the hill. Once there the other soldiers helped me carry him up to the camp that was already set up. The hill was some twenty meters high. After getting my brother safely to the camp, I went back to look for our guns, and returned with them a short time later. Sanguily, the rest of the officers, and my assistant were already there at the camp; they had crossed at the famous road from Camarones.

On the Hill of Pan de Matanzas: Camp Bolaños, Battle of the Hill of Pan

After staying there five days, Sanguily, ten others, and I left to go to Canímar in search of some two thousand rounds of ammunition that they told us Nicolás Zamora had; he was a commander without a regiment, camped on the hill called Liaño. The munitions were there, not at Canímar; so we went to Liaño with Commander Zamora, whom we met at Canímar.

We got some one thousand rounds for Remingtons and returned the next day to Canímar. Afterward, we left for Pan because we had left the force almost completely without ammunition.

We arrived after three days, late, I believe, on one of the last days of September. When we arrived, we had received information about Molina. He was planning an attack, so we got ready and waited for him. Clemente Gómez's force and ours were united for this battle, the two bravest regiments in the province of Matanzas at that time.

Two days later, while Sanguily and I were eating lunch, Félix Larrinaga, the lookout, advised us that he had seen the first Spanish column on the road from Ceiba–Mocha near the old store called La Catorra. I gave my equipment to my assistant and left with Sanguily in order to get a look at the column the lookout had spotted. It was just as he said; Molina was right in front of us!

Molina was in front of the camp telling his soldiers his strategy for the battle. This was an important moment; our patriotic hearts were swollen

---

17. *Jolongo:* A backpack used for carrying a rifle and ammunition.

with the sacred love of our ideal, and our resolve was hardened by our faith in the cause. The impending risk to our lives was of no concern to us. We only longed heroically for the terrible moment to arrive and to enter into combat. It raised our hopes to know that justice was on our side and that we would defeat the enemies of freedom; that's how I felt as I looked on.

Our commanding officer ordered the lookout to tell the other officers to take the armed soldiers to the trenches. And he ordered the unarmed to retreat.

The armed soldiers and their officers were already in their positions, waiting for the Spanish column in front of us to advance, when we heard shots from the back of the camp on the other side of the hill. Sanguily and I went to assess the situation because we only had a pair of lookouts on that side, and the shots sounded like another column. As we left, Sanguily ordered the officers of each company to hold off the Spanish advance at all costs.

Meanwhile, we left to find the two lookouts and to see what the situation was. When we had almost gotten to the lookouts, the enemy fire rained down on us like hail. Given the circumstances, I said to Sanguily that since we were the only two, if we were wounded, there wouldn't be anyone else to notify our troops. He agreed with me that this was a problem; so I said to him, "Call an officer to come with some troops and follow us."

I went back to the camp, and when I saw the first officer, Lieutenant Pedro Marrero, I ordered him to get ten armed men and to follow us.

We got to our lookouts' position quickly and found those two heroically firing on an entire column. The column was becoming bolder with their thunderous fire, as if they were shooting at a large company; so we opened fire on the column in order to prevent the column from advancing so that they wouldn't ruin our plans to punish the bold Molina.

The climb up the slope was difficult; so, with fifteen or twenty men shooting with discipline, we were able to keep the Spanish from advancing for the entire day. After ten minutes of firing, Sanguily and I went back to get some thirty or forty troops from Clotilde García's regiment, from Cárdenas's brigade. The regiment was passing through our camp. Because they were armed and their commanding officer relished a good fight (he was the older of the Mayato brothers), he wanted to charge the Spanish position so that we could go back to the other side of the hill to fight the two columns that were still approaching the front of the camp. We accepted his generosity. I didn't want them ever to forget how bravely we fought; so I said to Sanguily that because Mayato was going to fight with us, we should order someone to look for the brave Captain Abreu; it would be through his example that the entire force would be judged.

"Good idea," Sanguily said, and at that moment, with the two look-outs, we sent for the captain. When he arrived, Lieutenant Marrero was ordered to the battle of the camp. Just then a soldier next to me, Isidoro Cárdenas, was wounded.

At the same time, the battle for the corner of the hill began; it was in front of Corral-Nuevo, Clemente Gómez's campsite. Sanguily and I wanted to go there not only to see Clemente Gómez, who had the temperament of a brigade commander, but also to take part in the fight and to make a strong show of force wherever shots could be heard that day.

In order to get to the other battle, where Gómez's headquarters were located, we had to go through a very dense part of the woods; it was so thick with undergrowth that it took a lot of time just to cover a short distance. But because the unarmed soldiers of Gómez's company had gone through there before, I said to Sanguily we should get one of them to serve as our guide; in this way we could save time in getting to the new battle.

He took my advice and we went looking for a guide. We found the unarmed soldiers protected in a location out of reach of the Spanish fire. We asked who was in charge of the unarmed; they indicated that it was a sergeant named Desiderio Piloto. We asked him to guide us to the place where the troops had divided because we wanted to take part in that battle, and to support one of our positions in that battle that had now divided into three parts. The way the sergeant responded to us, indicating that he didn't know the way, we could see that he was scared to go to the fight. A *mambí* who doesn't know how to get back to where he just came from, and at noon no less, now that's strange! Sanguily wanted to force him to serve as our guide, but I argued that he wasn't suitable. He had already demonstrated that he was scared, so he might pretend to get lost, and we would lose time getting there. So I asked another soldier if he wanted to be our guide for just a short distance. We were then given a corporal named Antolín Hernández who took us. We left with him, and when we got close to the battle we sent him back, just as we had promised him. When we arrived at the battle, cries of "Viva Cuba Libre!" filled the air. Just then, in a state of frenzy, came reinforcements for the Spanish column that was fighting our forces whom we had left on the other side of the hill. We opened fire on the column and they responded; for a quarter of an hour both forces exchanged deadly, relentless fire. And Sanguily and I were pounding away at those soldiers. The commander of that position was Alférez, called Basilio.

Two soldiers next to me were wounded; they had been fighting outside the trenches because there wasn't enough room inside for everyone. One of the wounded was a youth who began his baptism by fire when I took him out of the trenches to aim and shoot more accurately. At just that moment he was shot. An Andalusian sergeant who was in the trench protested and said that it was my fault that the youth got shot. I responded that he should come out where I was, if he was so brave, and stop criticizing from inside the trench. The sergeant came out bravely shooting with great accuracy back at the enemy fire that flew around our heads like a swarm of flies.

But as the sergeant was firing, one of the enemy's shots hit his Remington, and a piece of the rifle stock flew off and hit him in the eye. What a sad sight of the war!

At that moment Sanguily told me to follow him to our camp to see how the others were doing and to see Brigadier Clemente Gómez. We had been informed that he had marched to our camp. We were able to retrace our steps to get to the other side of the hill, but there was a dangerous spot along the route that was clear of trees and undergrowth; so we risked being seen by the soldiers in the two columns facing our camp. They could see the spot perfectly. But we went anyway. When we got to the clearing and began to run across, Sanguily's hat flew off as they opened fire on us. He wanted to leave it because one crossing was dangerous enough, and we had luckily crossed safely. He didn't want to go back to look for the hat, but I decided to look for it and bring it back to him. I made three trips across that spot, and they shot at me each time! But they didn't hit me; they just filled my pants with holes; three shots also went through my shirt but didn't touch my body! Finally, we arrived at 1 p.m. at the camp that we had left at 11 a.m. By then we had covered all of the sites of the battle, and had the satisfaction of having fired on three different columns.

There, we met Brigadier Clemente Gómez, with two of his assistants, and we met Colonel Regino Alfonso as well. He didn't have a force then because it had been divided and put into Colón's brigade. But for about a month he had wanted to take part in that battle, and he did. So Brigadier Clemente Gómez and two aides, Regino Alfonso, Sanguily, and I all took up positions in a trench. Captain Jaime Plá was also there; in 1896 he had been the bugler for the María Cristina unit in the La Antonia forts at Canímar. He had spent the day before our attack at those forts. And already on the date that I just mentioned, he was a captain in the Liberation Army. This captain served us by advising us of the enemy column's movements by playing the bugle.

I also had occasion to watch the best marksman whom I knew during the war: Colonel Regino Alfonso. We were ordered to stop shooting for a moment so that we could see him firing on the target. He fired fourteen times, and we saw fourteen stretchers retreat from the columns in front of our camp. This was the column that Molina led. Unfortunately, he was at his headquarters, out of range of our gunfire, though close enough for us to see him clearly.

The aides came from the other side of the hill in order to deliver orders. As soon as the fighting commander received them, Captain Plá told us the new movements of the enemy by playing the bugle. The bugle was played every time an aide arrived and gave a new order to the fighting commander. And we delivered Captain Plá's orders to the troops in the trenches.

At three o'clock we saw an aide to one of the Spanish officers. After he talked with the officer, he passed orders on to the soldiers fighting, then retreated. Then the Spanish forces divided as they advanced on the hill. Just twenty paces from our front to the south, there was a climb to a cave, the only cave on the hill of Pan. Taking a train from Havana to Mantanzas, it is invisible as a cavern midway up the hill, on the far north side.

When we saw their approach, we stayed in our trenches without firing, sure that once they reached the middle of their climb they wouldn't be able to cross over the cavern toward us. It appeared that Molina thought that we had our headquarters in that cave, because it was the only cave in which sixty or more men could protect themselves. But he outfoxed himself! That cave was at too high an elevation to install a headquarters, because it would set a bad example for the soldiers who would see their officers located in a safer spot than they. You just can't do that in a war like ours. Discipline and authority can be maintained only through leadership by example.

We stopped firing because we wanted to see, as best we could, how many soldiers had been able to climb to a higher position than the one from which we were fighting. It was dangerous to approach the areas where the Spanish were climbing so boldly, but I offered to do it, and I counted ninety-eight infantrymen, the *práctico,* and the captain. They had climbed up to the cave. There was a small force of ours in the cave under the orders of Lieutenant Colonel Vicente Jorge and the Commander Julio Miró. Some time before, the force had been dismantled and now was maintained with only eight or ten men.

That day made for a great feast of Cuba Libre. The soldiers in the cave were also firing, but when they saw those devoted descendants of Pelayo climbing, they stopped shooting and climbed up above the cave. The Spanish got up to the cave then went back down to the point where they had divided. When they got back down, we opened fire on them again and our troops, now back in the cave, opened fire too. Being in the cave was like being on the flat roof of a house. You see everything, but the others can't see you. So the Spanish went to the cave, and our troops stopped shooting; and when the Spanish left, our men started shooting again.

Now Molina, who was a good ways away, didn't know that his troops had gotten up to the cave. But when that heroic captain had climbed back down, he saw shots coming from it again. At first we didn't understand it either until after the shooting stopped, when our troops who were still in the cave told us how they had climbed out and back in. We criticized them for what they had done because those ten men could have just kept firing, and kept one hundred or more of the enemy from climbing up to that spot in the first place.

But let's get back to the action. After a pause, we opened fire again and the battle began again. For a quarter of an hour it had been silent, and as the fighting resumed, Sergeant Bernardo Elisea arrived. He was a young black man, a giant in all the liberation forces. (He couldn't have been older than twenty or so, and out of four hundred men, not one could equal him in stature or heroic strength.) He came with a message from Alférez Basilio. Basilio had only a few rounds left, and so was requesting more ammunition. Both the great Clemente Gómez and Sanguily told the messenger that the soldiers were to fire at intervals in order to hold their positions for the rest of the afternoon. Then, as the sergeant was about to return with the order, he paused a moment to watch Regino Alfonso shoot; he was about to hit his target, Molina's aide who was on a golden horse coming to deliver an order to the fighting commander. The Spanish front line was about half a mile away. Just as the assistant finished giving the order and turned his horse, Regino shot him twice with his celebrated Mauser, and that *cipayo* fell. The fighting infantry recovered him; then Molina gave orders to another mounted assistant. He was coming to the battle lines with a long rifle and when he got there Regino said to us, "Lower your rifles; this man's a marksman. Let's wait until he shoots to open fire."

We saw him talking to the fighting commander, frantically asking questions. Then we saw that they signaled him toward a tree where our trench was and he opened fire in that direction. He indeed was a great shot. All of his shots on our trenches put us in great danger. On the seventh or eighth shot, Sergeant Elisea refused to wait any longer to fire, and stood up to shoot back at that monstrous sniper. But unfortunately, when he rose he couldn't fire his rifle, and from his horse that aide shot him through the head; the bullet entered his left temple and exited three centimeters or more behind his right ear, as a mass of his brains splattered on my right arm. All of us lamented the death of that sergeant; he was the bravest of the brave! Clemente Gómez shed tears over the body and later made a cross with our spent cartridge casings; he put the cross on the brush of a ceiba plant that grew amid a pile of rocks we moved to make the trenches.

When that damned sniper of the enemies of liberty stopped shooting, in the middle of a new charge, we all stood up to see if we had had the luck to avenge Sergeant Elisea's death. But Regino Alfonso implored us to leave the sniper to him, that this would be his last target because he wouldn't fight anymore that day. So we left him. Alfonso shot twice with his blessed rifle and we all gave a cry of "Cuba Libre!" because we saw the horrible Bernardo lose his balance on his horse and the rifle fall from his hands. The nearby infantry auxiliary came to his aid. His horse was terrified and turned galloping toward the spot where the force had divided. But as he ran off, the sniper fell, he who moments before had killed a great champion of freedom for our country.

It was about four in the afternoon when we saw the stretchers leave with the wounded; they had been in constant use since eleven in the morning when the battle started. We counted more than eighty wounded; a part of Cuabal's column followed them, and we left them fighting with Mayato and Abreu, who didn't let them advance despite having only fifty men, all spread out after falling down the slope to the west of our camp. On the orders of the superior officer, the column turned to come back, to take the stretchers back, we supposed. Night fell before they were able to collect such a great number of wounded. The rest of the two columns remained fighting until sundown, when most of us stopped shooting. The unarmed were an impediment for us. They had already come down from the top of the hill, four hundred meters high, to join up with us before dark because it was a certainty that we were to march that night to another camp.

It was assumed that the cowardly Molina would follow us from Cubilinganga. He would bring all of Spain against us to avenge the defeat we had just handed him. Indeed, we didn't have sufficient ammunition, nor could we go looking for food because the Spanish were in the area where we usually found food.

Now I must return to an unusual incident that occurred at three o'clock that afternoon. The commander of the day, Fernando Naranjo, climbed up to check on the conditions of the troops fighting on the west side of the hill. We were already on the eastern part of the hill (our camp was on the eastern side, although at a different elevation on the hill). When Naranjo returned from his check, the following occurred.

Everyone who had the position of "commander of the day" wore red ribbons. But our cavalry forgot that, so they took Naranjo for a member of the Civil Guard. And when our infantry saw him approaching, they began to abandon their trench positions in a frenzied retreat. Clemente Gómez and two aides, Regino Alfonso, Sanguily, and I were close to those "fugitives," and seeing all of this, Sanguily and I ran after them, cutting them off and firing everywhere to make them go back to their positions. Our work was very difficult among those craggy peaks, but as soon as we ran all around chasing them, they returned to their positions.

After we got our troops back in the trenches, we directed our shots at the Spanish infantry that had been advancing the farthest. They were approaching in an attempt to take the trenches and to make us retreat. But we prevented this. Because they were so close, we shot low in order to do as much damage as possible. And they had to fall back to their original positions, a city block and a half away. Then, Sanguily and I positioned ourselves behind the trench Lieutenant Fernando Naranjo was in. Sergeant Manuel Castillo was in front of the trench, and Captain José Aballí was also there. He was on commission to our camp, and had come from the Southern Brigade, Colonel Clemente Dante's force. He had just been wounded in Jicarita, during the retreat of the contingent at Cama-güey.[18] I said to the captain that if he wanted to complete his commission, he should get away from there because there were so many bullets and he could get wounded. He replied by asking if I were braver than he for being there, and I replied that if I got wounded there it would be in my assigned fighting post. For him it was different; he was in transit, and what's more, he was on commission; so if he got wounded, he wouldn't be able to complete it.

He wanted to prove his courage, but he couldn't because he was shot down, as I assumed he would be. The bullet entered through his face and exited through his neck, just below the ear. He was shot because he was obstinate. I called two infantrymen in the trench to come help take the captain behind a nearby rock so that we could pour water on his head and try to stop the bleeding. He was bleeding profusely from

---

18. Camagüey: A province in the middle of the island, between the provinces of Santa Clara and Oriente. This "theater of military operations" was famous for a number of important battles, and was also the site for the Jimaguayú Assembly in 1895, where the first war constitution was adopted.

the nose and mouth and soon died of asphyxiation. Fabián Elisea and Rogelio carried out my orders; they were two valiant and good soldiers, never wavering in their self-sacrifice.

Later, Sanguily and I went to the trench where Brigadier Clemente Gómez was positioned. There we found one of his assistants, Francisco Castañer, who was sick with fever; this was his baptism by fire.

The gunfire ended at nightfall. Molina came to the camp closest to the front lines and this conversation was overheard. He chastised the infantry commander, saying that he hadn't climbed to the cave at the hour when he ordered him to do so. That officer, who had in fact climbed to the cave, as I described, with the very real danger of being killed, faced up to the general, his commanding officer, and said that he was a soldier of honor and that he did not lie! And he said that he had in fact gone to the cave, and all his subordinates knew that with him they led the fight.

While the subordinate commander and that coward of a general were arguing, I begged Sanguily and Brigadier Clemente Gómez to allow us a volley of fifty shots to see if we would have the luck of killing that parasite and enemy of liberty. He made us suffer so many of the tragedies of war, while he suffered none. He was very careful to stay out of our range and away from any danger.

(This was true except for the times when he thought that he could attack the sick and women, like that day at Cubilinganga. He went there to satisfy himself by seeing the defenseless die beneath the blades of his birds of prey.)

But neither Sanguily nor Gómez allowed us to shoot because our unarmed men were coming down that very steep slope. If we had opened fire on Molina, the infantry that surrounded that vile man would have fired back. So they would have probably wounded many of our unarmed and our assistants who were climbing down, and so we would have had more wounded after the battle than during the battle.

For these reasons and more, we gathered the unarmed troops; we weren't going to start another march that night, but we were to go to another camp where we could rest from so much confusion and intense fighting. This made sense.

At four o'clock, the Spanish began their march to Mantanzas, where they could take their wounded. They left after the discussion between the brave Spanish officer, who we had been fighting since eleven o'clock in the morning until sundown, and that bloodthirsty commander who kept his distance from the battle to avoid getting shot.

After they retreated, we took our wounded to a safe location nearby, and we divided the two forces. Clemente Gómez marched to Canímar in the direction of Camarioca, and our forces marched to Purgatorio.

The Arrival at Purgatorio: Camp La Hierba Guinea

After eight or ten days at Purgatorio, Sanguily, ten soldiers, and I returned to Pan to check on the wounded and to deliver orders to Cayetano to give to a group of patriots in Matanzas. We also brought two Spanish coins that General Betancourt gave to Sanguily in Purgatorio.

Up until then, Cayetano had served us loyally at great personal risk, bringing us orders, when it was possible, by sneaking out from the city of Matanzas by night. In exchange for his sacrifice, he was given food and money. He arrived the same day that we got there with ten infantrymen. Sanguily gave him the money for the orders and so much food that he could barely carry it all. This was because our troops had just come back from Ceiba-Mocha where they had gone foraging, and they returned well stocked.

The orders were given to Cayetano, and the following day, in the morning at seven o'clock, he came back with orders, riding on a blue mulberry mare. Vicente Jorge's men admired this guy who, like Regino Alfonso, usually came on foot. But this day he came mounted and with so many orders. However, I wanted to hang this man because it appeared to me that he was working for the Spanish. But when he gave a ridiculous explanation for why he could move so freely and why he was so well equipped, everyone believed him. I was less convinced. Because of Weyler's invasion, at that time no one who was suspect was spared persecution. So it would be impossible for him to infiltrate a Spanish-held town so easily.

But most people chose to believe the stupid explanation from that reptile, who even had the nerve to have lunch with us before we marched.

Everyone had a big party in the camp with the delicious food brought by Cayetano. And people had reason to celebrate given that it was a time in which food was scarce and we often went hungry. Indeed, it had been more than a year since we had even seen food of that quality; usually, we saw very little food of any quality, for that matter.

I was the only one not to take part in the feast, and I happily stayed in my hammock.

Sanguily saved a little of the food for the sick, who were close by, as well as half of a meal of *jutía*[19] that I had killed the afternoon before. Sanguily invited Lieutenant Colonel Dr. Sigarroa and Colonel Regino Alfonso to eat with us. Dr. Sigarroa had just used some old pliers for shoeing horses to pull four molars from Regino Alfonso's mouth without tearing much flesh. He usually extracted teeth like that, with blows to the gums, because he didn't have any other tools. The doctor horrified us with his dental practices.

When everyone else was having lunch, I was in my hammock disgusted by a man whom I held to be a traitor.

Sanguily came to tell me that they were waiting for me in order to have lunch, but I told him that I wasn't going to eat. This was inconceivable, given what there was to eat, and that I wasn't sick! He asked me why, and I responded that the only way I would accept lunch was if he would promise to march that afternoon to Purgatorio. He told me no because he had given his word to Cayetano to wait until the following day. Cayetano was to bring a mule for him and a horse for Regino Alfonso, who didn't like the infantry that he had been in for two months because he had traveled by horse his entire life.

Then I repeated my proposition to Sanguily. But when I heard that he wanted to wait to get the mule, I said to him that if we left at nightfall we would arrive at Purgatorio at eight at night; and I would return at twelve o'clock in order to get the mule. Then he asked why I didn't want him to wait. I replied that I would go back for the mule because if an ambush took place, as I expected, and I were killed, it wouldn't hinder the war effort in the province because he would continue to lead the force. But if he were killed in an ambush, it would destroy the only active force at that time in the province. His death would result in the pacification of the region that Weyler so desperately wanted. With this clarification Sanguily gave me his word that in the afternoon we would march, as I

---

19. *Jutía:* A small edible rodent unique to the Antilles.

had asked, even if he looked like a coward for not waiting for the mule that that traitor Cayetano was going to bring.

I ate lunch, and afterwards we started on our march to Purgatorio. I was the *práctico* on that march, and we arrived at eight o'clock with ten infantrymen. Before I tied up my hammock, I called the corporal of the reserve guard, Evaristo Estalella, and asked him who would be relieving him. He told me that it was Corporal Fabián Sotomayor. I ordered him to call me at twelve or one o'clock in the morning because I had to get back to the hill of Pan.

Perhaps the day of my death hadn't arrived, or maybe what really happened was that the corporal forgot to wake me. In any event, because I arrived there very tired, I slept until sunrise, the hour when Sanguily was going to General Betancourt's headquarters close by to see how the wounded were recovering.

When he passed by my hammock, he called me. When I woke up and saw that the sun was already up, I was angry at the corporal who was supposed to have woken me up, and I wanted to have him punished. But Sanguily wouldn't allow it.

He said that perhaps my presumption concerning Pan and the man and the mule were right, and if so, then the corporal's having forgotten to wake me was a blessing.

Given his reasoning, I stayed in my hammock, seeing that I couldn't fix anything in respect to the trip to Pan at that hour. Because not only was it necessary to cross the same trail without the cover of woods, but it was also necessary to cross the rail lines that were close to the forts at the town of Ceiba-Mocha.

While I was lying in my hammock, reflecting on all of this, Sanguily returned from the headquarters and gave me a big hug. Seeing that he was so emotional, I asked him why, and he said that they had just killed Regino Alfonso; the murder was carried out by Cayetano, who had offered to bring Sanguily the mule. And just as I had thought, my premonition had turned out to be real.

At first, I just couldn't believe it; what I had speculated had actually come to fruition. Because I didn't believe it, Sanguily made me come with him to the headquarters to hear the news for myself.

When we got there, I saw Commander Guaracha (Gallego), who had just arrived to tell us what had happened. How unlucky and sad that news was! I wanted to know how the betrayal had happened, and Guaracha related the following account.

At daybreak Cayetano came to the hill, still very wet with dawn's dew, and he told Regino that he had brought the horse and the mule for Sanguily and that he was already tired from struggling with the two animals when he arrived; they had become too difficult because they were of Spanish breeding. Because the animals had been difficult, it took him longer to get there and so to avoid being exposed by the dawn, he had tied them up in a little stand of trees nearby. He came to tell Sanguily and Regino where the animals were; he had gained time in bringing them to the hill because he had gotten the best pony that they had (Captain Hurquia's golden pony). When he heard this news, Regino was overjoyed because all of us liberation fighters knew about the captain's celebrated pony. The brave owner showed off all of his war regalia on that horse.

So when Regino went to look for this alleged pony, that vile traitor kept asking insistently for Colonel Sanguily. But Regino said to him, "Don't worry about the mule. I will guard it, and perhaps this afternoon he will send for it."

They both left; Cayetano went in front as he knew where he had left both animals. The evil traitor had planned an ambush with one hundred Civil Guards hidden in a stand of trees close to the hill called Pan.

According to Morito, a soldier whom Regino brought to take the mule to the hill until I came looking for it, Regino didn't want to go into the stand of trees because he was suspicious. But the traitor said to him, "Don't be afraid, Colonel; here's the horse, so just come on and have a look."

How beautiful was that pony! So Regino decided to go in, but Morito, the soldier accompanying him, didn't. He made the excuse that he had to go relieve himself, and he took a long time.

Meanwhile, they took the path into the grove, with Regino following the secret traitor. They were walking along a path for two lines of soldiers, with one on either side of the path. When they had entered the grove at about a city block's distance, a line of those miserable guards rushed in between the two of them. Morito heard Regino say in a loud voice, "Oh, the miserable enemy! This is not the way that you betray a man!"

Successive voices from the Civil Guard then said, "Surrender, surrender!"

Morito, who was watching from outside, pretending to go to the bathroom, crawled into the weeds so that he wouldn't be their next victim. From his hiding place, he said that he heard the fight that Regino put up, although the one hundred soldiers eventually killed him with their machetes. Regino fought and he even bit a sergeant of the Civil Guard who cried out and let go of the machete he had just plunged into Regino's back. Regino pulled the machete out of his back, and even with such a wound he defended himself with the Civil Guard's machete until they hacked him to pieces.

Morito was able to discern all of this as he saved himself miraculously because of the denseness of the fog that morning and because he was able to hide in the high grass. But the fog and the high grass, I deduced, also hid the Spanish well; this is why Regino didn't see those villains, and so they were thus able to surprise and kill him.

And then Morito said that from his hiding place he could hear the comments by the Civil Guard when their commander admonished them for not having taken Regino alive in order to take him to the bloodthirsty Molina, who would have made his life hell as an insurrectionist. The subordinates justified their killing him by telling all that I have just described.

After the soldiers reported all that had happened, according to Morito, they still hadn't satisfied the Spanish commander. In fact, he rebuked the traitor Cayetano, too. He said to him that he hadn't told the truth in respect to Sanguily, whom Cayetano had assured would be there too to be captured or killed. Molina had offered two hundred gold pieces for the two of them. Cayetano tried to vindicate himself as best he could, saying that Colonel Sanguily had deceived him, and that he had told him that he would come with Regino to wait for the mule.

After Guaracha finished relating these events, I was still shocked that I had seen beforehand so clearly what would actually happen.

Two days later we received news from Matanzas that Colonel Regino Alfonso's body was there. They had thrown it in front of the jail and defiled the body all day; those despicable Spaniards, especially the traitor, kicked it in the face. They said that Cayetano had said, "Here he is, and this victory is owed all to me. After ten years as a bandit and two as an insurrectionist, the Civil Guard hasn't been able to defeat him. And in the war the Spanish Army wasn't able to capture him. So his death is owed all to me."

They gave him only five hundred pesos because in order to have gotten the other five hundred, he would have had to have captured Sanguily.

If they had listened to me, the despicable Cayetano wouldn't have had the time to carry out his plot because we would have hanged him the day before the betrayal. The war, at the time, was at its cruelest and bloodiest; so it was inconceivable that he would be able to make so many dangerous trips without arousing suspicion. But after Cayetano left, Regino was the first to criticize my doubts about him. It was so bad that when he found out that I had asked Sanguily not to wait for the mule, he ridiculed me, saying that I had embarrassed myself.

After the bad news of Regino's death, we left Purgatorio on a march to the woods of Canímar, in the direction of Clemente Gómez's forces. According to General Betancourt, they were already short of ammunition. For us, the mission was to resupply them even though we had used a lot of our own in the battle at Pan de Matanzas.

When we arrived, we camped a quarter of a league away from Clemente Gómez's camp, which was close to the pass of the Canímar River, known as Tumbadero. There were ten soldiers camping with us.

The Arrival at Clemente Gómez's Camp and the Battle That Took Place There

We arrived at Clemente Gómez's camp at Las Piedras, close to the pass of Tumbadero to which I just referred. It was around nine o'clock in the morning when we got there. We ate a meal with the ten soldiers from our camp, and we had been there no more than an hour when the guards started shooting. It was those damned *Panchos*[20] who had come for a new feast. But it had been quite a few days since we had roasted *el corojo*[21] (that's a *mambí* saying we used in anticipation of a long-awaited fight with

---

20. *Pancho:* The enemy.
21. *Corojo:* A palm tree bearing an oily nut.

the enemy). Everyone got into their positions. The trench, made of loose rocks, had already been prepared. Indeed, we made one wherever we went, whenever we camped for more than a day.

So the shooting started. After ten minutes of fighting in the trench with Clemente Gómez, I saw that the order to retreat was going to be given because our positions weren't advantageous. The Spanish were at a higher position and the trenches were hollows in the ground; the Spanish could therefore shoot at us easily. Sanguily told me to retreat to see if I could find María, his wife who had come on the march with us but whom we had left behind at one of the *ranchos*[22] near the trenches. When I got there, I found her calmly seated despite the falling rain of bullets. There was a pile of cane stalks next to her; I took one of them and began to peel it; when I pulled off the last piece of husk, one of the bullets, flying by like mosquitoes all around us, split the cane in two. Seeing the damage it did, I said to her, "I bet you won't eat that stalk of sugarcane that that bullet just split."

She said she would, and when she picked up the cane from the ground Sergeant Pedro González, of Clemente Gómez's force, came to her side and said, "*Mulata,*[23] those bullets are really buzzing!"

He had just finished pronouncing the word when one of those bullets hit him in the chest and he fell on María's dress without even crying out. I took his rifle and ammunition to take it to the commander of the company to whom it belonged.

At that moment, the soldiers from the trenches went by and recovered the body of that valiant officer. Just moments before, he had retreated from the trenches where he was fighting in order not to use the little ammunition he had left; he took his last breath just a few steps from the trench.

We retreated to the center of the woods called Piedra la Viña, and during our retreat the shooting stopped. But we heard shots in the next camp. We were very concerned because we didn't know how our compatriots were faring. But we didn't know which way to go through the

---

22. *Rancho:* A makeshift hut made of palms leaves and scraps of wood, used by insurrectionists and poor civilians living in the countryside.
23. *Mulata:* A woman of mixed white and Afro-Cuban parentage. Here the term is used as a term of endearment for Gómez's wife.

woods in order to get to the other camp. So we had to resign ourselves to the situation and just hope that luck would take care of them.

When we finally did find out something about them it was already the afternoon; they had been in a very dangerous situation in that grove of trees that wasn't advantageous for them in a fight. To make matters worse, our soldiers were there with barely any ammunition.

So we went to Gómez's camp looking for ammunition, but they didn't have any. Then we crossed the river looking for ammunition in the area of Camarioca. There, we ordered a commission, and waited with the force there in Canímar until the commission returned. Then we went back to Purgatorio.

A new infantry regiment was already at Purgatorio: Betances. (It began as the general's escort infantry.) They brought ammunition that they had found in the province of Havana, in the woods of Machado, close to Canasí. The general supplied us with ammunition, giving us half of what he had and keeping two or three whole boxes of one thousand rounds.

The Plan for the Battle at Camp El Infierno (Purgatorio)

We waited there when a company of infantry arrived from the Cárdenas Brigade; they were from the "Clotilde García Shooters" regiment, under the command of two bold fighters: Captains Daniel Tabares and Mayato (the older of the Mayato brothers who helped us at the hill called Pan, the day we gave Molina a beating). They came looking for ammunition, and General Betancourt stopped them and ordered them not to march any farther so that they could take part in the banquet we hoped to celebrate at Molina's expense.

Mayato's forces camped with one of the Betances infantry units and they formed General Betancourt's headquarters on the front of the mountain. Sanguily's headquarters, along with Captain Juan Abreu's company, covered the position through which the Spanish would have to pass. Another one of our companies was positioned at the corresponding exit; it was Captain Manuel Quintero's company. Facing him were two more companies: Tabares's force and another Betances under Martín Duen's command; he was the commander of the new regiment.

We formed a perfect triangle, and at its center was a savanna that perhaps looked like a park covered with vegetation. We burned it so that we would be able to find all of the bullets and arms that we were supposed to take from the Spanish that day during the beating we were sure we would be giving them.

It was February 7, 1898, my seventeeth birthday,[24] and I was already a frontline veteran. It was about seven in the morning, and I was lying in my hammock that was hung on a slope by the road that was the entrance to where we were waiting for the enemy. I heard coughs from a great many people who had colds; so I leaned in the direction of the coughing in order to see who it was. Then I saw a line of Spanish soldiers approaching. Right away I told our force so that each soldier could get to his position. At the same time, I asked if there was anyone at the bottom of the hill. They said "no," but I said to Sanguily that we should see if there were other companies delayed below. I also told the little general's escort squadron (being of the cavalry) to accompany us so we could protect the infantry. This way we would be able to protect the camp, because given their small numbers, they weren't able to put guards at the four extreme corners of the camp. In fact, they had posted only one lookout.

I showed up with some rocks, which I threw at the escort and showed him the sign, so that when they saw it they would know to mount and retreat.

Captain Tabares went across the center of our triangle (the *placersillo*) with three men who were going to the headquarters. I threw a rock at them and had the luck of hitting Tabares on the shoulder. He looked up and I signaled to him that twenty steps from him was a double column of Spanish soldiers. He changed direction to go to his camp, but unfortunately he didn't have time to warn the sublieutenant and the other soldiers, who were ten steps ahead of him and too close to the column. Those two ran into the enemy, who already had their arms at the ready; the fresh tracks had indicated that they had them in their trap. We saw that those *cipayos* had opened fire, destroying those two patriots, a sergeant and a second lieutenant; so we opened fire on them, and our soldiers shot back from the twelve positions we had prepared.

---

24. Because Batrell was born in 1880, February 7, 1898, marks his eighteenth birthday. It is unclear whether this error is a simple oversight or a more deliberate attempt to emphasize his youth.

I should explain why I didn't sound the alarm, particularly why I didn't alert the escort for the cavalry and Captain Tabares. If I had warned them, the Spanish would have heard me and wouldn't have entered the triangle where they were supposed to enter. They would have suspected a trap and would have been happy just to open fire on our camp. And from where they were, they would have been firing at the back of our camp, where we didn't have trenches, and therefore we would have lost more men. Furthermore, we wouldn't have been able to fight at our other positions. Indeed, it would have destroyed the plan that we had conceived and planned for so many days.

Therefore, there was the supreme order that under no circumstances was the column to enter until the *placersillo* was burned. There would be a severe punishment if this order were disobeyed. So whoever sounded the alarm before the Spanish arrived would have been judged and punished.

That month was also the anniversary of the other great battle of Oito in which Commander Rosell and several other brave compatriots were lost. So our positions opened fire on that brave and stalwart Spanish infantry. They were under the command of the heroic Aparicio, second in command of Molina's column. At that point, he was only a commander of a column, but because of his heroism in battle, Aparicio was promoted to military commander of the province of Matanzas. That day he did what he always did in battle. He stayed in La Mocha and ordered his troops to take our position at the fixed bayonets. It was easy to give orders, but when it comes to leading by example, it is more difficult, and he was incapable of it.

That battle would have horrified anyone who hadn't become accustomed to the war machine and its destruction. It is controlled by usurpers with their fingers on the trigger of the arms. So many fell like a house of cards blown by the wind; the sheer number of dead was horrible!

Many of the Spanish shot from a prone position, a newly improvised technique. This was the first time that I took this precaution too, shooting while lying on my chest with my head up. They fought like a cat defending itself against a dog; it moves with great dexterity, and with its claws it kills an opponent attacking from above. So it seemed as though the Spanish soldiers were shooting in all directions. I had never seen a column defend itself so ferociously as that column defended itself that day.

When the battle was at its loudest and bloodiest, I could see the Spanish Lieutenant Colonel Aparicio calmly sitting on his golden horse casually giving orders. Because I knew him before I went to the war, I said to Sanguily, "That man sitting on the gold horse is Agustín Aparicio." Then I shot at him with great accuracy; he fell with his horse to the ground. I had shot the horse and wounded him in the arm, this according to the newspaper reports that we later received from Matanzas where they related the events of the battle. The horse lay there dead along with several other horses; they later served as meat for our meals.

The shooting went on from 7:30 to eight o'clock in the morning. We were pounding them relentlessly, largely because our positions were right on top of their heads, you might say. They tried to punish us by attacking our rear guard. Because there was an angle in the ridge that we were using for our position, a point that jutted out, the lookout and I could see what was happening. I could see the courageous Justo Hernández, who was killed a few minutes later. We fired in that direction. It was difficult to climb further up the slope; so many of us tried to climb trees, trying to reach the necessary height. The Spanish contented themselves by showering a torrent of bullets on us. An entire company had run to the area. Justo then said that he didn't want to die there like a suicide. And I shouted to him, "Hold on and I am going to tell Sanguily," who had left; "he trusts you in this position because he recognizes your bravery."

I arrived at the trench where Sanguily was fighting and told him about the position. He replied, "It's very dangerous there, let's go there to bring Justo back to the trench."

Within ten minutes of his arrival at the trench, a damned bullet hit Justo in the navel and all of the food that he had eaten came out through the wound. When Sanguily and I arrived there to hold this dangerous position, there were so many bullets hitting the position that Sanguily now fully realized the danger there that Justo had reported; he had shielded himself in the only spot protected from the shots. There was room for only one man. There was a hollow in those hills called Cásimba. But because I didn't have a place to hide and protect myself, I stayed on my feet, trusted luck, and continued firing. The Spanish shot back, given their failure to climb to my location, while shouting "Viva María Cristina!" Meanwhile, Captain Estanislao Abreu arrived to tell Sanguily that the company had used up all of its ammunition, that at most his soldiers had four rounds left. Sanguily told him, from his hollow, to make one grand volley of shots to see if it was possible to hold the position until our soldiers could retreat from the other position.

In the brief moments Abreu was there receiving orders from Sanguily, he saw how thick the gunfire was, and said to me, "Cousin, you're in danger here."

I replied, "I'm going to do God's will." And I asked him, "My brother, who's in the trench with you, has he been hurt?"

"No," he replied. "The only one who is seriously wounded is Justo Hernández, who couldn't be saved."

I asked him, "Where was he standing when he was wounded?"

"Behind the trench where you are standing," he replied.

Abreu went back to the trench, but after a few minutes, the Spanish soldiers realized that the shots had cooled off a bit from the trench; so they tried to take it. When they saw that the gunfire didn't increase in intensity, they started to climb following the María Cristina's Filipino lieutenant. He was the boldest of the officers of that column.

We had no other choice but to retreat because we didn't have a single bullet left to shoot. We had already run out of ammunition when they got to the top of our position. They dislodged the rest of our forces that were at the same altitude. They also attacked some troops who were higher than Tabares's forces, and higher than the first Betances company, which was under Captain Martín Duen's orders. That day he received six shots from the waist on down.

If we had had the same ammunition that was given to the other forces that day, we would have been able to do what we had hoped, to take all the dead and wounded Spanish, with all their arms, as had happened a year before with Aldea.

But it appeared that petty rivalries made it so that we would receive less ammunition than the other regiments without being told why. So, because we didn't have enough ammunition to fight, we didn't succeed as we had hoped. It was so bad that when we ran out of ammunition, the other regiments had enough rounds to keep fighting for half an hour longer. If we had had the same amount of ammunition, the Spanish would have been forced to retreat. Indeed, when we exhausted our ammunition, the entire *placersillo* was covered with the Spanish dead and wounded. And under fire, they wouldn't have been able to recover so many dead and wounded, nor their arms. There were so many bodies that it would have impeded the retreat that they would have had to make. And we would have continued to fire as they retreated, and we would have pursued them. It would have been a colossal victory.

When the Spanish column, which unfortunately was able to carry away their dead and wounded, retreated, we came down from the *placersillo* very sad because we hadn't carried out the plan that we had devised. We were only able to be content with the great number of their dead. We could see a distinct trail of blood, pieces of clothing, and all kinds of medicines.

When all of the forces regrouped at the bottom of the hill and began talking about what they saw during the battle, we could see that Tabares's regiment had been hit the hardest. It suffered the most casualties because they made a trench just below the level of the *placersillo*. And we had called his attention to this danger, and he had replied, "What I want is for them to charge at our bayonets so that we can break their formation."

We had responded by asking, "How important could breaking their formation be if in the end they took your position?"—as they succeeded in doing.

We pointed this out to him and went on to talk about the savagery of the fighting and how those monstrous Spanish didn't seem to be human. If their bugler played for them to charge the bayonets, they charged decisively at the designated position without regard for how many men they were losing.

Because we already knew this through the experience of so many battles, we had advised Tabares on Spanish warfare. But Tabares didn't listen to us. Not only did he allow them to take the trench with the bayonets and gunfire, he also let his most courageous fighters get hurt. Among them was one of the Cárdenas brothers; they both were called the *jimaguas,* because they were twins. They were so similar in appearance that in the camp you couldn't conduct pressing business with one of them because you couldn't tell them apart. One twin was shot in the groin in such a way that the wound drained his bladder. He had to be given water constantly so that he wouldn't die. Despite the severity of his wound, he survived.

Also, Captain Mayato was shot in the arm. He was at General Betancourt's position, fighting beside him and Colonel Fernando Diago.

In the afternoon, the general distributed the two thousand rounds that he wrongfully declined to give out before the battle. If he had done so, we would have been able to take the arms from the dead Spanish soldiers, and their ammunition too; so perhaps we would have had more than the two thousand rounds he so preciously guarded.

The wounded who couldn't march were left at Purgatorio in a prefecture that was near camp El Infierno; the area had been liberated in the battle.

From there, we marched to the hill called Pan. Having arrived ahead of us, Tabares marched from there to Camarioco, his zone, to unite with the Cárdenas Brigade. The Betances and our Matanzas regiment stayed in Pan.

After a few days there, an infantry company from the Southern Brigade arrived; they were from Eduardo García's forces, coming for ammunition and medicine. But when Brigadier Pedro E. Betancourt arrived in the province, García was already being called Brigadier; this was in June 1896. In February 1898, he was already the commissioned commander of the province, and later the title officially went into effect. This happened because the criminal Avelino Rosa was removed from office; he had been governor of the war. Commander in Chief Máximo Gómez decided that General Betancourt was the best suited to be commander of the province. Although he wasn't the oldest commander of a brigade, he was the most successful in the province in fighting the Spanish. And this was true for our forces in general (Sanguily's forces), in that during Weyler's ruthless invasion we were nearly the only ones who truly felt the spirit of Cuba Libre in that province that was the most dangerous of the war. Matanzas was so dangerous because it was the most densely populated province. It also had more railroad lines that helped to transport both *mambises* and Spanish columns to reinforce their respective troops who found themselves in trouble. Commander in Chief Máximo

Gómez found this to be so true that he said that a *majá*[25] who fought in Matanzas, always under fire and always harassing the enemy, was worth more than a general in any other province.

Brigadier García was there with us when the Spanish came with formidable columns and all of the equipment necessary to fortify the hill of Pan and to put a telescope there in order to see a great distance away. That day we had a skirmish, then retreated. During the skirmish, the Spanish killed a corporal known as Prieto. And some of our troops remained in a small spot on the hill facing Palenque; the Spanish controlled the rest of the area.

That night we went down the hill in order to march to Palenque, the headquarters, with the Betances infantry escorts. They then marched to Purgatorio, accompanying Brigadier García, who went on to his brigade.

After a few days at Palenque, we also marched to Purgatorio. When we arrived, we found out that the enemy column that we had left in Pan had followed our trail the following day to Purgatorio; they wanted to see if they could attack the wounded and the very sick whom we had there. So the very sick got into the trenches with the general that day, and alone General Betancourt, the courageous Colonel Diago, and the very sick fought back an entire column. The Spanish tried to reap their revenge on them, but they failed. They couldn't imagine that those sick men, all of them black, could defend themselves. Indeed, almost all the soldiers for liberation who fought in 1897 in that bloody province were black.

Those sick soldiers were leaning in the trench, those who couldn't stand up. Even while propping themselves up, they were still able to fire while leaving patches of skin in the trench. Although the soldiers had green pockmarks that looked contagious, General Sanguily and Colonel Diago, without fear of getting sick themselves, defended them until the Spanish infantry got into its position. Then they had to retreat because of the crushing number of the Spanish forces. But the Spanish could only

---

25. *Majá:* Literally, a large, venomless snake indigenous to Cuba. Known for eating small chickens and chicken eggs, it is regarded as harmless to humans. During the War of Independence, "*majá*" became a pejorative for Cubans enlisted in the Liberation Army but who seldom fought—in other words, a coward.

satisfy themselves with taking Sergeant Fernando Alfonso prisoner. He had been custodian of the sick, and in the retreat he broke his leg. And because all of the rest could barely walk, no one could carry him; this was why he was taken prisoner.

The Spanish charged so aggressively because minutes before they had encountered fourteen or fifteen men who all were part of the escort company of General Betancourt's cavalry. This group of brave soldiers had gone in search of oxen for the sick in a nearby cane field. At that moment, the heroic Commander Escobar fell. He had been promoted to lieutenant colonel because of seniority and so he became commander of the escort. It was a little cavalry that accompanied the two Betances infantries. According to General Betancourt, the unit carried this title thanks to the patriot of that name, who was a personal friend of the general, and so sent from Paris as many supplies as was possible for the regiment. His supplies constituted most of what did arrive during that tremendous time! And we used them, since we were the force that fought with such valor. Molina's miserable guerrillas killed Escobar and took his body. They followed the escort in their retreat, as they went to inform the general about the sad events of the day. But those miserable guerrillas followed this group of heroic men.

Escobar's death encouraged the sick to take arms. A few minutes after the news, those murderers who had followed the escort arrived.

In addition to being a dear commander, as Escobar was because of his bravery, his death had had a purpose. He had gone in search of food for those very same sick, those who despite their illness didn't retreat. The sick were Julio Ibáñez, Félix Lombart, and others; they didn't want to retreat before avenging the death of their beloved commander, firing several shots at those enemies of Cuba's liberty.

We were there for several days and we saw that the Spanish left without being able to build a fort at Pan. They had failed perhaps because we had put up such stiff resistance. We stayed there until the end of February.

yo deje á la Audien
cia, puedes tener
la seguridad, que
saldras absuelto
por sentencia firm

Ya veo que has
adelantado much
en la letra, que
nes bastante cla
ra, sigue aplica
gescribe todos lo
dias una hora
do para que t
perfecciones her
oures la letra

III.

1898

In El Pan de Matanzas: March 1898

IN MARCH 1898, we had two or three very sick soldiers in our unit, among them my brother and the courageous Fabián Elisea. I helped him as much as I helped my brother because he was such a brave and dedicated fighter, particularly in the most dangerous situations. For example, when we were on a march and we suspected an ambush, Elisea and another soldier named Rogelio would go with me to investigate ahead of the unit. This way we could keep the entire force from being ambushed and so limit the number of casualties. I should say that during my time in the infantry, despite my rank as lieutenant aide to Sanguily, I was the *práctico* and always took this duty because of my experience. (Later, they took this rank from me when I had that argument with Sanguily and I went to the escort of the General Betancourt's cavalry.) My rank was then given to Juan Domínguez, who was only secretary sergeant to Captain Manuel Quintero. In the entire war he didn't learn how to fire a shot, not even with a 38-caliber revolver. In fact, he never saw what the battles were like. He only had a .38, and he always retreated with the unarmed before the intense fighting began; he never learned how to lead during combat or how to perform effectively under fire. The truth of his incompetence is borne out by the fact that after I left that force, it didn't have more than two skirmishes. And I am certain that Domínguez didn't shoot a single shot in either one.

As the *práctico,* I marched at the head of the force. It had gotten back to me that some of the soldiers were spreading rumors about me, but I didn't stop leading the marches because I was helping us to avoid attacks. Our missions were very dangerous, and our marches were often very difficult, owing to how quickly we had to move so that daylight wouldn't catch us in some dangerous area. That would have been our ruin, and at that time, being ruined was like saying "the countryside is pacified."

Now that I've explained why I protected Elisea as dutifully as I protected my brother, I will return to the events of the war. From our camp at Pan, Sanguily and I, along with ten other soldiers, went to the headquarters at Purgatorio to see if the general had received any ammunition.

General Betancourt told us that some few munitions had been ordered, but that they were headed to Canímar, a good distance away. It would take two marches to get them, one leaving at night and another for the return.

Because it was daytime, it was impossible to cross the railroad lines from Matanzas going to Guanábana. So we decided that Sergeant Manuel Castillo would accompany our usual ten infantrymen to go look for the ammunition. Sanguily and I stayed in order to return to the hill of Pan for the night, so that we would be with our unit. We didn't want the Spanish to attack the camp while we were gone. Then the general said to Sanguily that for the return march to Pan, he was to take two pairs of the Betances regiment, the general's infantry escort that had accompanied him there. Sanguily replied that with me he had enough men already. But that answer astonished the general. "You have that much confidence in this boy?" he said.

"I have so much confidence in him," Sanguily replied," that without him I know that I'd be deprived of a comrade even if the entire force went with me."

Amazed to see that I was beardless, the general said, "Well look, one of these days I'm going to have to send you on a mission to Pinar del Río to the headquarters of General Mayía, Commander of the Department of the West. They have to make a forced march and cross Mariel's *trocha* at Majana. I won't allow you to take this boy. He's so young, he's doing more than what he should have to; he has enough on his hands without having to risk the hazards of that *trocha*."

Sanguily paused for a moment then replied, "Look, General, he's the soul of my unit. So, if you, as my superior officer, order me to march without him and without Juan Abreu, I'll go. But I'll go without the necessary confidence in the men who accompany me. In all the hours of the worst fighting that I've been a part of, these two have taken the added responsibility to help me and to direct the force with the help of Captain Quintero."

The general then addressed himself to Colonel Fernando Diago, his commander of the headquarters, and said, "What do you think, Diago, of what Sanguily says about this boy?"

Colonel Diago replied, "If he says it, he must have a reason for praising the boy's bravery. He has a force of about four hundred men, and they have fought many times with those persecuting Spanish. His confidence in this man has been tried and forged in battle."

The general called me to approach him and asked, "Which town are you from?"

"From Sabanilla del Encomendador," I replied.

"Why did you come to the war so young?"

"Because I believed that I should, General."

"When did you enlist?"

"Six months before you came to the war, General," I replied.

The conversation ended at this point. He ordered me to take two packets of cigarettes and a can of condensed milk. I didn't smoke the cigarettes and took them to my brother, who, as I said, was very sick at the camp at Pan.

Sanguily arrived at the dinner hour and was invited to eat with the general. But he saw that he was the only one invited, so he told the general that he couldn't accept the invitation if I weren't invited too. The general accepted and I ate with them and Colonel Diago as well. So the four of us all ate together. After so much of Sanguily's talk about my bravery, the general fully appreciated my military service to the Matanzas regiment. Because the Liberation Army lacked any real organization at that time, there hadn't been much notice of my role in carrying out the position of lieutenant aide. And for my part, I wasn't overly concerned with the official designation of my rank, because I had complete confidence in the loyalty and honesty of my commanding officer and friend, whom I loved as much, if not more, than my father.

By the end of the day, Sanguily and I had returned alone because, as I said, he didn't want to take the two pairs of infantry that the general wanted to give him in exchange for ours who had gone for ammunition. Sanguily had said that the two of us were all that was needed for the return; because I had experience for this kind of march, it would be as if he had the entire force with him. But during that damned return march, we destroyed our friendship forever!

There are things that crush a man's spirit and make the heart grow indifferent, even more so when it is as young as mine was at the time that I describe here. My soul lived for love and hope. I saw in the love of my commanding officer a father, and in him I recognized an honest and loyal friend. I held him in such high esteem that I dreamed of better days together with him, although the future for me was still unsure. I dreamed of being at his side, helping him in the fights we would face in war; I dreamed of being with him as his most faithful soldier and his most affectionate son!

But that damned return march! Something serious, very grave, happened between us on our way back to the camp. But I didn't shoot him because I would have had to give up the glorious ideal of a liberated Cuba, and I would have had to surrender to the Spanish. But I did load my *tercerola*[1] to prevent him from following me. No one would have understood the reason for my killing him, if I had done it. I told him this and he agreed not to follow me. He hadn't walked half a league before he got lost, because of his lack of a sense of direction. In my entire life I have never seen anyone so inept in learning paths and roads, not even after we had walked that road more than fifty times. So he got lost, and I arrived at camp alone. The guard was very alarmed to see me without him.

My heart was filled with sorrow because of that argument, and I swore to him that our break would be forever. Everyone in the camp bombarded me with questions about Sanguily, and I responded to them with insults and curses. I walked off and camped alone; I was resigned to stay there, then to go to help my brother until he was better. Then I would leave for another force.

A few minutes after I got to the camp, we heard shots fired by Sanguily; he fired to call for help because he couldn't find the road to the camp. The guards responded with a shot, a signal that they were coming to help guide him back to the camp.

When he arrived, everyone was alarmed and tried to find out why the two of us were fighting, we who were regarded as one person in two. But he declined to give an explanation. And because he was their superior officer, they didn't continue to ask.

They came to my solitary camp to ask me what had happened, and I too refused to explain. At sunrise, I took the milk and cigarettes to my brother and Fabián, and I stayed in my own solitary camp; I left the

---

1. *Tercerola:* Short carbine rifle used by Cuban rebel infantry and cavalry.

force of the man who was no longer my commanding officer, as far as I was concerned. He did try, though, through several intermediaries, to get me to change my mind. He didn't come to talk to me himself, but he did send Captains Juan E. Abreu and Manuel Quintero, who tried to intercede.

But I didn't provide any kind of explanation, given the possibility that once again I might be friends with the man for whom I had had great respect until that day—respect not as my commander, but as a beloved friend, like a son for a father. Because of all of the hardships of the war, I had believed in him, and had been his greatest admirer. I believed in him so because he was the highest-ranking officer under whom I had fought, and I believed in him because of the bitter days and many liberation battles in which we fought together. In those most dangerous moments of battle, in those supreme hours, we were always inseparable. How I was deceived!

After three days of this situation, General Betancourt arrived at our camp. When Sanguily went to meet the general, he immediately asked about me. The general really didn't know what to say when he saw me. He was just astonished because he thought that the Spanish had killed me at the crossing of the rail lines at Bahía, close to Ceiba-Mocha. There was a strategic crossing there, going from Purgatorio to Pan or vice versa. What's more, the day that we returned, there was an enemy column camped at Mocha. Usually, when they were camped there, they would make an ambush at the crossing, because they knew that we were going to cross at that point. But thanks to my quick decision making, we were not their victims that day.

Believing what I just described—that I'd been killed at the crossing—the general didn't understand why Sanguily looked perplexed when he asked about me. Sanguily responded, with his head tilted, saying that nothing had happened to me, but that I didn't want to be in the force any longer, that I was so adamant, in fact, I was camped alone a short distance from the main camp. The general immediately asked what was the reason for my wanting to leave. He was astonished because on the same day of our disagreement Sanguily had declared how highly he regarded my company and loyalty.

When the general arrived, he wanted to know the reason for my resolution, and why I was away from my post. I said to him that I couldn't explain why, but that there was nothing that would keep me in that regiment of Matanzas under Sanguily's command.

Then the general wanted Sanguily to explain my position, but Sanguily said that he had already asked and he wasn't going to ask again.

Then the general asked me what decision I had made. I told him that if he didn't allow me to go to his escort unit or another force in another province, I would go to the province of Havana.

The general didn't have another solution, so he agreed to my request that I go to his escort squadron. There my services as an experienced and tireless fighter would be useful.

From that day on, I remained an assistant to General Betancourt, still an enlisted soldier, because Sanguily didn't want to clarify my rank. He thought that I would return for the privileges and rank I had achieved as a lieutenant aide in his force. But he was mistaken. When I take a position, I don't waver; nor does the price for my convictions concern me, no matter how high it may be—such are the casualties of war.

The same day that I enlisted in the general's escort, Colonel Diago asked to speak with me privately. During the conversation, he asked me as a gentleman to tell him what had happened, that he was going to be in the war my commanding officer and my new friend. And if we survived the war, perhaps he would hire me in peacetime. I don't know why I believed in this officer, whom I really did admire as a good protector and friend. I told him why I had taken my position to leave and what had happened with the man whom, until that day, I loved like a father.

My brother had improved when the general marched from the camp; so I then marched with him to Canímar. It was still the month of March.

From Canímar we marched to Purgatorio, where we received news of the armistice. When the news came, Estanislao Lamadrid and another youth came from Matanzas to enlist; and they had brought two good horses. It was about nine o'clock at night when we heard the amazing news that the peace of Cuba Libre had come! That day we were all so happy. I'd never seen such intoxication without alcohol! Everyone shot off their guns and fired all the ammunition we had. It looked like a great battle all night long. We even knocked together cooking cans; we didn't use very many for cooking.

The next morning, we went to the center of the woods to a clearing where we would receive families. Those who had family close by, and even those who didn't, went there to see the people from the town. It seemed as though we would never see them again.

Later, it was necessary to go looking for the Matanzas regiment that was in Viajaca, and to get there we had to cross the plain of Labata. This area was dangerous because of the guerrillas from Cabezas, Madruga, and Palos. No one knew if they had received the news from the Spanish forces that were operating in the area, that there was a cessation of hostilities. And because we didn't have more than the two horses that had just arrived with the new enlistees, no one wanted to risk crossing the plain. Everyone was saying, "The war's just ended; I'm not going to get killed because of carelessness."

Given this situation, I went to the general and said that I would go across the plain of Labata to Viajaca. I only asked for one of the horses that arrived the night before.

I was given the horse and I left for Viajaca. I was unconcerned with crossing the plain, what to others was a great danger. I crossed it in order to take the horse to my brother so that he could cross the valley on it. I had been told that he had a delicate leg, impaired by the illness from which he had recently recovered. I knew that if I didn't go and the force was attacked by some column or by the guerrillas, one of the first who would be endangered would be my brother if he were on foot. So I went to give him my horse, and I returned on foot.

When I met the guard for the camp at Viajaca, I told him that the war had just ended, that the news of the armistice had been given. (The Havana regiment was also there at the camp.) When they heard the news, they too were drunk with joy and showed it by shooting off their guns, playing bugles, and shouting "Cuba Libre!" In the midst of this merrymaking, the camp had to organize itself because I told them that they had to start a march at that hour, nine o'clock in the morning. They had to march to Mogote,[2] where the general was awaiting the reconcentration of the entire Northeast Brigade.

---

2. Mogote: A town in the province of Matanzas approximately twenty-five miles southwest from the city of Matanzas.

I gave the horse to my brother, who didn't appear to me to be strong enough to make the trip on foot, the danger of which, even with the armistice, was difficult to estimate. We arrived at Mogote at one o'clock in the afternoon.

Consider this "coincidence": while I was in the Matanzas infantry regiment, that unit beat the record for the number of battles fought. After I left, it had no more than two skirmishes. Also, before I joined the escort for General Betancourt's cavalry, because of its meager size it didn't have many skirmishes, and not a single machete charge; nor did they achieve any significant victories. Because of their small numbers, they maintained only defensive positions. In my first mission, with the escort of only sixteen men, we took four prisoners and killed thirty guerrillas who attacked us.

There at the camp at Mogote we received families who wanted to visit and to express their gratitude. After being there many days, the general sent a message to the owner of the nearby farm, called San Ignacio (the farm belonged to the merchant Cañizo, who now lived in Matanzas), to request that he sell some pairs of oxen to the force. His response was insulting; so the general ordered the cavalry from his escort to go there and take the oxen.

So sixteen of us from the cavalry went in search of the oxen.

We came to a place where two guerrillas were letting some oxen graze. We took the guerrillas prisoner, and we took the oxen back in the direction of the camp. But because the forts were close by, the Spanish soldiers in the forts started shooting at us. We didn't return fire and continued to drive the oxen we had just taken.

In reaction to our contemptuous attitude toward their gunfire, they ran out of the fort insulting and threatening us with a lot of gunfire. Just a short distance separated us from those impudent guerrillas. But as long as they didn't harm us, we didn't shoot or pay them any attention, even though their bullets flew by us like menacing flies.

But they did split the hoof of one of our horses, and a bullet went through the rider's clothes. So we turned our horses toward those impudent provocateurs. There were thirty of them on foot and sixteen of us on horseback.

Maybe they were so bold and insolent because they outnumbered us. They thought that we were scared of them and that after they shot a few times we would leave the oxen and run away. But they were wrong and their impudence cost them dearly—the lives of all of them, absolutely all of them!

We turned our horses directly toward them, without firing a shot, and we galloped toward the hill where they were positioned. They concentrated their fire on us, but we didn't stop galloping.

Once we got to the top of the hill, they were positioned in a tight group against our cavalry and ready to defend themselves in hand-to-hand combat.

So, as they stood there in their formation, we attacked with fifteen men (we now had fifteen because when we got close one of our men, Martín Molinet, was shot in the side). But we didn't stop, not even for that. We fell on their formation, a group of thirty men well formed in an "O" and shooting from every side. Every time that we killed one of them they closed the "O" more tightly, so the formation looked like a wheel sprocket.

We charged the horses at them, wielding our blood-soaked machetes, but they didn't stop shooting at us as we broke apart their formation as one would shuck an ear of corn. In this way we hacked through their formation until only one man was left standing: Lieutenant Romero. We couldn't kill him with a machete because this one fought like a lion with rabies. Surrounded by the bodies of his soldiers, with his hair flying wildly, and with a machete in his hand, he stood defiantly, challenging us with his gaze and his stance.

A number of us galloped at him and tried to hit him with our machetes. With skill we had never seen before, he waited until the blow of the machete was close; then he jumped down on the ground and the machete just hit empty air. Then, with the skills of an artistic equestrian, he leaped up, grabbed the tails of the horses, and stabbed them with his machete.

Then three of us tried to attack him in succession. The first to rush that man-lion was the heroic Corporal Liborio Martínez; he missed Romero in the way I just described. The guerrilla inflicted two light wounds on him with the machete he yanked from the tail of the horse. And he inflicted two wounds on the horse that Martínez was riding. Corporal

Filomeno Hidalgo then took a turn, and Romero did the same thing to him. Hidalgo received two light wounds, also from Romero's machete, when he went by him without being able to take the lieutenant's weapon. Then Ezequiel García Benavides took a turn and was wounded in the same manner as the two before him. Then it was my turn. Reflecting on the situation, I said to my comrades, "Let's shoot this guy; he's crazy. A man who sees twenty-nine of his comrades dead all around him and thinks that he alone can fight those who just killed all the others can't be in his right mind!"

Then the young soldiers naturally began to make jokes. We were all very young, not yet twenty years old. But I objected to the jokes and to more hand-to-hand fighting, because it was impossible to touch him. It was just impossible to kill that man with a machete. My comrades listened to me, and our commanding officer in that attack, Secundino Alfonso, agreed with me too.

While I was explaining my sense of the situation to my comrades, this man was standing like a statue, defiantly. With eyes as wide open as his eye sockets would allow, with those fixed blue pupils and bloodshot corneas, he looked like a raging wild beast, ready to devour his attackers.

When he saw us point our two Mausers at him, he flexed his arms and tightly clutched his machete in expectation of the shots. They simultaneously hit him in the chest and went through his back. That valiant Spaniard lingered for a moment, then fell to the ground.

While he still had breath, he continued cutting and slashing with his machete in all directions, so that nobody could get near him. We kept our distance from him, commenting on how this man died. We had never seen anyone else die with such heroism as that lion showed.

When he exhaled his last breath, we came close to the body to take his machete, but it was as if it had been nailed to his hand. In fact, I couldn't pull it out of his hand because he was still gripping it so tightly.

But this was war, so we didn't lose time with scruples; we cut off his fingers to take the machete from him. While we finished this gruesome work, two of us left with the one seriously wounded we suffered. As our one wounded retreated, twelve of us remained behind to take the guns and supply belts from the dead. All of them had Remingtons with yellow bullets;[3] they make horrible wounds because they break open such a big opening when they exit the body.

After taking the guns and ammunition from the bodies, we went to the headquarters that was at Mogote, very close by, on the hill. Because the headquarters and the general were on the hill, everyone was able to see our fight perfectly.

Those guerrillas paid for their audacity with their lives, but it did amaze us to see those thirty men fight to the death without surrendering, not one. Of this group, the majority of them were Cuban.

When we arrived, the infantry had killed some of the one hundred animals; they had already driven to the fort the three oxen we captured when we took the three prisoners without firing a shot. It was because we took those animals from the pasture that those guerrillas ran from the fort and tried to frighten us with their shouts and insults. This was very expensive because they all paid with their lives for their audacity. Only the lieutenant and a few others were Spanish; they had been in Cuba before the war. The lieutenant worked for many years in Cañizo's store. He joined the army, was made a lieutenant, and made the destruction of the sugar mill, San Ignacio, his top priority. That had been our camp in 1896, when we were in the cavalry. But in the middle of the terrible year 1897, when we were in the infantry, we had had to retreat to the woods. Like so many of our other camps, it was converted into detachments of small forts and used by guerrillas. The small forts protected the owner's farm and produce. When they found our abandoned camp, they turned the area into a series of paths going in every direction. Meanwhile, the big Spanish columns went after our camps of infantry installed in the woods and mountains.

Let's return to our arrival at Mogote with all of the booty from our victorious fight; our return turned into a great big party. Meanwhile, we took the three prisoners to the headquarters surrounded by our infantry,

---

3. Yellow bullets: Ammunition for the Remington carbine, used by guerrillas and Spanish regulars. Because the bullets were tipped with a casing of copper alloy, they were particularly destructive when penetrating flesh. Upon impact, the bullet expanded or "mushroomed," creating an exit wound much larger than the entry wound. The destructiveness of the bullet was much greater than that of the Mauser ammunition.

who amused themselves by making fun of them. After our soldiers ridiculed them for a while, two of them became enraged; they stood up and began to shout insults back at our infantrymen. To restore order, the general ordered the infantry away from where the prisoners were being held. And in response to the insults, he ordered the prisoners to get used to being prisoners. But they cursed the general too! In fact, he was so insulted that he ordered the two insolent prisoners executed by machete.

A sergeant in the Betances infantry, Félix Lombar, volunteered to kill one of them, and the other was assigned to Ezequiel García Benavides. Some of us went to see the execution of those two who went looking for their own death by being so insulting and disrespectful.

Both Félix Lombar and Ezequiel Benavides were very large, strong men. They argued on the way from camp to the execution spot about who could deal the most forceful machete blows. Lombar was first, and made good use of his size and strong build, killing the soldier in two blows. Ezequiel Benavides went next. Before he started his work, though, he wanted to smoke a cigarette with the prisoner who was to be his victim. With this gesture of kindness, he led the prisoner to believe that he wasn't like Lombar and that he wasn't going to kill him. He asked the prisoner for his underpants, shoes, and shirt. The prisoner gave them to him, believing his promise that he wasn't going to kill him. Ironically, it was this prisoner who had heaped the most insults on the soldiers and who had cursed the general. His curses were followed by those of the one who was already dead on the ground without a head. Seeing this, the second soldier, the cause of the two deaths, begged for his life.

Benavides continued to talk and to deliberate, as we expected, until we saw the result of this drama of blood.

The prisoner asked his executioner if he could return to the camp. Benavides said "yes," and as the prisoner turned to go, Benavides hit him with the machete. In reality, he put his rival executioner to shame because he dealt one of those machete blows that we *mambises* called "*balvitarro.*" The blow sliced through the shoulder at a slant to the other side, almost cutting the man in two. The machete rested in his right shoulder after entering and cutting through from the left side. "Tremendous blow!" everyone exclaimed. (Those dead guerrilla prisoners were Cubans; they were traitors!)

When the executions were over, we didn't bury those two who died for their insolences. If they hadn't been so insulting, they wouldn't have met such a fate. As for the third prisoner, he was of greater importance because he had been in charge of the supply store for the farms as well as an administrator for Cañizo. Because of these responsibilities, and because he remained respectful when his two comrades began shouting their insults—even telling them to shut up at one point—nothing happened to him.

I say that we didn't bury those two because the coffins in similar cases were the hill and its soft breezes; these hills were bloated with corpses, as there had been many similar executions!

When we returned to the camp, there was more partisan debate over the two macheted men. Some argued that Félix's blow was tremendous. Others said that Benavides was the champion. I was on Benavides's side because he had done it in fewer blows, as everyone saw. But all of the discussion stopped when the big party began. There was lots of dancing for those who wanted to dance, and grilled meat for those who just wanted to eat. I didn't want to be near all the noise and merrymaking, so I went to lie down in my tent until nightfall. Then we spent the night in an area where there was abundant pasture for the horses. Earlier we had passed the day in the *batey* of the Mogote sugar mill; it was a quarter mile from where the infantry was camped and where the headquarters were at the foot of the hill. Before we returned for the night, we received orders that those who hadn't gone on the victorious charge were to stay with the infantry to search for supplies from the San Ignacio sugar mill supply store. The prisoner whom we did not execute volunteered to take charge of the store; this was his attempt to thank the general.

As it got dark, two companies of infantry began to march with a group of the escorts from the cavalry vanguard. As they approached the Mogote sugar mill, they saw that it was on a very high hill. Before they climbed, they were at a river where they heard a loud conversation that wasn't coming from the families that were living there. It couldn't have been coming from the forts for the sugar mill either, because they had destroyed all of the little detached forts when they left to avoid our taking the oxen. That conversation was suspicious because of its noise and because we would be exposed on the climb up the hill, in that there was no grass to hide us along the way. I assumed that the noise was coming from some reinforcements who could have come from the nearby town of Cidra. Given the short distance, they could have heard the gunshots from the fight that ended with our machete charge.

When they went to get the supplies from the sugar mill store, a prisoner named Florentino volunteered to investigate the sounds. He promised that if the noise was from enemy forces he would return and tell us, but we doubted his promise. He objected, saying that now, after having treated him so well, eating with us and so forth, was he going to repay our kindness with betrayal and ingratitude? Finally, it was agreed that he would go to investigate. When he got close he was supposed to make certain that they were enemies and then he was to return to tell us, so that we could retreat. He got to the spot and saw that they were guerrillas from Cidra. They had come to collect the bodies and to guard the effects that they had abandoned when we made our charge and killed their guards. Not only was Florentino dishonest in respect to his promise to us, but when he got inside the guerrillas' stone masonry fort and had the protection of those old demolished sugar mill buildings, that liar shouted, "Viva España!" His shouts deafened the area, and they were followed by more shouts of "Viva España!"

Because of Florentino's lies, the bugler played to call their soldiers to their positions to defend the fort. Given the situation, our men returned to their point of departure. We lamented that in that moment we hadn't known to kill the guerrillas that morning, because there was no one left in those forts. That's how we should have approached the sugar mill. And so we would have taken what we most wanted, which was salt, although the *pacíficos* did bring us some during our reconcentration at Mogote. We didn't think that it was enough, since we assumed that the hostilities could break out again, and we wanted to have enough salt on hand that we wouldn't be without it again, as we had been before. But the general didn't want to lose men attacking those forts, an effort to which the entire force was dedicated. Although they probably had trenches, we didn't think that the guerrillas from Cidra had the ability to put up a real fight, not inside the fort. But seeing that they could wound or kill some of us, and because none of our veterans (each one of whom was worth all the guerrillas put together) deserved to be wounded in that situation, we returned to our camp at Mogote. The following day, Colonel Enrique Loinaz del Castillo arrived; he was commissioned, according to what was reported by the government or by the central command (Jefatura) of the western department. He camped at our camp or at the headquarters' camp. The day after he arrived, Brigadier Eduardo García, commander of the Southern Brigade, arrived, and presented seven guerrillas who had joined those columns.

Because of the armistice, we all relaxed and got comfortable while we were camped at Mogote; it was a place where we could sleep and let the horses loose to graze in good pastureland near the Magdalena sugar mill. Our soldiers let them run free without their saddles or riders. Many of those men didn't want to listen to my warning that from the moment that we killed those guerrillas by machete, we shouldn't trust the armistice.

Those who refused to listen to me unsaddled their horses and let them run free. But the majority of the troops listened to me, kept their saddles on their horses, and didn't let them run loose.

At about seven in the morning, some men tried to slaughter a cow, but it gave them a lot of trouble, and in the end they couldn't kill it because it kept getting away. It was nine o'clock by the time they caught the cow for the last time. They called me to come deliver the coup de grâce with a dagger, because everyone knew how skilled I was at that kind of thing. I went to kill that surly cow with only a dagger, and it fell with its throat cut. And at that very moment we heard the alarm, and the entire escort unit wanted to run for cover. Lower down on the hill close by, we could see a group of eight or ten men in the cavalry dressed in blue. They were bringing back the horses to those riders who didn't listen to my advice and had let them loose. First, I thought that the approaching men were Brigadier García and the guerrillas. Moments before, he had left along the same road with those guerrillas, all dressed in blue; they had just surrendered. While I was thinking about the situation, we signaled the new group of cavalry to halt in order to be recognized. They stopped, but they were waiting for the vanguard and the bulk of the force to come down the hill.

It was a steep hill, so a big force would have to come down slowly. As it turned out, the eight or ten soldiers were scouts from Colonel Alfau's Spanish column. We realized this after I had said that it could be

Brigadier García. The realization gave me a wrenching feeling in my gut, and I shouted, "To the horses! It's not Brigadier García!" But there was a good deal of confusion that naturally arises among such young soldiers, as we all were. Most of them said that I had already said not to run and that we should all stay there on foot. I didn't listen to them and mounted my horse that was nearby, already saddled. All of the others who had heeded my advice not to let their horse loose followed my example and mounted their horses too.

Eight or ten of us mounted our horses, among them Secundino, the commanding officer of the escort. We saw that the suspicious soldiers were following us, so I shouted to them, "Halt! Who goes there!?"

It looked as though their vanguard had already gotten down to the bottom of the hill. It was a group of about one hundred cavalrymen galloping toward us, and being convinced that it was a Spanish column, we opened fire on them; and they fired back in response. Then they tried to attack our flank to cut off our retreat to Purgatorio. But the flank that they approached ran along the border of Mogote toward the west. Mogote, you see, is connected to Purgatorio by a range of hills and mountains. And when they threw their horses along that range, they were going to run into the infantry camp along the way, but they didn't know this. Despite the fact that we fired alarm shots to alert the infantry, they didn't understand, thinking we were still shooting in celebration of the armistice.

All of them were in the camp; some were cooking while others were lying down in their tents, when suddenly the Spanish were right on top of them, trampling them or butting them with their horses' chests.

In all of this confusion, the fighting was hand to hand, as only a few soldiers in those first moments could open fire on our attackers. They were trying to cut off our retreat, but didn't know that they were going to run into our infantry.

They were trampling the *ranchos* until they ran into the headquarters, just at the moment when Colonel Fernando Diago, General Betancourt, and Loinaz were coming out. The last one out, Loinaz, ran into the Spanish Lieutenant Ruiz, and it looked as though he were drunk. If he had arrived sober, perhaps Cuba would have lost one of its fighting forces. For when Ruiz hit Colonel Loinaz with the chest of his horse, he fell under the horse and Ruiz could have struck him with his sword. But as luck would have it, Loinaz received only a bump. He grabbed the horse's reins, pulled out his revolver, and shot the bold Ruiz, who then fell from his horse. So Loinaz escaped certain death.

I should mention that when that Spanish cavalry tried to cut off our retreat, they didn't know whether or not our infantry had returned from its "maneuver." Because if they had known for certain, the destruction would have been tremendous for our infantry! Because, like us, they weren't expecting the Spanish.

They fought the Spanish cavalry as they ran surprised from their huts toward the commanding officers of the respective camps, all looking for their arms. All of the guns were stacked in a row in front of the commanding officers' tents to prevent the men from shooting their guns off in the air. There was also emery paper there because the men were required to keep their guns clean and well lubricated.

So, even though the Spanish knocked our soldiers over with their horses, and even though our troops couldn't defend themselves, they quickly ran to where they needed to, each one to his commanding officer's tent.

Despite the dire circumstances, they killed only two or three of our truly venerated men. All of the dead were war-hardened veterans; among them was Sergeant Nicolás Polledo, Colonel Diago's orderly, and Corporal "Congo" of the escort. It was he whose horse's hoof was split the day of the oxen incident. That was the reason that we turned on those bold Spaniards, until not one was left.

They killed Corporal Congo because of his misplaced altruism. When I mounted my horse, several others did likewise. But there was a soldier at my side, Victor Naranjo, who didn't have time to cross the entire distance to get to the infantry. (I assumed that getting there would have saved him.) I signaled to him that the general's horse didn't have a rider for the moment. This was because the general was encamped with the infantry. The horse that I pointed out to Naranjo was closer than mine, so he could have mounted it before I got to my horse. But he was too scared, seeing that the enemy was so close. While I was getting to my horse, he went behind me rather than going to mount the general's horse.

I had signaled to him and said, "Mount that horse, Victor! When those soldiers charge at us, I'm not going to mount you on the back of my horse, because there are other horses running loose. If you don't ride one of them, the Spanish will take it!"

So, when I mounted my horse, it looked as though the vanguard was right on top of me because they were charging right at us. Some of our troops began firing at them, while the rest retreated toward Purgatorio. These were the ones who could do nothing more than mount the horses that were within reach but had no saddles or bridles. This was because the Spanish soldiers who were just a short distance away saw everything, and tried to cut off the retreat to Purgatorio that the first group had begun, certain that those of us who were firing would also head in that direction. With the first shots that Secundino Alfonso fired, Victor Naranjo threw himself at me and grabbed my leg; he was standing on the ground close to my horse. I could feel the man's terror as he grasped my leg, and I realized that he was paralyzed with fear. Trying to avoid getting killed too—knowing that he was not going to let go of me—I hit him with the butt of my gun, and he had to let me go. Then I opened fire on the Spanish as I retreated.

But poor Congo. He was retreating along with me, but he stopped to mount Naranjo on his horse, despite having the Spanish cavalry closer than a city block away. Naranjo jumped down to the ground and grabbed Congo's waist, pulling Congo to the ground with him. Panic-stricken, Naranjo grabbed Congo so tightly that he couldn't break free from Naranjo's grip until two soldiers from the cavalry got there. They were part of the group that attacked us from the front while the rest went around trying to cut off our retreat. They had gotten caught up in our infantry camps. I was now a short distance away when I turned my head and I saw the two soldiers dismount their horses while the rest of the cavalry surrounded the victim and his helper. Congo couldn't defend himself because Naranjo was holding on to him, trembling with fear and cowardice. And the Spaniards struck them with their machetes, the two already on the ground and defenseless. I stood up and opened fire. Then the group that was standing there watching the mutilation charged at me.

They chased me hard, shooting at me and riding with their machetes hanging in their sheaths. I had to ride hard while firing back, as I retreated toward Purgatorio.

I should say that this path ran parallel to the infantry camp. And because I was close to the crossing point of our two paths of retreat, we could see everything that happened with all the confusion of the Spanish cavalry soldiers and our infantry. So when the Spanish Lieutenant Ruiz knocked down Colonel Loinaz with his horse—and given that it happened as Loinaz was leaving the general's *rancho*—I thought that it was General Betancourt who fell under the bold lieutenant's horse. I opened fire on the lieutenant, and shouted the alarm so that Secundino Alfonso would do as I did and shoot in the same direction. The Spanish officer then fell from Loinaz's shot. (Loinaz fell on his back, grabbed the horse's reins to avoid being trampled, then shot Ruiz; all of this happened in great confusion.)

The soldiers had arrived in Purgatorio in order to exchange places. The Betances forces were going to Matanzas and the forces there were coming to Purgatorio. Because all of them were war-hardened soldiers, they were able to get to their arms under the conditions I just described; less experienced troops wouldn't have been able to do so. There was a soldier in the infantry who was knocked down three times by Spanish soldiers on horseback before he could get to the company's armory. Trampled so by the Spanish horses, the troops somehow got to the armory, got their weapons, and defended themselves by shooting at close range. Because the Spanish were right on top of them, they couldn't use their machetes. For example, the moment that the soldier fell under the horse, he grabbed his gun.

General Betancourt protected himself that day, something he knew very well how to do in situations like that. He fought between the Spanish soldiers' horses, hitting some of the soldiers on the right and left. He then stabbed Second Lieutenant Sabino Céspedes, who didn't fight with real gusto.

When we reached Purgatorio, we reorganized ourselves into our proper divisions and then we left for the hills of Camarones. There, Captain Martín Duen withdrew from General Betancourt's forces because Duen was extremely upset. When Escobar, commander of the Betances regiment, was still alive, Duen was second in command of the regiment. When Escobar died, Duen, for legal reasons, remained the commander of the regiment. So, during the bloodiest period of the war, when it was necessary to try the capabilities of potential commanders for their courage and leadership, Duen was tested. But as soon as he received the news of the armistice, when families of the town came to visit us, I don't know why, but General Pedro Betancourt gave the order to look for Guillermo Schweyer, who was then only captain of sanitation. And Betancourt gave him the command of that courageous regiment. It was then that Captain Martín Duen left and went to the Havana regiment so as not to suffer the insult of being ordered around by someone who passed the entire war on the banks of the Canímar River, close to the city. Shweyer didn't know what a strategic location it was, even though it was his own camp.

Here Duen's example well illustrated the kind of racial injustice that a great part of white Cuban society practiced. Martín Duen was black, and blacks made up all of the Northeast Brigade in the province of Matanzas, with the exception of General Betancourt and Colonel Fernando Diago. As courageous soldiers, they withstood the vicissitudes of the war in 1897, as we all did. Indeed, for the most part, we were all black, and so each time, on the battlefield or in an ambush, that a soldier of the Liberation Army in the province of Matanzas died, it was some poor black. In the hour of sacrifice, we gave our lives.

And as I said earlier in this historical narrative, some of our white compatriots in the war didn't participate in racial discrimination. That's why, at the hour of sacrifice, the black was inspired to lift his heart like a brother to the height of the sacrosanct ideal of liberty. Black and white embraced each other, and so together they celebrated victory; and together they fell under the enemy's steel.

But at the end of the war, or as soon as victory was certain, it became necessary to ignore or to obscure the heroism and valor of those with dark skin. For white soldiers, it wasn't possible to present blacks as commanding officers to the privileged white families who visited us.

What a hard lesson, given by a country that boasted that it aspired to breathe the intoxicating air of eternal liberty.

To construct a magnificent building of weight and stature, it is essential that the foundation be perfect and solid. When a solid foundation is lacking, the entire edifice will fall to the ground because of its weakness.

Let's return to Martín Duen, who despite the injustice he was made to endure, still felt grateful that his case came to the attention of General Pedro E. Betancourt, who was one of the few "good" generals who didn't execute soldiers. He was different from many of the generals who, to justify themselves in a case like this one, would deny the soldier the right to leave or to protest by hanging him.

So Captain Martín Duen left the regiment, and later, there in Camarones, Martín Moliner died of his wounds. Despite the fact that he received a serious wound the day of the battle at Mogote, we were able to retreat with him. But on the retreat march they absentmindedly left him unattended, and this turned out to be his death. Although his wound was serious, it was healing, and he had stopped feeling the cruel pain that the wounded always feel.

Colonel Loinaz left Camarones to go to the province of Havana. His going there resulted in the division of the Havana and Matanzas provincial forces.

Those of us in the cavalry escort went to the north on the border of the two provinces, Havana and Matanzas. After a few days, the general ordered us to go on a reconnaissance mission. We arrived at a stock of arms that was left there because during the days we were in that area, we went to the town of Caraballo, where the Spanish had left their posts. They did so because the blockade by the American naval fleet had forced the Spanish to concentrate their forces on the coasts and on the population there.

So, given the situation, we were able to stay in the area freely, with only the guerrillas around. Although they were in the area in greater numbers than we in the cavalry, the quality of our fighters outweighed their numbers.

We arrived at Purgatorio and we met the force there; it hadn't moved since we left because the general had already received the news that the Spanish columns wouldn't attack us because of the blockade. Because of these circumstances, the infantry didn't have more battles to wage after I left.

From Purgatorio we went on to Viajaca, where we camped. There, the infantry camped in the mountains while we in the cavalry camped in an old company store, also called Viajaca. The following day, we saw the guerrillas of Cabezas and Palos coming through La Vija, and so we got into our battle lines and opened fire on them.

That day there were two small groups of the escort regiment, called the squadrons. I say "called" because in total we barely had thirty men;

we were divided fourteen or fifteen in the vanguard—under the command of Secundino Alfonso—and a group of the rear guard, under the command of Andrés Martínez; they were both mestizos,[4] and showed the bravery in battle that is typical of their race. I was in the vanguard because from the day that I joined the escort, I wanted to be with a group of real fighters. But those in the infantry told the older members of the escort that I was going to take the glory and fame from everyone in the cavalry. They started the rivalry between the two groups of comrades. So that day the rear guard wanted to compete in the battle to prove to me that they were also brave, and could kill with machetes like us. They were so eager that on the second volley of shots we invited them to charge with machetes on the cavalry that was directly in front, shooting at us. The cavalry was about two hundred men, a larger number than us. But they were positioned badly in that we were on a hill and they were in a hollow made by the old bodega of Viajaca. Despite the fact that they tripled us in number, they were content to shoot at us for more than ten minutes without advancing. At that point, we attacked with ferocity with our machetes, forcing their hasty retreat. That day I was the *práctico* in the escort pursuing the Spanish retreat because I had done the job since 1896.

In regard to their retreat, I thought that it was a false retreat, so I ordered our troops to slow down to avoid their trap. We advanced slowly so that they would only see our horses advancing at a trot as we fired on them.

But when I told our troops to hold their horses—not only to avoid an ambush, but also so that we could block the cavalry's retreat—our troops at first didn't want to slow down. But I was the *práctico*, so I was responsible for any defeat we might suffer for lack of precaution. So I turned my horse to retreat, but we were already heading down to the hollow where the Spanish were, so we opened fire on them. We had stepped into their trap, and the shooting was the signal for the column, Mocha de Madruga, that was coming to combine with the guerrillas in the hollow. They would have taken the position we abandoned for the charge.

---

4. Mestizo: A person of mixed racial heritage. In this context, the term most likely refers to a person of mixed Spanish and Indian racial heritage.

If they had combined their forces at the hill, and so had added to their superior numbers, we would have been totally wiped out because we had no means of escape. And although I didn't know that they were trying to combine forces, my experience in war taught me how to react to suspicious situations.

When I started to retreat, the rest of the troops had no other choice but to follow me, because they couldn't stay there without a *práctico*. There were two possible retreats: the first to the infantry camp, and the other in the direction of Madruga or Pipián, going through the only pass for the cavalry that ran along the Charco-Hondo River. I chose the latter in order not to bring the enemy to the infantry because it wasn't able to retreat to Madruga or Pipián. I also refused to charge as we arrived at the Charco-Hondo River in the retreat. We passed by an old house with no roof, in fact just a skeleton of a house, behind which we saw the cavalry of Mocha de Madruga posted, observing us, from behind.

They were posted there without firing a shot, waiting for us to charge. The two guerrillas invited us to charge with their quick retreat, and if we had shot, we would have fallen into their noose. Those detestable fugitives would have taken the hill that was at their back when the shooting started. And so those miserable bushwhackers would have taken our original position, and not a single one of us would have been able to save himself.

When I entered the old house, as we retreated, in the drawing room I ran into four or five soldiers in the enemy cavalry. I was carrying my loaded Mauser, and so in the moment they were aiming at me, I shot at them and then turned to take the other retreat to the infantry camp.

When those first two guerrillas saw that we didn't follow them immediately, they attacked with ferocity. Since we didn't allow them to combine forces, they probably wanted to see if they could make us rush into the other column, at our back. So I, the *práctico,* was shocked at the extremely dangerous situation for my men who trailed behind. Nevertheless, they came firing in retreat.

When I got on the path to the infantry camp, I saw that it was the infantry of Lieutenant Colonel Cuevas, belonging to the province of Havana and of the Southeastern Brigade. Because I was wearing new clothes, they confused me with the enemy. The path curved around where they had dug a trench; there they fired twelve or fourteen shots at me, but miraculously I escaped with my life, because the saddle and equipment protected me from the bullets. They also couldn't hit me because I ran at the trench very quickly to make my escape. I was able to grab the rifle of one of the soldiers, because he got tangled up in a vine. I yelled, "I'm Cuban! The Spanish are coming behind me!"

And I followed him to the trench without stopping because my comrades were coming behind me in a very dangerous situation, bringing the enemy down on top of us.

They returned to their positions in the trench in order to withstand the pressure of those two forces that had now combined.

As the last of my troops got into the trench where Cuevas's infantry was positioned (this is the same infantry that mistakenly shot at me), the enemy turned that same curve, and in one volley we killed eight of their horses and four or five of their riders. This forced the Spanish to move back and to begin the fight again on foot. But in addition to attacking us, they were attacking the infantry of Matanzas, with their headquarters that was stationed nearby. They opened fire and hammered the Spanish flank, so the Spanish had no choice but to retreat after two hours of fighting. But they didn't retreat before one of their soldiers climbed a tree on a hill that they held at their backs. From there he could see from which direction our cavalry was coming. And from the tree the soldier was yelling to his commanding officer, "They are going toward Las Vegas. What a *práctico* they have, the one on the black and white spotted horse. He's still the *práctico* and he's not wounded, even though the sergeant had said that he had injured him in the fight at the old house. If he had been wounded, he wouldn't still be the *práctico*. They owe it only to him that they were saved."

I was the one on the spotted horse. And it was I who eluded that soldier. We retreated through the field called Matriato. I stopped close to the town of Pipián until the shooting with the infantry stopped; it had lasted an hour at full force. And the Spanish had no choice but to retreat without having been able to dislodge the two infantry divisions from their positions. When the shooting stopped, I went with two men to see if the Spanish had retreated and to see the results of the fight. We were happy that we didn't suffer any casualties.

But I was amazed when I arrived at the trench where Cuevas's men were, the trench where they had shot at me, and later at the same distance at which they fired on the Spanish. There, in addition to the dead horses, I found many trails of blood and three or four broken watches, broken by our bullets. I examined the situation and the soldiers were dead from the damage to the watches. The guerrillas, like all the soldiers in the cavalry, wore their watches on their belts around their waists. So when a bullet hit a watch, the wound was always fatal because of the glass and metal. There were others killed, in addition to those killed by their watches.

After seeing them fight, I changed my opinion of Cuevas's infantry that mistakenly tried to kill me. Before I arrived at headquarters, I followed the retreat to see if I could see the Mocha column at the Charco-Hondo River; the column had to retreat toward Madruga, their headquarters. Actually, they were in the Cayajabo sugar mill, on the road to Madruga. It was close, and from there you could glimpse the hill that was pretty high. I counted more than twenty stretchers, not including the stretchers the two guerrillas carried; they retreated in a different direction. I left one of the guards there and ordered the other to go looking for the rest of the escort that I left at the end of our retreat.

While my orders were being carried out, I went to headquarters to inform the general that despite the despicable enemy's combined forces, there had been no change in circumstances for us and that we hadn't lost a single horse.

As it turned out, I didn't have to tell him anything about the difficult situation we had been in. He knew everything already; he had heard about the soldier whom the Spanish officer had ordered to climb a tree in order to observe our retreat. It was then that they told me that it was the *práctico*'s commands that had saved the cavalry. Also, the general knew about my bravery in the trench of Cuevas's troops. If I hadn't done what I did, our last soldiers to arrive would have had to abandon their horses and run for the woods to escape.

As I said, I didn't need to explain what had happened. When I arrived, the general greeted me with a letter of commendation, on the orders of the head of the general staff: Colonel Diago, and with the signature of Gabriel Villada, secretary of the general staff, and sanctioned by the general. Among other things, the letter stated:

In recognition of the merit (and excellence) and military attitude and of services lent by you to the cause of Cuban Independence. The general deservedly confers on you the rank of . . . In the homeland and liberty, Camp of Viajaca, on the . . . day of May, of the year one thousand eight hundred and ninety eight.

General of the Division

Pedro E. Betancourt

Commander 5th Corps, 1st Division

Matanzas

That afternoon we left and went to Purgatorio, and Cuevas's forces went with us.

General Betancourt left Purgatorio, with a part of the escort, to go to the province of Havana, to Alberto Nodarse's camp. Nodarse was commander of one of the Havana province brigades.

When the rest of the escort left with the general, the part that stayed went on a mission to look for livestock for the infantry because they had killed the last of their livestock near San Ignacio. I was one of the twelve who should have left with the general. But knowing that there was going to be a mission that would surely run into guerrillas, I gave myself permission to go, thinking that the general would let me. I also wanted to find a horse, if I were so lucky, for my brother to ride. He was in the infantry and I wanted him to go to the cavalry escort, so that he wouldn't be under Sanguily's orders. I was still very angry with him, although he tried to get me to return to his regiment. Indeed, he didn't stop petitioning Captains Quintero and Abreu for my transfer.

The general allowed me to go on the operation because he didn't want to quarrel over it. In the war he didn't want to restrict me or be overbearing, an example of the ideal of the freedom for which we fought.

The next day the general left on his trip, and we left for Viajaca. There, there was a *presentado* who had returned to the revolution because, with the armistice and the North American blockade, even the guerrillas surrendered, seeing the certain loss by the Spanish government. We went with twelve riders and Sanguily, who volunteered to go with us. We went through an area that was a shortcut between the towns of Cabezas, Palos, and Nueva Paz; it also went through the Josefita and Central Nueva Paz sugar mills. These were all fortified areas with guerrillas of the cavalry at each one of them.

This mission was very dangerous; nevertheless, with fourteen men, we tried our luck in order to find oxen. We arrived at Viajaca at eleven in the morning. From there we wanted to get to our next destination in fifteen minutes.

When the *presentado* who went with us as our *práctico* saw that we had only fourteen men, he asked if the rest would be coming soon. He asked for two reasons: first, he didn't believe that this little group was the entire number of riders we were going to have, because in all probability we would have to fight with 150 or two hundred guerrillas of the cavalry, positioned in the places just mentioned; the second reason was that this *presentado* dishonored himself by surrendering to the enemy in our zone, which had a lot of cavalry regiments. One regiment was, like the escort, under the command of Escobar; another was under Rafael Águila's command. So, we responded to him that no more troops were coming than what he saw, and he changed completely. He was scared to death. Although he returned to the war, he hadn't enlisted in the army; he simply came to our side but with another *presentado,* Justo Ojeda, who returned to the revolution and was made prefect in Viajaca. The *presentado* then looked for a pretext not to go. He said that the cattle hadn't gone out to the pastures that day. This was a lie, although he convinced everyone but me; in fact, Andrés Martínez, and Alférez of the escort were in agreement that we should go back to Purgatorio, even though the mission was under Sanguily's command.

When they started their return march, I remained sitting where I was; when they saw that I wasn't following, Andrés Martínez came back to find out why. I said that I thought the return was cowardly and that I would tell the general that we had returned without getting any oxen in order to avoid a fight with the guerrillas. He responded asking how we could go into a dangerous zone without a *práctico*. I told him that I was a *práctico* because I knew the area well. We had operated there the entire year of 1896.

Given my threat, there was no other choice for them but to continue the search, because they didn't want to be accused of cowardice before the general. So Andrés went to inform Sanguily of what I had just said.

Then everyone turned around and Andrés told me that Sanguily had stopped and gave me the responsibility of the *práctico* and that we were to go toward the towns and sugar mills as before.

It was around one in the afternoon when we began marching from the woods of Teresa Rueda toward the valley of Valera Acosta and Sangroni in the vicinity of Palos and the Josefita sugar mill. We all arrived at the border of the Josefita region, near the sugar mill, at the same time, and then proceeded toward the *batey* of the sugar plantation. Although I didn't know where the oxen were grazing that day, I really wanted to exchange fire with the guerrillas. I was so intent on fighting with them because during all my time with the infantry in his force, Sanguily had never gone on a mission with the escort of the cavalry on any operation. And now, on my second mission with the escort, he volunteered to go.

So I wanted to find out why by getting into a fight with the guerrillas. A short distance away, I met a man out traveling with his young son, and I asked him if he knew where the cattle of the sugar plantation were grazing. While he was telling me that he didn't know, I noticed that he had just left the *batey* that was very close by. So it didn't make sense to me that he didn't know where the cattle were.

We found ourselves in a situation where the Spanish had us covered from the forts and we only had the cover and protection of guinea grass. Despite the fact that they had a sentinel on top of the sugar mill's condenser, they didn't try to shoot us, even though we could see him perfectly, and it was a very short distance separating us from the lookout. The man whom I had just questioned was seized with terror, and responded to me in a low voice; so I took out my machete and hit him twice, turning the blade of the machete and just wounding him in the head. Blood gushed from the wound, covering his face so that this supplicant had to wipe the blood away. And, still nearly whispering, he said that he had told me that he didn't know where any cattle were because he didn't want to put me in danger; very close by, on the other side of the wall, there were fourteen guerrillas guarding the grazing oxen. I replied, "Why didn't you tell me that the first time I asked?"

In the war in general, but especially on this day, I was very eager to get into a fight with the enemy, and to find out why Sanguily had come with us. So I didn't appreciate this man's hiding the fact that guerrillas were there. I told him, "Hide yourself and your son in the grass because I'm going to stir up this wasps' nest."

It would have been prudent to wait for the larger group of our troops that had stayed with Sanguily, but I didn't. Instead, I said to Catalino García, my younger compatriot, "Do you see the guerrillas that the *pacífico* says are behind that wall? I'm not going to wait for the rest."

So, I crept up to the wall very carefully. When I got there, followed by Catalino, the only one who would go with me, I heard whispers and the sounds of money on the other side. The guerrillas were playing cards. That's why they didn't see us when I was talking with the man whom I hit. I heard one player exclaim, "It's the king of spades and it's the winning card! And because I bet twenty reales, give me five pesos."

The guy he was talking to responded, "Quiet! Quiet! Out of respect for the card played."

The other exclaimed, "Here you all don't value the play card, nor . . ."

Then I said to them, "I am covered by the shade of the same tree (the ateje tree) that protects you, but your immorality is going to cost you dearly."

Then I jumped over the fence and into their midst; they didn't wait to see if I was alone or accompanied. Out of shock, the sergeant threw his *tercerola* at me, without shooting. If he had hit me in the chest with it, I would have fallen from my horse. While I was chasing the sergeant, I told Catalino to call the others and tell them to come, that there were more guerrillas. The rest of our troops arrived, but they were unable to overtake the guerrillas who were shooting at them from behind the sugar plantation's *barracones*.[5] They fled on foot because they didn't have time to mount their horses. In fact, they left them to us saddled, and some with their *tercerolas* still in the side pouch of the saddle.

Those guerrillas had gotten behind the wire cover that protected the *batey*. I then caught up with the sergeant, charging with my machete. But I saw that I couldn't kill him that way because he was very large, and I

---

5. *Barracón:* Slave quarters. A semipermanent structure, usually made of dried mud, used for housing slaves.

was rather frail for my age. So I decided to shoot him; I did, and left him for dead.

The other guerrillas shot at us while we tried to get the horses they had left behind. There were some twenty-eight of them; some were free in the pasture, some had belonged to the riders whom we had just surprised.

Frightened by the noise of gunfire, some of the horses tried to run to the vicinity of Palos. My comrades only wanted to herd the cattle; there were about one hundred of them. And they wanted to let the horses escape because the herd of cattle was so big and because of the shots flying by. We assumed that they were coming from the Spanish cavalry from all their nearby locations. But in these kinds of difficult situations, I am of the doubting Thomas sort. I wanted to know who I was afraid of and to know if there was a real reason for fear.

So, I tried to see what the situation really was. I jumped behind two horses that were going toward Palos; I was lucky to have been able to intercept them and to have gotten between two of the best of the group.

When I got to the other troops, some of them were taking the cattle in the direction of the mountains, Sierra de Brito, close by, and I cursed the ones who wanted to leave those horses! Then Sanguily said to me, "I know that you're a good soldier and very brave, so do what you think is best."

At that moment, the buglers from the sugar mill were heard. That's when the trouble started with herding the cattle. I had some harsh words for those who were handling the cattle, and I exhorted those who wanted to fight. I asked them to wait with me for the guerrillas who were about to leave the sugar mill. So Ezequiel García Benavides, Catalino García— my devoted friend from the escort—Alberto Betancourt, and I stayed and waited. The others left with the higher-ranking officers, Sanguily and Andrés Martínez.

When we got close to the cattle in the woods and hills of Brito, the guerrillas had already left the wire covering of the sugar mill and were coming toward us. In fact, they were just a short distance away before they opened fired. We counted eight or ten of their riders. All of them were on the move, and they all wore the clothes of the *pacíficos* and had Remingtons for weapons; these were infantry weapons, and that made us laugh. Despite the fact that we were only four in number, we didn't fire on them because we wanted to see their reaction. So, when they saw that we were going to leave without shooting at them, despite being close enough to use our revolvers, they started shooting at us. We then turned our horses toward them without firing a shot or attacking; so they stopped and were content to just keep shooting. Then we turned onto our path, lamenting the fact that we hadn't had six more men. Our men had climbed the hill with the livestock. But if we had had six or more we would have been ten in total, and so they wouldn't have had time to reach the sugar mill before we overtook and killed them all with our machetes. Those guerrillas were bold then, but cowards nevertheless.

From the hill, our infantry saw our brash decision not to take the hill, even though we estimated that we could have killed them with our machetes without firing a shot, had there been more of us. They waved to us with their hats to hurry and to get closer so that they could fire on the enemy from the hill. We went up the hill because we saw that San-guily and Andrés were not coming down, which was their duty. With the other four riders, they should have made a nice little feast of those eight or ten cowardly guerrillas.

We had to retreat by the hill for them to cover us, because Sanguily and the others were at a higher elevation. So, from above us they could fire on those miserable enemies, as they did. So the enemy was able to escape because Secundino wasn't there in the other group of young machete-wielding fighters (those in Cañizo's group), the group with which Andrés did not go.

When Quintero's infantry, along with a company of Betances un-der Lieutenant Chacón's command (Chacón was known as "the Orien-tal") began to fire, those of our four who didn't have much desire for a fight turned to go. When I arrived on the hill, the better horses had al-ready been taken. But if it hadn't been for me, the operation would have been lost.

Seeing that they were taking all of the best horses, I was indignant and stated something not fit to repeat. They didn't try to argue because they couldn't. In fact, they did not argue; they agreed with me and said that I should choose a horse that I liked. So I selected one and the dis-pute was over.

Then we went from Brito toward Purgatorio. A torrential downpour started, and those who didn't have a cape to protect themselves from the rain got sick. They had been burned by the sun that entire day in June, so when they got soaked they were wracked with shivers.

When I saw that the officers hadn't given any orders about the operation, I put myself in charge so that we would avoid the night taking us while marching with the cattle. If it got dark, some of the cattle would get lost, and we presumed that the Spanish would come looking for us the next day to take them back. It was a good idea to avoid losing any so that the Spanish wouldn't have the pleasure of taking a "sample," because later they would say that they had run us off—their usual lie to make themselves feel better.

I divided the livestock into two groups because I thought that it would be easier to drive them this way, and it was. So, with six other riders from the vanguard, we drove some fifty oxen and horses and arrived at Purgatorio before nightfall.

When we arrived, the hard work of caring for those beautiful steers had begun. The rest were kept in the extensive woods and hills of Purgatorio where they could be easily defended. We took the whole area for ourselves since the Spanish column didn't want to be bothered with pursuing us that far. They only came as far as La Loma de Brito, and then contented themselves with taking the "card player," the sergeant's body.

The guerrillas didn't attack us, as we expected them to from the towns and sugar mills just mentioned. This was according to the *pacíficos* who informed us. While we were on our mission, the Zapata guerrillas, along with the *pacíficos,* went out foraging for food, to avoid being seen with *mambises*. They didn't bring us salt or other small provisions; those isolated few whom we encountered brought nothing except for a plug of tobacco that smokers enjoy.

Of the twenty-eight horses we took, only eight or ten were useful. The other ten served as meat for the infantry when they finished the oxen. The useful horses were left to help the escort.

After we changed our horses, those of us who went on the operation weren't satisfied with what we had. Some of the new horses were better than ours, and so those of us on the mission had the right to choose.

When the general arrived, he was to select the soldiers who should to go the escort. It was always the blacks who made up the infantry, and all were less than twenty years old. He ordered me to choose those from the infantry whom I knew to be courageous and who were young, as we all were. In this selection I chose my brother, Bernabé, and several others who I knew would be to the general's liking, keeping in mind the age factor. Choosing youths made sense because they were too young to really think about the situations in which we fought. So their youth was a benefit, given the unequal numbers of the enemy against whom we always had to fight.

Half of a squadron of the Havana regiment arrived in the same week that there was the addition to the escort. The half squadron was coming from the province of Havana, escorting General Roberto Bermúdez. It was said that Commander in Chief Máximo Gómez had summoned him. The escort of the Havana regiment that arrived at General Betancourt's headquarters was to return to their province. I was summoned to the headquarters and told to prepare myself to join General Bermúdez's escort to the Northeastern Brigade of the province under his command. And according to a communication that the lieutenant colonel of arms[6] carried, the forces of the brigade under Clemente Gómez's command were in charge of the mission. I responded to the general that I understood, but that someone else who hadn't gone on that recent operation should go on this trip. But he responded that I should go. I chose four men, and the following day, before we left, Sergeant Alberto Betancourt was ordered to go too. At five in the afternoon, we started our march. It was the month of June 1898.

When we left the woods of Purgatorio, Alberto, who was the lead rider, came back to where I was so that in case of an ambush or some other dangerous situation, we could be in communication. This was important, given the fact that we were going with a small number of escorts. While Alberto and I were talking, the general called the *práctico,* Bernardino, and talked with him in private. But when we finished our conversation, Bernardino didn't dare tell us what he and the general had been talking about.

---

6. Lieutenant colonel of arms: An officer in the Military Policy, here responsible for delivering General Bermúdez to Máximo Gómez's camp.

The conversation between Alberto and me went something like this: If I heard gunfire on the vanguard, I was to reinforce them with my men. And if he heard gunfire on the rear guard, he was to reinforce us with his.

At eight in the evening, we arrived at Cuatro-Caminos at the old company bodega of Grima, close to Matanzas. This area was suspicious because of frequent ambushes by the guerrillas of Matanzas. We were in a narrow pass that from San Francisco de Paula leads to the Cuatro-Caminos, as I just mentioned. I heard the *práctico* shout "Halt!" three times, and immediately afterward, gunfire. I began to ride hard with two of my men from the rear guard in the direction of the shots to reinforce the vanguard, as we had discussed. But in my haste along that narrow, dark stretch, I collided with the lieutenant colonel of arms. Because my horse was bigger and stronger than his, I knocked him over onto the wall. But I didn't stop until I arrived at the shots from the vanguard. When I got there, I shot at a grove of trees in the same direction that the vanguard was shooting. But because I didn't hear any enemy fire, I shouted for our troops to cease fire. Just afterwards, the general, revolver in hand, yelled at us to resume the march. And immediately I said to the general, "Look, the lieutenant colonel of arms isn't with us; I think he fell with his horse back along the road."

He responded, "Silence! And continue the march."

Because he made all of us march directly ahead of him, we didn't know how to explain why we had left the old man. But when we arrived at the Arroyo La Vieja River, General Bermúdez's pack mule fell. While we were putting the harness and equipment back on the mule, Armas caught up with us. He had followed the sound of our horses' hooves that made a lot of noise on that terrain. When he arrived, he wanted to reprimand me, saying that I was responsible if he had remained separated from the regiment in such a dangerous area. I explained why I had run into him, but he continued with his threats. Then I took out my Mauser and said that when he heard the shots from the vanguard he should have reacted as I had, and that I wouldn't have run into him in the darkness if he had. He wanted to continue the argument, but General Bermúdez, who stood some distance away, stroking his mustache, commanded him to be silent, and he did so. We continued the march in silence.

At twelve midnight we camped close to Guanábana, after having crossed the border of Sabanilla, close to the farm called La Reunión, which was close to the Canímar River.

At four in the morning, we began a march toward Commander Remigio Landa's camp and got there at about nine in the morning. He had this rank of "commander" only because he was in a secure wooded area La Armería, where he prepared and repaired guns. Most of them were broken in the wooden part of the butt, and some others had broken a small piece called the "*votador*."[7]

We only found guns that were to be repaired, and those guns that were commissioned for the infantry regiment of Matanzas were there too. We also saw kettles boiling on the cooking fire and sacks of food, all left unattended—testament to the retreat of these soldiers who hadn't even given us a "halt." We were amazed at that retreat and that they left the thing most sacred in war: guns. Guns were so important that when we were on the battlefield and the Spanish killed one of our courageous soldiers, we always asked if his gun was recovered. If the answer was no, then the loss of the gun would be mourned as much as the loss of the compatriot. For days afterwards, not much more was said than, "Have you seen the lost gun of so-and-so who was killed? What a good gun that was!"

So you can see the value we placed on our weapons. That day, when we saw twelve or thirteen guns abandoned there without any owners having fired them once, we were all astonished; and for me, the embarrassment made my blood boil, because General Betancourt had told General Bermúdez that although he commanded a small force, he had always appreciated the way in which the *mambises* of Matanzas carried themselves in the heat of battle. Looking at this scene, General Bermúdez turned to me, because I was the one with whom he talked the most during that march. I had been cordial with him, but I don't know if he talked to me because I was so young or because they had told him about my heroic exploits. Now he said to me, "Is that a sample of the glorious epic poem of Matanzas?"

Embarrassed, I replied, "I don't know, but it will be, General! Because there is a commission from the Matanzas regiment here, and it is

7. *Votador:* A small mechanism in rifles that ejects the spent cartridge.

a war-hardened force with which I fought before I came to General Betancourt's cavalry escort."

"How do you know that there is a commission here of that force?"

"Because I know all the weapons for that force, and its equipment, and here I see Corporal Luis Cartaya's cache of arms."

"Call them and we'll see if it's true that you know just by this simple insignia whose cache of weapons this is," Bermúdez replied.

So I began to call them, saying my name. And high up from the hills and woods in front of us, two responded, among them Luis Cartaya. Then they came down the hill with Major Landa, commander of the camp. When they got to the bottom where we were, those of us from the province were indignant to see that those cowardly riders were making an awful impression of us, the fighters of Matanzas.

Major Remigio Landa met General Bermúdez, famous not only for valor beyond belief, but also as a harsh punisher of cowards. Landa was dumbfounded by the imposing stare of that man! Bermúdez asked him, "Who made you a major in the Liberation Army?"

He couldn't respond to him. He only dried tears. He said it was because he was so upset that his riders didn't give the alarm (Halt!) before they retreated. But Commander Nicolás Zamora and I saw that General Bermúdez had pulled out his revolver, so we moved our horses in between Commander Landa and General Bermúdez, interrupting him and saying, "Look, General, we can camp near here because there is good grazing for the horses and a good water supply for bathing them."

When the general realized what we were doing by intervening, he spurred his chestnut-colored horse, the one he rode during the day. A golden mule followed him, but was untied; he rode it at night. He had a chestnut-colored pony as well that followed him untied. The two free ones never got separated from him, even when there was gunfire.

Even after the general yelled at him, Commander Landa still wanted to follow the general, trying to explain his inexplicable retreat. We stopped him, saying, "Stay in your camp, and you should know that this was a very dangerous day for you in the war!" And we followed the general. A short distance away, we camped in order to eat and to rest the horses; we resumed the march in the afternoon.

We were camped out of General Bermúdez's view when Ezequiel García, our lookout, came back. Then Corporal Luis Cartaya, of the infantry to which I belonged, called for me so that he could explain why they had retreated so quickly. This was the explanation: They were out foraging for food at night in the Limonar zone, a town near where we were camped. Given the destruction in that enemy area, they assumed that guerrillas from the town were around (this is the area of the daring Lieutenant Cojizote), and they began to follow the guerrillas' trail. But when they heard our horses' horseshoes on the rocks, they retreated too quickly.

I criticized them, despite their explanation. Actually, the reason that he gave me proved that they should have been in a good position higher up on the hill. So, if the guerrillas had arrived just as we got there, Cartaya's men could have fired on them from the higher elevation without the guerrillas being able to attack them. And if they hadn't been so careless and negligent, they wouldn't have besmirched the reputation of such a courageous infantry as the Matanzas regiment.

After having duly reprimanded Corporal Cartaya, General Bermúdez sent for me to join him for lunch. After receiving the message, I told Corporal Cartaya to go back along the edge of the woods from which he came so that General Bermúdez wouldn't see him, since the general was still very upset with him and his corps.

As for Bermúdez, he should have survived the war, which didn't last more than two months after the day that he went to his own execution at the hands of his own army.[8] Fighting in its lines, he couldn't stand up because he had broken both legs. He moved from the hammock to the horse and back. After the war was over, it would have been a great idea to have that man travel the civilized world as a symbol of the glory of Cuba Libre. He symbolized the self-sacrifice on the part of the Cuban liberators in service to the sacrosanct ideal of "independence or death."

---

8. Bermúdez's execution: Bermúdez was court-marshaled on three counts: first, that he made one of his men kill a *pacífico* with a machete; second, that he had taken a horse and a quantity of *tasajo* (jerked beef) from an infantry officer; and third, that he had given passes to Cubans to go into Spanish towns.

At three o'clock, General Bermúdez ordered us to begin a march to Limonar; there he said that he wanted to give the celebrated guerrillas of the town, La Niña, a good fright.

We arrived at the entrance to the town at four in the afternoon. We rode fast and hard to the vicinity of the Francisco sugar mill, where we all would wait for death. We could see the movements of the guerrillas in the town and knew that if they came out, none of us would survive, because there were one hundred or more guerrillas, almost all of them war-hardened Cubans, and good riders. And we were only fourteen in number, counting General Bermúdez, who, after mounting his horse, was worth two men. But still, it was inconceivably reckless to be there, given the number of the guerrillas and the threat of attack.

All of them remained mounted on their horses. Some one hundred came out and got into formation, just in front of our position. But when they saw that we didn't move, it appeared that they thought that it was a trick like the others we had pulled on them. Often we would show a small force so that they would attack, thinking that they would slaughter such a small unit; but we would have our larger force close by for an ambush, and so we would give them a great scare. So perhaps their memory of this trick saved us from death that day. When we told the general about our previous exploits with the guerrillas, so that he could take into account our small numbers and the fact that we were on commission, he responded that this was what he wanted. We weren't going to leave the province of Matanzas without having a fight with those irregulars who were known from as far away as Pinar del Río.[9] Given his desire to fight, who was going to argue with him? The history of Cuban independence will glorify the exploits of that fierce lion. In all of the dangerous situations he was in, he was always the same, with either a small unit or a large force. Either he would be wounded or he would leave unharmed. So we all resigned ourselves to certain death if he persisted in staying there.

While we were standing there in front of the town, the soldiers of the fort could see us, as could the mounted guerrillas in the formation of a line next to the fort. For close to two hours we raised a fervent prayer to heaven for the sun to go down so that the ghost of death would

---

9. Pinar del Río: The province at the western tip of the island.

disappear. At every moment it seemed as though that specter would devour us; we were there defenseless and without hope of salvation. But it was God's will that it got dark without those guerrillas daring to attack us. We were separated by barely a kilometer without anything blocking their view. There were only some sweet potato patches in the area.

And, as we stood there, General Bermúdez, who was at the front of the line, passed the entire time just gazing at the town. He sat on his horse with one of his broken legs resting on his saddle, smoking like someone who was simply enchanted looking at a pretty view.

It seemed to all of us that that man was chasing death; he finally met it at the hands of his own compatriots when he returned from that trip to Máximo Gómez's headquarters.

Now let's return to the day of our trip. On the general's orders, we resumed our march, as it was getting dark. He called the *práctico* to his side and we followed them toward the town. We were all nervous and bewildered because we didn't know why we were going toward the town, and so we all got ready for whatever emergency arose. We were greatly relieved when we saw, as we were arriving at the fort, that they had given up. We were so close to the sentry that we heard him say, "Corporal, a group is approaching!"

And we heard the corporal say, "To arms! Everyone to their posts! Silence!"

At that moment we passed in front of the fort, but they didn't fire on us, perhaps because even they thought that we were going to enter. In fact, in response to our approach we heard the bugles throughout the town playing "Attention." But thank God they were mistaken, just as we were, except for the *práctico* and the general. Only they knew that in those first moments the Spanish troops were going to abandon the town. But the rest of us held the same assumptions as the guerrillas defending the fort. They thought that we were going to enter; if they had thought otherwise, that we were just going to shoot and run, they would have opened fire on us. And if they had fired on us, it's possible that some of us, whom bullets had respected for nearly three years of continuous fighting, would have been endangered, right at the end of the war. We might have been shot for having provoked them recklessly, even though it had not been our decision to do so. But because of our military discipline, we endured the circumstances that were imposed upon us.

But when they didn't fire on us, we continued our march, and then camped half a league from Limonar; it was eight in the evening. We set up camp in an old coffee plantation that was between Limonar and Sumidero (it had been burned at the beginning of the war).

We camped there until 1 a.m., and then resumed our march to Sumidero, two kilometers away; there we slept for a short time and the horses were able to eat. When we arrived at Sumidero, the general remembered that he had left his files where we had passed the night in order to let the horses rest for a few hours.

While the general's aide went back to look for the documents, we stopped and waited for him at Sumidero. While we waited, I stood at a distance from the general and his assistants, and I reflected on this order, because I saw that there was some mystery that hadn't been explained to us.

I had already noticed that General Bermúdez didn't get along with the lieutenant colonel of arms, and the general wouldn't follow the LCA's rules. Indeed, because of these irregularities, I tried to refuse to have meals with him, but he was so insistent I had no choice but to accept. For example, in the middle of a meal he would often take out his revolver; and, sitting in his hammock, he would tell me how many men had been killed while fighting with him, and how terrified a man was, totally riddled with enemy bullets. And given that we had to hear these kinds of stories during the invasion, it was impossible to digest one's meal! So I would be sick and pensive at these meals.

While we were waiting there for the officer who had gone to retrieve the documents, the general called me in a loud voice: "Little Sergeant, come here!"

When I approached, he said to me, "Why are you always lagging behind on these marches when you're supposed to be accompanying me?"

"General," I said, "I was standing over there because there was some good guinea grass that I wanted my horse to eat while we waited for your papers."

"I'm not referring to this time," he said, "but ever since we left Purgatorio, I've noticed this habit. If I call you to eat with me, it's because

General Betancourt has said something to me about you. You look to me to be quite young, but comrade Betancourt tells me that you are one of his most trusted soldiers, and that you have served your commanding officer well in the most dangerous province. He says that after two years of war you are a subordinate to be trusted, and that you have earned everyone's respect. You clearly love your country, and more, you love the independence we're fighting for, the independence that we've already achieved in fact."

When I tried to make another attempt to apologize, the general interrupted me and said, "Listen closely and never forget what I'm about to tell you. This commission in which the governor or the commander in chief, Máximo Gómez, is cited, I imagine is a deception or obfuscation. During my recent trip through Las Villas, I found out that several brigadiers were leaving to secure autonomy for Cuba.[10] Among them is Massó Parra, who escaped from me because I couldn't put a guard in his own regiment to watch him. If I had put Cayito Álvarez and Vicente Nuñez in place as guards, they could have prevented him from carrying out this treason—treason against the cause of Cuba—this after having sworn on the Cuban flag in those historic mangroves of Baraguá![11] And this after having served for more than two years with devotion to the cause."

The general's voice vibrated among the palm groves of Sumidero. It was two in the morning during the first fortnight of June.

He went on: "So it appears that this accusation comes from my true, resolute love of Cuba. It has cost me my falling into a trap, perhaps the reason for this citation at the headquarters of the commander in chief! But I am resigned and confident that the law of the Revolution will protect me and because I have the firm conviction that the Revolution will not last more than two months. But even if the Revolution were to last

---

10. Autonomy for Cuba: The moderate position of being neither a colony nor an independent country, but a self-governing region of either Spain or the United States. Because the Liberation Army was fighting for full independence, negotiating for autonomy was regarded as treason, and thus was an offense punishable by execution.
11. Baraguá: The 1878 meeting location for insurrectionist leaders dissatisfied with the Pact of Zanjón. There, Antonio Maceo and other rebel leaders vowed to continue fighting, thus making Baraguá symbolic of steadfast commitment to Cuban independence.

even six months longer, I would make them know what Roberto Bermúdez is capable of!"

"But, General," I responded, "what responsibility could I have in this? I'm only a subordinate who is accompanying you on the orders of my superior officer in the escort; and I don't even know the objective of my accompanying you."

"Yes, I know that," he said. "But I want you to know what I am telling you and never to forget it!"

The officer who had gone to retrieve the forgotten papers returned, and we continued on our march in the direction of Coliseo. At nine in the morning, we arrived at the camp of Brigadier Clemente Gómez, camped close to Coliseo on the hill called Mata Negro. There, Brigadier Gómez came out to receive us.

When we left to go make our camp, the lieutenant colonel of arms and Gómez talked alone. I don't know what they talked about, but later the brigadier said to us that after resting the horses we could return to General Betancourt's headquarters. I asked him if it was essential that we stay there in the camp. He told me no, that he had already ordered his troops to guard the general in the camp. They were also placed on the road from Coliseo to Limonar; nevertheless, it was a major passageway, and he told us that it was the crossing point for the enemy forces. But I said that that didn't bother me. Given all of this, I didn't even want to rest my horse there at the camp.

I began my return march after saying good-bye to the general, and he told me to remember what he had told me that dawn. Because of what he had said to me, I didn't want to be at his side. He was right, but I excused myself, and we began our march back, despite the fact that our commander, Nicolás Zamora, and the rest of our comrades on the trip wanted to have lunch there. But when they saw that I was setting out on the march with my close friends Ezequiel García and Serafín González, the rest waved me down with their hats in order to stop me. They caught up to me and we all went on the return march together. On the way, we found out why there were shots at Grima the first night of the commission, and what had been the objective—that General Bermúdez would be able to talk with the *práctico,* Bernardino ("el mocho"), when we left Purgatorio.

When we left General Bermúdez, the *práctico* told us this, that when the general called him to talk privately when we left Purgatorio, this is what he said: "We have to cross close to Matanzas, right?"

"Yes, sir," replied the *práctico*.

"Isn't it true that there in Cuatro-Caminos the guerrillas of Matanzas usually conduct ambushes because they have their headquarters close to there?"

"Yes, sir."

"Well, good. When we get there, shout, 'Halt! Who goes there?' three times, even if you don't see anybody. After the three 'halts,' shoot your gun, even if no one has responded or shot. Don't tell anyone else on the commission about our plan."

This is what Bernardino, the *práctico,* told us. He didn't tell us anything about this at the time because the general had ordered him not to.

When Bernardino told us all of this, we realized what the real objective had been. Because of the shots, the lieutenant colonel of arms would stay back, since, according to Bermúdez, he didn't really like gunfire. And the reason that I ran into the LCA was that I was going to the aid of the vanguard that I thought was caught in an ambush; but I didn't know that the general had prepared a trap for the LCA, to leave him and to continue on his own to the government or to go to the headquarters of the commander in chief.

On our return, we crossed through the eastern part of the burned-out town, San Miguel de los Baños. The first camp that we made was on Commander Zamora's farm, in an area called Río de Auras, the terminal point for Bolondrón, Sabanilla, Limonar, and Corral Falso. There, there were some old yams, and we were able to take some, and we fortunately found a nest of guinea eggs. With thirty eggs and the yams we made a good stew, our favorite meal during the war.

After the meal, all of us lay down in the shade of the palms that grew in that area, because we were so weary from a lack of sleep because of the forced march of that commission we had just completed. It was one in the afternoon of the day after we left General Bermúdez in Clemente Gómez's camp. I awoke covered in sweat because the shade had moved, due to the movement of the sun. So I had been sleeping at the mercy of the burning rays of June's harsh sun. But I woke up fully because of a heavy downpour that started. And because I didn't have anything with which to cover myself, and I was already sweaty, I sat there shivering from the rain that had started while I was sleeping.

In order to cover myself, the only thing I could do was to go into a banana plantation that was close by and that was guarded by my comrades. When I found shelter under the new leaves of a grove of banana trees, that made me feel worse. My shivers worsened so much that when I left there I felt that something was lodged in my throat when I tried to swallow.

My comrades told me that I was having a spasm because of the combination of the hot sun, digestion after our meal, and finally the unforeseen downpour. After we camped at four in the afternoon, we left on another march to cross the rail lines between Cidra and Sabanilla, intending to arrive at Purgatorio by dawn.

As we were passing close to the Saratoga sugar mill at about five in the afternoon, we saw four or five armed men guarding a herd of cattle grazing near the sugar mill. I wanted us to charge and attack those wretches, but my comrades thought that it would be ill-advised to attack because we would stir up the region. Since we had arrived in that area, our movements hadn't been detected, and the number of Spanish cavalry had decreased. Also, because this was a zone that the enemy crossed often, there could be guerrillas nearby returning from any of the surrounding towns. We were going to have to return through that area anyway, so if we attacked those miserable guerrillas and killed some, the others would go on a forced march to the town that they left and telegraph back to the rest. And so they would cover the rail lines and make a triangle of hiding places. They would wait to see if we were going to cross the area that night. If we crossed, they would attack us in an ambush, and if we didn't, they would leave the next day, combine forces, and then pursue us.

For these two reasons, I gave in to my comrades and we resumed our march without attacking those five reptiles. When we went by close to them along the road, they were withdrawing, without even firing a single shot toward the sugar mill that was close by. We crossed right through the cattle, but we didn't take any because the march was already difficult enough and we wanted to avoid the sun coming up while we were still far from Purgatorio.

When we arrived at the Vista Hermosa farm before it got dark, we found the fresh trail of the guerrillas of Sabanilla who had just passed through there moments before. So it had been the right decision not to attack those five guerrillas guarding the animals. We continued the march, and we arrived in Purgatorio at seven in the morning. There, we met the regiment of Havana that was with General Mayía Rodríguez, who was camped with General Betancourt.

The following day, we charged the guerrillas of Empalme, who frequently camped for several days in Ceiba-Mocha. During those days, they committed all kinds of crimes against the women of the town who went out foraging for food. When we shouted "Halt!" those ladies would respond with curses and insults because those crude guerrillas had ordered them to. We were able to kill only one guerrilla by machete.

The following day, my sickness worsened, so much so that even General Betancourt saw how bad it was and wanted me to remain in the field hospital of Purgatorio to recover. I gave in to his demands because the pain was unrelenting. In fact, I was so sick that I couldn't mount my horse; I couldn't even stand up.

But when the general told me that he had to give my horse to another soldier because he, the general, had to travel across the province to examine all of the brigades, and that he needed to take as large a number of escorts as possible, I said that I wouldn't stay behind. No one rides my horse. He objected, saying that I was in a delicate state. But there was no argument that would make me stay, and I told him that I would try my best to follow on horseback.

And so, sick as I was, we began the march that afternoon. We accompanied General Mayía to Labatá, at the border between the provinces of Havana and Matanzas.

From there, we turned back with Brigadier García, who was also going in the direction of Zapata. At five in the afternoon, General Betancourt hit the bull's-eye with his Winchester, killing a guinea hen that was perched on a palm branch.

We continued to march toward the woods of Tinajita (Zapata). There, we were going to cross the railroad lines of Villanueva and go through the demolished La Lima sugar mill. But at this point I couldn't stand the pain any longer; it was so sharp that it wracked my entire body.

I got off my horse in an act of desperation, and went to the commanding officer, General Betancourt. I'm not sure exactly what I said to him, but what I apparently said was, "Shoot me, General! This pain is killing me!"

With kindness that during the war had no limit for the truly courageous—he treated us as a father would a son—he comforted me in my state of desperation, and said, "Go to my assistant, and he will give you a liter of cognac. Drink as much as you can and see if it stops the pain."

I went in desperate search for this medicine, and when I got the liter of cognac, I opened it and drank it all!

After that, I wasn't aware of anything, from that hour (eight at night) until eight the next day, when we were going to leave the place where we camped for the night; this is according to what my comrades told me at nine in the morning.

So, after I drank the bottle of cognac, in order to get on my horse, they said that they had to tie me on my horse so that I wouldn't fall off; they did this because I did fall off once.

Yet, when I woke up I didn't feel that cruel pain; it was almost all gone, although I was slightly injured from having fallen off my horse.

We continued the march. Just a few minutes after leaving our camp, we came across a fresh camp made by Spanish soldiers. We inquired and found out that it was Molina's camp, and that he was there with three thousand soldiers.

We continued marching east to avoid running into such a large column. We arrived at Jagüsito, and as we were watering our horses at this old farm, the guerrillas of Nueva Paz opened fire on our rear guard. The guerillas had completed their mission of escorting the bloodthirsty Molina, who didn't move without a military escort.

When the guerrillas started firing, I couldn't raise my gun to shoot back, given my weakened state. I simply had to be content just watching those despicable guerrillas. Then we had to retreat without charging those impudent reptiles because the terrain was too rocky.

We were retreating along a stony footpath through the woods toward the south. Doctor Panchón Domínguez, who was with the general, stumbled and fell because there were lots of branches lying across the path. He was ahead of me when he fell from his horse, but he was still able to get to the woods on foot while the guerrillas were close behind shooting at us; and the bullets were thick, falling like hail!

We didn't leave Doctor Domínguez's horse there because, sick as I was, I was able to lead his horse forward until we were clear of the danger; then one of the healthy soldiers held it. We went on from there through the woods with no more gunfire, because the guerrillas didn't dare to follow our retreat.

We camped in Guanamón de Armenteros in the Hato de la Manteca campsite. There, the general gave me half of the guinea he had killed the day before and a little bit of rice so that I could make myself some soup, because I was still so weak. I hadn't eaten a thing since the spasmodic attack I had in Río de Auras in the rain.

I ate the nourishing soup and began to sweat profusely, but I didn't have anything to protect myself from the storm that was brewing. It began to rain in a torrential downpour with bolts of lightning, and we began to march at two in the afternoon toward Guanamón de Herrera under these conditions. Before we arrived at a place known as El Asiento de Guanamón, lightning struck close to my horse, making it bolt wildly; I stayed on it, not knowing what was going on. My comrades told me that my horse calmed down quickly, but I remained unconscious for a good while, for a quarter of an hour I came to realize.

Then I saw the entire escort—my good comrades—along with the general (at that time one couldn't have asked for a better commanding officer, although in peace he changed somewhat). The valiant Colonel Fernando Diago was also there. He was an equally compassionate commander in the war, and a faithful and consistent friend in peacetime. They all surrounded me, thinking that I wasn't going to come back to life, but I opened my eyes, and they saw that I was back again among the living. But I couldn't yet respond to the different questions they were asking me. I could only respond with signs until we made camp for the night at El Asiento de Guanamón.

My devoted friend Catalino García made sure that I could rest in solitude, and at all cost he wanted me to eat the mangos and roasted sweet potatoes that he had.

Even though I kept telling him that I didn't want to, he kept trying to make me eat at least one of the two. He insisted on the food consistently and lovingly, and I said the first words that he welcomed with joy: "Don't tire me anymore, Catalino!" I was very grateful for his insistence, and that's why I spoke that same day.

In the morning, we began our trek, going close to the town of Güines, to the Providencia sugar mill. There we camped close to Caraveo, the camp of Colonel Camejo and Cuevas. We were there three days. Afterwards we got back on the trail to Zapata, to the Tinajita camp, where again we saw Molina's trail—indeed, a good reason for us to go to Tinajita's camp at Guanamón.

The Camp at Tinajita

We were there a week, and during that time I went on several missions in search of livestock, since I was almost completely recovered by then, if still a little weak.

Colonel Diago went out with us on one of the missions when we went to the area near the town of Cabezas; Brigadier Eduardo García also went with us. It was during this mission that we took ex-Captain Toribio prisoner. He had surrendered to the Spanish more than a year earlier, and after three months he had returned to the Revolution without enlisting in any force or regiment. In order not to be discovered, he would walk through the woods and mountains of Brito, and at night he would walk through farming areas where some *pacíficos* were living since the first Armistice. On the night that we surprised him, he was ordering the farmers to roast a chicken that he had sent to be cooked. When we caught him red-handed, he couldn't run away, and we took him prisoner. And after the family of farmers finished telling us about how much time he had been there (and because he had committed that crime), he was condemned to the ultimate punishment for criminals in the war. The commander, Colonel Diago, and Brigadier García wanted to execute him right there; they wanted to kill that man who when he was a captain in the Liberation Army—before he surrendered—was cold-blooded and cruel, executing his own comrades for the slightest offense. He tried to show his steely resolve right up until his death. He asked that they not kill him there, that we go back along the road that we had left; he said that he would show us a good spot. We arrived with him at Cuatro-Caminos of

Cabezas going toward Esperanza de Domínguez; he said, "Here is a good spot." And there he was killed, that *presentado* captain.

We got back to Tinajita, our camp, at dawn. With the news that fifteen guerrillas from the town of Cabezas had surrendered, the general ordered Sergeant Alberto Betancourt and me to go out looking for them. He said that if we found them, he would give us first and second command so that, as the squadron added to the escort, we would work together.

We spent four days in the surrounding area of Cabezas, and he found out that maybe the guerrillas had never surrendered. So we returned to the camp and informed the general. The following day, Andrés Martínez and I had an argument; he was one of the higher-ranking officers in the escort, not because he was more courageous, but because of his age. Most of the rest of us were practically boys.

The argument was because I had been on three or four missions during our stay there, and the major part of the escort had not gone out as many times. Martínez wanted me to go out again with the other group. I refused and told him that my horse had suffered more injuries than the others. The argument got so heated that he had to leave for the protection of the headquarters. I didn't go on the mission and the general and Colonel Diago took my side.

The following day, the alarm was sounded in the camp because a band of guerrillas was apparently approaching through el Cuco (Juan Pedro Baro's colony of Central Conchita). We formed a defensive line of fire and waited for them, as fifteen or twenty guerrillas appeared all dressed in striped cotton. Before we opened fire on them, we recognized the first soldier in the front; it was Colonel Pío Domínguez. When they got closer we could identify the group. They were a part of the irregulars of Bolondrón who had passed by earlier. Almost all of them were insurrectionists who had surrendered, except for about nine or so who were guerrillas from the beginning of the war.

They camped apart from us. They were on their way to form the only cavalry of the Southern Brigade united with another ten or twelve *pasados*.[12]

---

12. *Pasado:* One who has "gone over." An insurrectionist who surrenders, then fights for the Spanish.

Some of them came to our camp wanting to find out about the famous escort.

Talking with our troops in our camp, they began to change some of our impressions, particularly for those of us who didn't fully understand the agreement to let the guerrillas pass through our area. During the conversation, they began to recount the disaster at Oito the year before. When they began to talk about the events of that day, I paid close attention because I was almost killed in that battle. They were quite frank and honest, assuring us that there was no lingering animosity on the part of the veterans. Then they told how they had fought, and came to the part where they had left me; I was on foot going from Jagüey Grande the day of that fight. If they hadn't wanted to make such a show of killing me with their machetes, perhaps I would have died that day. But because they did make such a display of trying to mutilate me, I was able to kill two or three of them. I escaped because every time I aimed my gun that day, I hit the mark. It was as if the supreme hand of God was guiding the bullets in to the bodies of those traitors.

As they related the story of the shooting, at one point one of them said that he thought that Providence was protecting the insurrectionists that day; they went on to say that one of them, almost a boy, mounted a spotted-blue horse and rode alone into the midst of twelve of them. Not only were they unable to take him prisoner, but he succeeded in wounding four of the bravest guerrillas. At this, I perked up my ears. It seemed as though the assistant to the general, Pelayo Alfonso, was just cold and heartless because you'd have to be to talk like that about so many of our dear comrades whom they had killed. He asked, "Did any of the wounded from that day come here with you?"

One of them answered, pointing to two of the wounded: "Look here's one, and there's another."

They started to pull up their shirts to show their scars, but they didn't have time because I jumped up from my hammock and almost wounded one of them. I had been sitting there listening to the unconscionable questions that soldier asked, but I was enraged when I learned that it was he who had put my life in such danger. I was the soldier who rode on the spotted-blue horse that day!

My comrades in the escort kept me from attacking that man because they knew that the general wouldn't allow the killing of a guerrilla in the camp, after having let them pass. If a guerrilla were killed, it would make it impossible for the rest to pass through peacefully, and the policy had already been set that they would be allowed to pass through the area on a regular basis.

The following day, we moved our camp, or, more precisely, we went on a march to review the brigades in order to avoid a fight with the guerrillas passing through the area. And the threat of a fight was very real because it was the guerrillas who were the vanguard of Pavía's column, the column that was fatal for us in the battle of Oito in February 1897.

From Tinajita we marched to Hato de Jicarita, stopping there to eat and then continuing our march toward Brigada de Colón (Montaña de Prendes).[13] On this march we had a skirmish in the old Europa sugar mill, at an improvised *trocha* made to prevent communication between the brigades of the southeast and southwest.

The Arrival at Prendes

There at Prendes we found the camp of the brigade under the command of Colonel Rafael Águila. We were there for several uneventful days until we received news of the enemy. General Betancourt ordered a battle plan, so we in the escort and the cavalry got ourselves in our positions for battle in a pasture. Meanwhile, the general went with the infantry to be in place in order to open fire on those tyrants when we retreated. We in the cavalry waited for half an hour, but the Spanish didn't appear. The general then ordered the cavalry to retreat to see if the Spanish would approach. We retreated, and no more than fifteen minutes had passed when we heard the explosion of gunfire. The general, Colonel Diago, and Águila were fighting with the infantry against those Spanish who didn't want to approach while the cavalry stood waiting out in the open. When we returned to check on the camp, we found a great trail of blood, and a trail where the wounded were treated. Our infantry didn't have more than two fallen. What a great satisfaction! We stayed there long enough for the general to inspect the brigade.

---

13. Colón: A town in the province of Matanzas, approximately fifty miles southeast of the city of Matanzas.

During the first days of August we marched toward the center of the province to inspect Brigadier Clemente Gómez's and Carlos Rojas's brigades. We found the forces together camped in the hills of San Miguel de los Baños.[14]

After the general spent three days inspecting the forces, he ordered us, his escort, and Clemente Gómez's troops to go out looking for cattle for the infantry. Twenty of us went out toward the town of Jovellanos,[15] and we spent the night in the Peñalver sugar mill, near that town. At four in the morning, we positioned ourselves for an ambush in a grove of trees near the sugar mill. And right at dawn five guerrillas approached, I think to get horses for their commanders. They dismounted their horses close by where we were hiding. Five of us ran out quickly with Águila, not giving them enough time to remount, and we took them prisoner without firing a shot. This took place at about seven in the morning.

We used their clothes to dress some of our men. And so, dressed like guerrillas, our troops went toward the town's forts and were able to avoid the sentries. In this way, we were able to get to the greater number of cattle that were grazing in the surrounding area.

When we arrived at the fort that sits on the bridge called Govel, two guerrillas came out. But when they were only a city block's distance away, those miserable guerrillas began to ride faster and harder, so that we couldn't overtake them. They thought they could get away. We had planned to proceed in pairs in the back until we got close to the cattle. The town's inhabitants could see us, so we wanted to herd the cattle in such a way that they wouldn't sound the alarm until we had the cattle on the road back to the camp. Also, in this way, two or three could follow the oxen while the rest of us would hold off the guerrillas of the town, who certainly would have come out to take back the cattle.

Despite the plan, I charged the two of them; they were carrying bread for the detachment at the Luisa de Baró sugar mill. When they saw me charge, machete in hand, one started to run away, firing in retreat.

---

14. San Miguel de los Baños: A town in the province of Matanzas approximately twenty-five miles southeast of the city of Matanzas.

15. Jovellanos: A town in the province of Matanzas, approximately twenty-eight miles southeast of the city of Matanzas.

Meanwhile, the other, Canario, was taken prisoner by my comrades. I caught up with the first one, and took him off of his horse with a machete stroke. Then Sergeant Matías, one of Clemente Gómez's troops, killed him; with him on the ground, Matías shot that traitor who was a native son of Matanzas. I took his gun and his ammunition pouch with seventy bullets for a Remington. And I ordered Catalino García to take the sack of bread that the traitor was carrying.

We began to gather the cattle that were close by where that guerrilla fell, but they were pretty spread out. In one of the groups of cattle we saw an odd kind of fort that was difficult to make out. They had tied five saddled horses there. And because no shots had been fired from there, some of us wanted to go take those good horses; my brother Bernabé was one of those who suggested this idea. He said this to everyone, but it appeared to me to be a trap, because it looked to me like a kind of mobile fort. They wanted to argue with me, but then I ordered them to get into position in order to open fire on that suspicious edifice where the horses were. Some listened to me; others didn't.

We fired on that strange fort, and the troops inside responded immediately with a hail of bullets. It was a steel-armored wagon that looked and functioned like a mobile fort; they were using it to protect the cattle in the pasture by yoking the wagon to the oxen. Every time they moved, the wagon moved along with them. While we exchanged shots with the wagon, the other comrades herded the cattle; there were some eighty oxen in all.

The enemy hit one of our men, Prudencio Vidal, with the first shots fired from the car. He was one of those who doubted my hunch that the saddled horses tied together without riders were a trap. He remained standing in a group of three, but my brother and two others heeded my advice and spread out. So, when I opened fire with my Mauser toward the wagon, those in the wagon fired back on the group of three, hitting Vidal.

Now back on the road with the cattle and our wounded, heading toward the Peñalver sugar mill, we heard the town bells ringing, signaling the alarm. They sounded the alarm because we were close to the town when we took the oxen; the alarm would hurry the guerrillas back to the town. But the guerrillas were foraging in the far east of the area and the town was in the far west. The guerrillas rushed back immediately, and as they crossed the town in hot pursuit, we heard them boast and mock when they saw how small a group we were. They shouted to their women, "So-and-so, I'm going to bring you fresh *mambí* meat." At that moment I was passing out the bread that I had taken for my comrades; we were fourteen. We delayed a bit in order to cut off the path of those loudmouths who didn't know what they had coming to them. I mean, they even dared to say that they were going to have some *mambí* flesh! They only took notice of our number, without realizing that we substituted quantity with quality.

When they passed beyond the town's last houses and forts, they spread out in order to start shooting at us. But those of us who were herding the cattle were already a good distance away, almost back to the sugar mill. Some fifty guerrillas on horseback opened fire on us. In the first moments of the shooting we didn't fire back, nor did we take our horses toward the path. When they saw this display of contempt, they started to charge at us, and advanced spread out, shooting as they came. As we saw them drawing closer, we turned our horses to face them and shot a volley back at them. They stopped, but continued to fire. We turned our backs to them and continued our march, shooting just a few times in retreat. We arrived at the sugar mill, where we had left the prisoners, and there we found them like Adam in Paradise. We told them that when their comrades arrived, they must take up arms and shoot at us too. They replied that they couldn't shoot at us because they owed us their lives. But we told them that it was the law of the revolutionary government to pardon all of the Spanish who were taken prisoner, but not to pardon any Cubans who committed treason against their country.

We continued to shoot as we moved from the western part of the grove into the eastern part, where those guerrillas were. We already had the cattle a kilometer away, so they saw that despite their superior numbers, they were going to suffer the embarrassment of not recovering those animals. So they made their last and most desperate attempt to overtake us when they left the grove. They charged at us with fury to see if we were scared, but they got more than what they had bargained for. You see, we didn't have a lot of ammunition. We were about a league away from the camp of the infantry, and we had to go along a bad road because it had been torn up by the horses; it was totally covered with the leaves and branches from the Panamá.[16] So, given the dire circumstances, if we hadn't fought our hardest, we would have been killed by those guerrillas. We had to throw caution to the wind, as it is often said, and that's what we did.

We turned our horses back toward them and charged after those insolent cowards. When we got to their lines, they turned in panic, fleeing, despite their superior numbers, and we chased them. They went back into the grove, and we went in after them, but we hadn't seen that they had brought an infantry unit behind them, and that the unit was already in the grove. The infantry opened fire on us with a thick round of shots from their Remingtons; they knocked one of our riders off his horse, and killed it with two shots to the head. Then we came to a halt, and, face-to-face, we exchanged gunfire with the infantry and the cavalry. Two of our men were shot in that exchange and fell to the ground. One was pinned under his horse that had fallen down dead on top of him. Some of us got him out and threw him on another horse, and we retreated. But they didn't dare to pursue us again; they just satisfied themselves with shooting at us from inside the grove, while we were still in range.

After we got out of firing range and away from the danger, we put the wounded man on a stretcher. At a distance, we could see the cattle and our men who had taken them, and we could see our first wounded whom they were already taking to the hill called Unión. We got there at eleven in the morning and met General Pedro Betancourt, Brigadier Clemente Gómez, and Colonel Fernando Diago there; they had come from a camp that was two kilometers away, along with Gómez's infantry and a company of Betances. They were desperate because they had heard so many shots so early in the morning, and feared that we had been attacked by a column. We were too far away from the infantry for it to help us, because we were two leagues away from the hill and in difficult terrain for a retreat. Indeed, the area was all high weeds and mire that can tire even a good horse, especially when it is spurred on to its limits. Bear in mind, too, our small number that had gone out on this mission.

---

16. Panamá tree: A tall tree with a large, straight trunk and smooth, yellowish bark. The leaves are large, with five pointed lobes.

Even one hundred armed men would have been too few against an entire column, to say nothing of only eighteen ill-equipped men like us. So, when they heard the gunfire, from early in the morning until about ten, they believed, with good reason, that we had been wiped out. They were so concerned that they were about to go out on the plain with the infantry when they didn't hear any more gunfire. But moments later, we arrived with our spoils of war: eighty oxen, two *tercerolas* (both with ammunition), and a Remington. And we sustained only two wounded, one soldier from Clemente Gómez's unit and the other from ours—General Betancourt's escort; they were wounded in our successful machete charge. It was so successful that the guerrillas didn't chase us anymore. And it was only because they had the damned infantry behind them that we were unable to cut down those miserable parrots that day. We proved to them that it wasn't so easy to get *mambí* meat, as they had shouted they would when they left the town in their attempt to take back the cattle. They cost us two seriously wounded men, but both were saved, although the second one was gravely wounded.

It was the first time in the entire war that we saw a wounded soldier with two such large wounds survive. The bullet entered an inch above his left nipple and exited below his right shoulder blade. The entrance and exit wounds were very large, but the heart of the wounded soldier continued to function perfectly, and this despite not receiving treatment for an hour after being shot. And after the war was over the soldier didn't have any disabilities from the wound. I saw him two years later; he was a tenant farmer near Jagüey Grande.

That day, the two wounded we suffered were well worth our heroic fight against superior forces. One of the wounded was from Clemente Gómez's forces, the other from General Betancourt's escort; thus the rivalry between the two forces was reduced, as neither group was braver than the other. This was the striking characteristic of that glorious day, August 17, 1898.

Camped at San Miguel

On the eighteenth day, the cavalry made a trip to the farming area of the sugar mill called Petrona. I went too because we expected a fight with the insolent guerrillas of Limonar, and I wanted to be in on it. We arrived at about nine at night at the sugar mill. While my comrades were getting some young corn, I remained nearby sleeping on my horse. After getting the corn, they returned without realizing where I was, or thinking that I had already returned to the camp. But my horse had wandered off eating without my guiding it. When I woke up, I was in front of the fort that sat at the entrance on the road from Limonar.

When I opened my eyes, not only did I see the large fort, but I saw the sentry outside. At that moment he shouted, "Halt!"

When I heard the "Halt!" and found myself in front of the fort, I opened fire on the sentry, and retreated without hearing if he shot back at me. It took a few seconds for the others to shoot back, but I had already gotten a good distance away. At that moment I heard my comrades shooting from another part of the sugar mill. I caught up with them and we all got back to the camp at four in the morning. We made breakfast and at about nine in the morning the general received news that the guerrillas of Corral-Falso, called La Muerte, were coming along the road from the Diana de Soler sugar mill.

We prepared to go out to meet them, since they were saying that they were coming to take back the oxen from Jovellanos. A section of our unit went out—all armed with Mausers—and among them were some of Clemente Gómez's men. The rest of the escort and the rest of Gómez's men stayed behind, prepared to reinforce the other men. Also, the infantry squadron of Cárdenas, the Betances, and Clemente Gómez positioned themselves behind the cavalry in case they needed to enter the fight.

Those of us who went to meet the guerrillas spread out on the hill that faced the road, Diana, at the sugar mill called Llince. We weren't there long when we saw the vanguard of the guerrillas appear. We let them get pretty close, close enough to be in range of our revolvers. They didn't see us because we were on foot and our horses were tied on the other side of the hill behind us. Also, there was some white *guano* where we were positioned that hid us. When they got close, we let loose a ferocious volley that stopped the vanguard, and they had to make a retreating maneuver until the main part of their force advanced. When the main force got to the battle, the Spanish made a titanic effort to advance, but our deadly fire didn't let them; so they turned in a different direction toward the Llince sugar mill, to the east of our position.

We chased them, firing while they were still in range. So we repulsed those cowardly guerrillas of La Muerte, and returned to our camp.

In the afternoon, we found out from the *pacíficos* that the sentry at the fort at the sugar mill Petrona had been killed in the shooting the night before. He was a *presentado* who joined the guerrillas after deserting the Liberation Army, and he met the fate that all traitors deserve.

On the twentieth day, the alarm was sounded in the camp because a large cavalry unit was coming along the same road on which we took the cattle three days before. All of us mounted our horses and took our positions, and a number of us went out to meet that cavalry. When we shouted "Halt! Who goes there?" they responded, "Cuba!"

It was strange for us to see two hundred soldiers and so many riders in the province, and more were coming from the same direction. We couldn't assume that they were from the Havana regiment. We ordered that one of them come forward to be recognized. And one of the five of us advanced to meet them, while the other four were in the line of fire. It was General Mario Menocal's unit contingent; he was coming as the commander of the two divisions of the 5th Corps, made up of Havana and Matanzas.

We turned to inform the general, and he went out to meet with General Menocal. The two forces camped together in the Santa Ana de Caballero Valley, where we slept that night.

News was already spreading about the peace that was signed four days later. During the short march to the valley I just mentioned, some in General Menocal's forces were commenting that they had heard in Camagüey about the famed Betancourt escort, but when they saw us they seemed doubtful; they couldn't believe that this group of boys could be the group that they had heard praised so highly as the pride of the liberating forces in the most dangerous province of the war. For our part, we were desperate to be attacked by enemy forces before operations ended, so that we could prove wrong those who dared to believe that "character comes in a big sword hilt."

At about one in the afternoon we received news that a cavalry unit of the Civil Guard was approaching on the road from the Saratoga sugar mill. Our reaction was foolish. By the time Menocal's men mounted their horses and got into formation for battle, we were already a kilometer from the camp going toward the location from which it was reported that the enemy was coming. We didn't listen to what they told us, that it was dangerous to go through the weeds and the mud of the valley to the enemy. But we were too intent on the attack. And more, because the camp was on higher ground, it was better to wait for the enemy there and to receive fire. In this way the enemy would remain in a bad position down in the marshes and the weeds that we were facing.

But we didn't listen to any of this, and left for that valley like the wind. The horses went into the mire up to their chests, but nevertheless we got within range of those we assumed were the Civil Guard. About two kilometers away, General Menocal's men stood watching as we went after the Spanish like someone going after a sumptuous feast. As it turned out, the Civil Guard was coming on our mission; they had deserted and had joined our ranks.

When we returned with the Civil Guard—now our new comrades— it was to the astonishment of the other troops and of General Menocal's officers. Because of our decision to attack without regard to danger, they were convinced of the escort's ability to fight. But because no shots were fired, many of us weren't satisfied with the appreciation that they had for us. We wanted to earn their respect in battle.

General Menocal's troops rested their horses and slept there that night; then we woke them up to go to another fortified zone in search of food. So we went to the Saratoga sugar mill, and approached the forts with those who had doubted our bravery. When we were very close to the forts, we opened fired on them. The Spanish fired back with a torrent of shots. Menocal's force, made up of men from Camagüey and Oriente, appeared to be unaccustomed to gathering their food under fire. Some of us kept gathering our corn, while the rest returned fire at the forts, but our incredulous comrades not only retreated, but lost two *tercerolas*. When we returned to the camp, it was satisfying to see that those who doubted us had to be there all night and into the morning looking for the two guns. And since all of our men returned with provisions, we had the pleasure of giving food to those who had dropped theirs in the chaos. And we all returned to camp happy and unharmed. They were convinced that our actions proved our valor. (I had proposed this plan and it was approved by several of my comrades.)

On the March with General Menocal: August 1898

That afternoon we continued to accompany General Menocal, who was marching toward the province of Havana. We stopped in Mogote because it was already the 23rd, that was said to be the day of peace, though in fact the peace was signed the day after, on the 24th of August.

We stayed several days in Mogote, during which time the general charged me to pursue those in the surrounding towns who were committing many outrages against the women of the towns. It was the *presentados* who had surrendered to the Spanish who were coming back now that the peace was signed, escaping from the towns. They didn't enlist in our camps, but continued to commit crimes. And because it was the law that the revolution should pursue and punish those who committed crimes, I was charged with this responsibility. In one of the trips I took across the area surrounding the town of Cabezas, I took a guerrilla prisoner near one of their forts. Not only did I not kill him, but I didn't allow my comrades on the commission to kill him either. And in protest they accused me of being scared to kill the guerrilla.

I was insulted, so I told them that they could come with me, just the five of us, and go into the town right then—at nine in the morning—to prove to them that I wasn't intimidated. And because we were all war-hardened veterans, they didn't hesitate, and we all left at a gallop with absolutely no concern that the war had ended, and that it might be more prudent to look to our safety. At that point in time, we didn't know the meaning of the word.

We crossed through the forts as if we were in a race, and at the railroad station we took two oxen and two yokes (they used the animals to move cars around in the yard). And we were lucky that the aforementioned guerrillas from the town weren't mounted, because the church bells began to ring, sounding the alarm, to call the guerrillas back from their foraging. Although the peace had already been signed, they still were around to protect property. But we left without being harmed, before the guerrillas arrived. The forts didn't open fire because, given the state of things, they were unprepared. All the soldiers were on foot, regardless of rank, and they only trusted the sentry in the church tower. But in a state of shock, he saw us, machetes in hand, in the middle of the town, and dropped his *tercerola,* making a loud noise.

We got back to the camp with the yoked oxen and without incident. One of the soldiers on the mission told Colonel Diago that as commander of the commission, I had taken a guerrilla prisoner and hadn't killed him, and that I had ordered him set free.

The colonel summoned me. Despite the affection he always showed me during the war—and also during the peace—he said that if someone else had done this, he would have been arrested.

For me this was the same as a severe punishment, because my commanders in the war had never said anything like that to me. Even more galling, this statement came from someone whom I admired and who, supposedly, admired me.

The province allowed the guerrillas of Cabezas to move around freely for two days, and the aforementioned guerrilla of the recent skirmish came to our camp with the *pacíficos*. He had the impudence to go to the headquarters disguised as one of the poorest and most wretched among the visitors. If it weren't for his evil intentions, no one would have noticed that he was there; I wouldn't have recognized him myself. But he was so despicable that he was going to tell the general that a commission of the escort had been through the town of Cabezas, and that two centenes had been stolen. He said this because he knew that this was punishable by the Wartime Tribunal, and almost always resulted in the execution of the accused.

After he made his accusation, Colonel Diago summoned Porfirio, the soldier whom the guerrilla had accused; Porfirio was called in order to see if he knew this complaining *pacífico*. Well, Porfirio, who was from Cabezas, could testify to the identity of that "bird" from the war. Despite the fact that he was disguised, he recognized him and said to the colonel that he was the guerrilla who had escaped after he had been taken prisoner that day. Then Colonel Diago wouldn't allow him to speak with the general. In fact, the colonel hit the guerrilla with his own machete. As a consequence, there was a great deal of alarm in the camp; we had never seen the well-bred colonel so upset.

The alarm was how I found out that there was a problem. I then came to see where the malefactor was, the one who had cost me two arguments: one when I saved his life after taking him prisoner, the second when Colonel Diago gave me my first and last reprimand in the war. I got close enough to see that it was, in fact, that vindictive traitor.

Later, Colonel Diago had to go on commission to the headquarters of the 5th Corps that was stationed in the province of Havana; so I went with a pair of soldiers to escort him. We reached the headquarters of the 5th Corps in Guayabal, between San José de las Lajas and Tapaste. The Corps was camped with General Mario Menocal, commander of the 5th Corps, and General José María Rodríguez (Mayía), commander of the Department of the West. We spent a week on this commission.

When we returned, our force, along with the general, had already left Mogote and had gone to the Majagua sugar mill. It was run by a brother-in-law of General Betancourt, Leoncio Supervieye. Because he was a French citizen, he could escape during the war, given the constant support he gave to General Bentancourt and to the cause.

The Arrival at Majagua

We arrived at Majagua and a part of the escort was there; the rest of the escort was with the general a league and a half away. He had gone to inspect the Southern Brigade, camped at the Olano sugar mill. He went there also because six unfortunate veterans had just been executed by firing squad in the Southern Brigade's camp. They had been members of Alfredo Wood's forces, and after he was killed, they had surrendered to the enemy. Then they repented and wanted to return to the Liberation Army, but the cessation of the hostilities had already taken place. And so they were in rebellion against both groups, avoiding encounters with both Cuban and Spanish forces. They were called "The Black Hand." There were eight of them, but only six were executed. The other two were defended by General Clemente Dantin and were set free. He argued for their exoneration because they had been some of the courageous, though unfortunate, ones who had fought for their country; and it was only because they were ignorant and uncultivated that they embarked upon such a tortuous path in life.

Because of this defense and because of General Betancourt's arrival, they were spared: Pantaleón Martínez (Cuba-bella) and Porfirio Guzmuri (Lloni).

Knowing General Betancourt as I knew him during the war, I am fairly certain that if he had arrived before the other six were shot, Cuba wouldn't have lost those other disgraced ones, who also fought for her.

The March to Olano

From there, we went to Olano. When we arrived, General Betancourt was already there, prepared to return to Majagua. It was about 4 p.m., and despite the fact that we had been marching since four in the morning, we returned with the general to Majagua, getting there at six in the afternoon. After having walked on a forced march for more than forty leagues without eating, we arrived at that hour very happy and self-satisfied, as if we had just returned from a vacation. What times those were, when the Cuban's self-sacrifice was unlimited, because he yearned only for the freedom of his beloved Cuba!

From Majagua we went to the sugar mill, San Cayetano, closer to Matanzas, but it had already been abandoned by the enemy forces. We then went from there to the San Juan River.

The few days that we were there at the river, we received visitors from the city; they were all overjoyed at our triumph, and came constantly to visit. On one of those days the alarm was sounded in the camp because it was rumored that the celebrated Cajizote was in disguise among the visitors from the town. He was the lieutenant of the guerrillas at the time and was reportedly there to assassinate General Betancourt on orders from the bloodthirsty and cowardly Molina.

In response to this information, General Betancourt ordered Cándido Rodríguez and me to search among the thousands of *pacíficos* for Cajizote. We started our search, and as we were getting tired, we spotted him on the other side of the river dressed like a peasant, in white pants and a white shirt. He also wore a Panama hat without a band, but we were able to recognize the mark the band had left. (The guerrillas of the Spanish cavalry used the band to attach adornments.)

He started running as soon as he saw that we were coming armed with three Mausers from the cavalry. We chased him, and when we saw that we couldn't catch up to him, we decided to open fire on him. But Prudencio Vidal, a soldier in the escort (he had been wounded in the charge at Jovellanos), was a childhood friend of Cajizote and begged us not to shoot him. Just then, he twisted his foot and fell, and then we caught him. We took him to the general, who ordered us to tie him up, and ordered the Wartime Tribunal to convene immediately.

After the tribunal had finished its trial, a squadron of the Civil Guard arrived with a María Cristina unit, all coming in search of the prisoner and coming with a document from the ruthless Molina.

The Spanish force stopped on the other side of the river. And we in the escort of the cavalry and the infantry were in formation on the opposite side watching them, trying to figure out the intentions of this enemy force that had approached our camp.

We shouted "Halt!" Then the commander of the Civil Guard came forward with a sealed envelope, rode to the middle of the river, and delivered it to our commander, who met him there. Upon reading it, General Betancourt immediately turned back and ordered Cajizote released.

When Cajizote arrived at the riverbank, the Spanish commander came forward so that Cajizote could get on the back of his horse, and they both rode to the other side.

As soon as that force reached Matanzas, Molina sent one of his thugs to deliver a threat to General Betancourt. The message said, "If you do not move at least two leagues away from the city within seventy-two hours, we will attack."

As soon as the envelope containing the threat arrived, I was ordered to find the general, who gave me an envelope to give to General Mario Menocal, commander of the 5th Corps (he was camped a good distance away). And the general said to me, "Although it might kill the horse, I want the response to the contents of that envelope within forty-eight hours."

I took a horse that wasn't mine, because it was better to lose that one on a forced trip like this one, and I had to take care of my own horse in case we had to fight the notorious Molina when I returned.

I arrived at General Mario Menocal's headquarters. As soon as he read the contents of the envelope, he consulted with Mayía Rodríguez, the major general, commander of the Department of the West.

Immediately, they sent an aide to the headquarters of the 2nd Division and the 5th Corps. And, obeying the received order, the commander in turn ordered the 1st Division of the 5th Corps (Matanzas), the two most courageous squadrons of the cavalry regiment of Havana, to go to the San Juan River with their commanders in front: Quirino Zamora and Manuel Antonio Martínez.

Within forty-eight hours I had already returned to the river with a letter for General Betancourt. I arrived at the camp headquarters in the afternoon, and the general asked me if the forces of which he was informed in the letter would be delayed very much. I said that I thought that they would arrive that very night.

In fact, they were all there by the latter part of dawn when the Spanish bugler of the numerous cavalry played reveille, and Molina with all of his troops were displayed. In fact, the two forces were so close that the only thing separating us was the river; the two squadrons of the Havana regiment also played reveille. Our bugler in General Betancourt's escort (one of the best cornetists that the Revolution had) immediately began to play reveille, showing up all of the rest of the other buglers who had preceded him. In fact, he upstaged both the Spanish and the *mambises* when he played all the versions of "Diana" known. And when it was daylight, he played a call to the cornetists in the Spanish cavalry to come to our camp. The Spanish cavalry had come on Molina's orders to "intimidate" us. But those poor cornetists who came to our camp came only to see our bugler. If the celebrated Castillo had known this, he would have taken them to the dungeons of San Severino.[17]

Six days went by, and I don't know why, but Molina refused to carry out his threats. It appeared that it was because our bold commander had terrified him. So the two regiments of Havana returned to their camps, and we stayed there until it was necessary for those of us in the escort to go with the general to review the brigades. The two infantry regiments left and split up to guard two different sugar mills. The mills needed armed forces for their security in the new regime of Cuba Libre because they had already discharged the guerrillas.

---

17. Dungeon of San Severino: A notorious dungeon in the San Severino castle in the city of Matanzas. Erected by the Spanish in 1693, the castle's dungeon was used to house newly imported slaves. During the War of Independence, insurrectionists were imprisoned and executed there.

On the March from San Juan

From San Juan we went to Varadero to inspect the Cárdenas brigade, which had its headquarters there. Afterwards, we went to inspect the brigade near Colón, but we had to go back into town before completing our inspection; then we camped nearby. General Betancourt was receiving, in the name of Cuba, two commissions of grand patriotic ladies from Colón; one of the ladies was black, the first to arrive. Those enthusiastic ladies bore the *mambí* insignia on their clothes, and when they came out, they were exposed to one thousand insulting Spanish bayonets. At this moment, we received a telegram relating the very sad news that Major General of the Liberation Army Calixto García Iñiguez[18] had died. The bugler stopped playing music and the funeral march began, and the flag was immediately flown at half mast.

That same afternoon, we returned to Matanzas to report to Perico and to the camp of Brigadier Clemente Gómez in the Madan sugar mill, close to Jovellanos. Afterwards, we went to Playa de Bellamar, Matanzas, where we stayed until the last boat of Spanish troops left on December 31, 1898.

When the last boats left, it was like a dream finally to see that colonial power destroyed—that power that for so many centuries had ruled this pearl of the Antilles of the Americas, at a cost of so much bloodshed and so many horrendous crimes.

While we were in Playa de Bellamar, it was I who had to carry out the important commissions at the headquarters of the 5th Corps that was stationed in the province of Havana, together with the headquarters of the Department of the West. I also took a commission from the agricultural engineers of the American Army from our camp at Playa, Matanzas, to the city of Cárdenas; the purpose was to make a map of the distance traveled.

On the return to Matanzas, we went through the Precioso sugar mill, to cross through Camarioca going toward the pass of the Canímar River

---

18. Calixto García Iñiguez (1839–98): General in the Ten Years' War, La Guerra Chiquita, and the War of Independence. He was second in command of the entire Liberation Army, and commander of the army in the east. He died of pneumonia while on a diplomatic mission to New York City.

(the pass was called Andarivel); there, we had to get off of our horses and take off the saddles in order for the horses to swim across tied to a boat, while the riders crossed over a very old bridge with the saddles.

On our return trip, the two American lieutenants on the commission asked General Betancourt to allow me to go with them to the American camp. They wanted me to learn how to send telegraphs and to learn English. But General Betancourt wouldn't allow it, stating that I was the only one he could trust with these important commissions; not only was I the only *práctico,* but because I didn't like games or pastimes, I could be trusted to carry out the commissions.

The Clash at Navajas

A few days after I had come back from the American commission, there was nearly a battle in Navajas between the Cuban forces of the Southeast Brigade of the province and the Spanish forces that had to go through the town of Jagüey Grande and others as part of the evacuation of the capital, Matanzas. The problem arose all because that idiot Molina didn't anticipate that our forces would be reconcentrated. So he ordered the Spanish forces to retreat and to stop guarding the town. The Brigade of the South immediately occupied the town and raised the flag of the solitary star.[19] After the flag was raised, Molina didn't want his forces to cross through under it because it would be an insult. He wouldn't allow his army to march through an area where the Cuban flag flew! He wanted the flag lowered, and he didn't want any Cuban troops camped there; so he made a great show of force, displaying the units' arms. After being vanquished he wanted to terrify the conquerors! When the news reached the headquarters of the province, General Betancourt, of the 1st Division of the 5th Corps, ordered, in response, that we in the escort prepare our horses to march to Navajas to punish Molina's impudence for the last time.

But some of our saddles were in the saddle shop in the city, in a central location on Manzaneda Street at the intersection with Cuba Street. And no one wanted to cross through twenty thousand Spanish soldiers who had come from Playa Judío and who were between us and the saddle

19. The flag of the solitary star: The flag of Cuban independence.

shop. What's more, we couldn't go more than one at a time because a group of us could be seen as a provocation.

All of my comrades wanted to avoid going to get the saddles, pointing out the danger. So I volunteered to go looking for them. I went carrying only a 44-caliber revolver hidden under my army jacket because we were supposed to go unarmed.

So I undertook my commission. I got on my horse, and because it had seen the enemy dressed in striped cotton so often, it couldn't look at all of those soldiers without getting scared. So when I got to Dos de Mayo Street where it crosses Cuba, my horse became very hard to control. There I saw eight or ten guerrillas from Sagunto just sitting there still wearing the uniform of striped cotton. I spurred the horse to move on; moving quickly, it kicked up a rain bath of mud on the corner, splattering those guerrillas. They started to curse me, maybe because they thought that the splattering was intentional. So they went off, protesting, to where the soldiers from the Cuenca regiment were. It was a regiment on the bridge of San Luis that I had just crossed and one that I would have to cross again. Those guerrillas told the soldiers that they were covered in mud because I had thrown it at them intentionally to humiliate them.

I then went to the saddle shop, got the equipment, and began my return. When I got back to the corner, there were more than forty soldiers gathered, all with their Mausers from the cavalry, and waiting for me.

When I got close, the entire group of soldiers pointed their guns at me. I stopped, put my hand under my jacket, and grabbed my revolver. Just then, the street vendors began to shout, "They're killing a freedom fighter!"

Fifteen to twenty vendors ran from the nearby butcher shop with their knives held high and ready to fight the Spanish as soon as they saw them threatening me.

A captain in the Spanish Army stood watching the mob on the sidewalk across the street with his arms crossed as if he were watching a grand comedy. I didn't say a word and only looked at the faces of those cowardly villains who didn't want to leave Cuba without one final act of cowardice.

But five minutes hadn't passed when the honorable Captain Filipino came out from the same plaza. (The captain was in the battles we fought when I was in the infantry; I saw his fearlessness during the battle in the camp of El Fierno in Purgatorio. I went there to get Justo Hernández, who died from the great wound he received there, and there I witnessed Filipino's bravery and decisiveness.) Hearing the shouts of the vendors, that honorable and courageous man left the plaza without his cap, sword in hand. In response to that officer's voice, everyone with a clear view took heed and stood at attention. In those first rancorous moments, if it hadn't been for the actions of those vendors, God knows what cruel drama would have unfolded. But when the honorable Captain Filipino arrived, he looked at me and said, "What's going on, young man?"

"Captain," I replied, "I have come from our liberation camp on the orders of my commander. And your subordinates want to kill me."

Then he said, "I don't believe that Spanish officers have sanctioned these acts. You see these villains are troublemakers by instinct. You can return in peace."

And because there were two sergeants in that group of criminals, they began to reprimand the group with slaps and then ordered them all back to the barracks. But on the other side of the bridge, there were about eleven thousand soldiers watching the punishment their comrades had just received. They blocked my path with campfires and firewood that they had piled up in the road so that I wouldn't be able to get by without running into them. The captain understood what was going on and came over to see. Then, as I got to the middle of the bridge, he signaled for me to stop, and he got a coach in order for me to go directly across, until I got by those wild animals.

As soon as they saw the captain coming toward them, they momentarily moved all of the obstacles they had deliberately put in my way. The captain arrived and dismounted, standing there until I passed through the center of all those eleven thousand men. I didn't know the city very well, so I didn't know another street to take.

As I went through the middle of those eleven thousand soldiers, I didn't pay much attention to them because of the captain's presence. But I did observe the movements of some of them who tried to avoid the captain's notice, and tried to detain me further away from where he was. In fact, I saw two men go behind the warehouses without the captain seeing them. But because I'd seen them go behind the buildings, I was ready for them. When I turned onto San Juan de Dios Street, those two good-for-nothings came out from behind the buildings to meet me. But I was already prepared, and as soon as I saw them I pulled out my revolver and fired at them. I don't know if it was because their arms were to be inspected to see if they had fired them, but whatever the reason, I do know that they didn't shoot back, but instead ducked into a nearby house.

In less than ten minutes, I got to La Playa, our camp. The troops were already in formation to march to Navajas when the general received a telegram from General Mayía saying that the trains filled with Spanish troops were allowed to pass freely through Navajas and not to fight them.

The following day, Molina and his aide, Lieutenant Colonel Jiménez Castellanos, son of a Spanish general of the same name, were going to inspect the castle of Peñas-Altas, and had to go along the same street that went by General Betancourt's headquarters. This was because the headquarters' house, La Monona, and the sea were separated by only some four meters. And this street was the only way.

When the news was received that day, that the criminal Molina was to cross in front of our camp, the patriots of the town assumed that it wasn't for a good reason or out of respect for General Betancourt. He sent for me, and I was told the news. He put me in charge of the guards at the door of the headquarters and advised me to exercise caution and restraint when Molina passed by. It was about ten in the morning when he was spotted, accompanied by the treacherous Jiménez Castellanos.

I placed a pair of guards there with their backs to the headquarters door and with their arms at rest, and I stood in the middle of the street with my Mauser.

When that miserable little man arrived in front of the headquarters, he saw that a Cuban coat of arms had been painted on the door. He stopped his horse and the despicable little criminal puffed up like a porcupine. He noticed that I was smiling and shot me a threatening look. I was very close to him, so close that a half yard didn't separate us. He spurred his horse and continued his march with such a rage that no one would have believed that he was looking for the soldiers of the castle of Peñas-Altas, his journey's destination.

When Molina returned, he crossed through our camp like a man possessed. In fact, his aide was barely able to keep up with him.

Three days later it was Christmas Eve, December 24, 1898. And that day I was in charge of order in the camp. At about eleven at night I heard desperate cries in the castle of Peñas-Altas. The cries turned out to be from a sick person in great pain; so I went directly there and when I arrived in the darkness where the gun-carriages of mounted cannons were, ten or twelve soldiers came out, Mausers in hand, shouting at me, "Halt! Who goes there!?"

"Cuba!" I replied.

They responded with curses followed by the sound of the cocking of their guns. I told them that I was coming to help them.

With caution and with Mausers at the ready, we approached each other, and then they asked me why I came there alone at that hour. I told them that I had come only because of the cries of anguish that I had heard, and because I trusted in the nobility of the Latin race.

I invited them to carry the sick man to our camp because they didn't have a doctor there and because the city was too far away to get to in a hurry at that late hour. Some of them objected because they didn't trust me. But there was a cousin of the sick man there, whom we had taken prisoner some time before. He remembered that in the month of December 1896 he was wounded with some one hundred of his comrades, and was taken prisoner. We didn't harm him despite his having been taken prisoner after a long battle. So he agreed that we should take the sick man to the doctor of our camp.

That poor soldier was desperate, but it took only one hour in our first-aid station to alleviate his pain, and to cure him almost completely. He had been carried to the camp, and when he returned to the castle he went in good health and on his own two feet. When they left our camp, I went with them until we got close to the castle. There, they insisted that I accept a token for their thankfulness, a gratuity. The sick man insisted as much as the cousin, but I didn't accept it. I told them that what I had done, as an act of humanity and military honor, was what we all owed to one another.

A few days later, before five o'clock in the morning, those soldiers evacuated and had to pass through our camp. And that soldier who had been sick risked punishment when he left his lines to give me a big hug to say thank you. As they went on the launches through the sea mist, we were on the shore watching what seemed like a dream, watching that line of boats filled with soldiers. Just months before, we had thought that we would fall under their bullets without seeing our beloved Cuba free from the yoke of oppression.

From their launches, they gave us an affectionate good-bye, waving their hats as if we had all been fighting for the same cause. In response, we gave them a hardy farewell, and I thought at that moment about what life really meant.

Just months before, these same soldiers had shot at each other in anger, with the mutual intent to destroy each other in the name of their respective flags. But afterwards, they not only helped one another but also gave each other truly affectionate good-byes.

The End of the Evacuation: The Period of Discharge

On the first day of January 1899, we made our entrance into Matanzas. The liberation forces were intoxicated by the flowers thrown from the balconies and the shouts of "Viva Cuba Libre!" accompanied by the "Invading Hymn" and the Cuban national anthem, "Bayamés."

It was in those days that there was truly a Cuban community. There were no worries or any races. Everyone was joyful and full of brotherly love.

Just imagine that a man could show his true heart to the world. That was what that group of patriots wanted to do through their yearning for an independent and free Cuba.

EPILOGUE

Here you will find a list of the highest-ranking officers who died in the province of Matanzas. They died either in combat, by wounds received in battle, or from sickness.

Generals

Juan Fernández Ruz: In command of the provincial forces in the Brigade of Colón at the end of the year of 1896 or the beginning of 1897. Died of sickness.

Ángel Guerra: Served in the Brigade of Colón (in Prendes) and in the crossing of the second invasion, with Commander in Chief Máximo Gómez and the infantry of el Oriente under General Quintín Bandera. This glorious paladin of the three wars of independence, who had crossed from the far east to get to Matanzas—that hellhole of a province—fell in combat.

Clotilde García: Served as Commander of the Brigade of San José de los Ramos. Died in combat in 1896.

Eustaquio Morejón: Served in the Brigade of Colón. Died from wounds received in combat on the trail from Peñón in 1896.

Enrique Junco: Served in the Brigade of Colón in 1897. Died in combat.

Regino Alfonso: Served in the Brigade of the Northeast. For being a traitor, he was exposed and killed in an ambush at the hill of Pan.

COLONEL CEPERO: Wounded in combat.

COLONEL LORA: Served in the Brigade of Colón. A valorous Dominican, dead.

Lieutenant Colonels

ALFREDO WOOD (Inglesito): While crossing through the province of Havana, he was mortally wounded in the charge on the guerrillas from San Nicolás (de Güines) in 1896.

SOSITA: Killed in 1897 in the mountains of Zapata, by his assistant, while leaving to surrender to the enemy.

ANDRÉS TAVIO: Killed by wounds received in combat.

JOSÉ ANTONIO MESTRES: Killed in combat.

BIENVENIDO SÁNCHEZ: Commander of the Brigade San José de los Ramos. Wounded and taken prisoner. Shot by the enemy in 1897.

Majors

MENÉNDEZ: Served in the Brigade of Colón. Killed in the attack on the town of Aguada de Pasajeros, in 1896.

EDUARDO ROSELL: Served as commander of the general staff to General Betancourt. Killed in battle of Oito, Zapata, on February 3 [Battrell does not provide a year with this date.], in the area of Recreo at Coliseo.

FRANCISCO GUEDES: Killed while on a commission with twenty-two or more men in la Margarita, in the Zapata Mountains, in 1897.

A MAJOR: Killed by a Cuban who was operating in the area of Recreo á Loliseo.

LORETO ESCOBAR: Commander of the infantry and cavalry escort for General Pedro E. Betancourt in 1897. Killed in intense fighting. His body was taken by the enemy to Ceiba-Mocha.

THE TAVÍO BROTHERS (There were five): Commanders of squadrans of the valorous regiments in the Brigade of San José de los Ramos. All of them died. They were among the bravest. One of them, Andrés (Noné), was so brave that he was wounded while being carried on a stretcher in order to lead the squadon on one of their ambushes. He was paralyzed by the effects of the moon, and later died.

From the account that precedes the officers of high ranks, reader, you can see the number of officials, classes, and soldiers who have perished in the theater of war in the most dangerous year, 1895.

It is well confirmed that in the province of Matanzas there were more fallen in the Liberation Army than in any other province of the island. In fact, our invincible leader, Commander in Chief Máximo Gómez, said as much: "One *majá* of Matanzas is worth more than a general in any other province." (*Maja* in the war was the name given to those who didn't fight and who stayed in the woods without operating in an organized force.)

Despite the antagonism between the different ranks of officers, when the war intensified in 1897, a great number of the commanders who surrendered were white, some already colonels. Of the ill-treated blacks, not one officer surrendered. It was not, for example, Cajizote's wish to surrender. He surrendered because all the other people who were tied up with him were to be killed. If you could escape, you did, as he did. He went to the safety and protection of the Spanish, and that was his salvation.

Below is a list of battles and the number of dead, to the best of my memory:

Oito	18 dead
Bellocino	12 dead
Bolondrón	5 dead
Purgatorio	14 dead
Vijas	1 dead from Dantin's unit
Vijas (the second battle)	1 dead from Tavío's unit

Lizaldes	5 dead from Sanguily's unit
El Pan	5 dead
Sabanilla	1 dead
Sabanilla (the second battle)	1 dead
Jabaco	2 dead
San Ignacio	2 dead
San Ignacio (the second battle)	1 dead
Mogote	2 dead
Mogote (the second battle)	2 dead
Ibarra	1 dead
La Antonia	24 dead
Liaño	1 dead
Valera Acosta	3 dead from Higinio Olivera's unit
With Castillo on a mission	4 dead
Sosita (Montes Pedroso)	22 dead
Jagüeisito	1 dead (assistant from Octavio's unit)
Canímar	2 dead
El Tomeguin	2 dead
Total	169 dead (those whom I can remember)

⌒

Below is a list of battles in which I took part and remember after the twelve years since the War of Independence ended. I have not included some encounters that were not battles but forts that we fired on.

1 – La Antonia
2 – Santa Bárbara
3 – Esperanza Domínguez

4 – Claudio
5 – Attack and taking of Roque
6 – Magdalena
7 – Bellocino
8 – El Ciervo
9 – Los Jardines
10 – Jabaco
11 – Manga Larga
12 – Unión de Fernández
13 – Julia de Molinet
14 – Valera Acosta
15 – Las Vijas
16 – San Ignacio
17 – Gavilán
18 – Oito
19 – La Josefa
20 – Ingenio Nieves
21 – Potrero Guacatá (Río de Auras)
22 – Ingenio Condesa
23 – Vista-Hermosa (Río de Auras)
24 – Vereda el Peñón (Prendes)
25 – El Lizaldes
26 – Cuatro-Pasos
27 – Las Vijas (the second battle)
28 – La Batá
29 – El Empalme
30 – Josefita
31 – La Gabriela
32 – Europa

While in the infantry from May 1897 to March 1898, I was in the following battles:

33 – Canímar
34 – Loma del Pan (de Matanzas)
35 – Sierra de Ponce (Picadura)
36 – Loma del Pan (the second battle, the Great Battle)

37 – Purgatorio

38 – Canímar (the second battle)

39 – Loma del Pan (the third battle)

While in the cavalry in 1898, I was in the following battles:

40 – San Ignacio (machete charge)

41 – Igenio Josefita (machete charge)

42 – Viajaca (my saving of the escort)

43 – Ingenio Europa (skirmishes with the forts)

44 – Jovellanos (machete charge)

45 – Ingenio Llince (encountering guerrillas and charging them, La Muerte, of Corral-Falso)

Attacks and the Taking of Towns

46 – Cabezas (twice)

47 – Nueva Paz (one time)

48 – Sabanilla del Encomendador (twice)

49 – Bolondrón (one time)

50 – San Nicolás (one time)

51 – El Roque (one time)

So, the war ended, and with it Spain's dominion over Cuba. But with sadness, I saw the rise of political intrigue and injustice, especially in Matanzas where only black men waged war against Spain. Immediately after the armistice, those little white officers who stayed in the camps and didn't fight began to come out of their hiding places. Positions of authority were being given to those *majases* rather than to those who had fought without rest.

To prove my point I refer to the case of Colonel Guillermo Schweyer, who was captain of sanitation in 1896. When the war intensified at the beginning of 1897, he sequestered himself on the banks of the Canímar River. Frequently corn bread was delivered to him hot as if it had been made right there. His family sent it to him from where they lived in the city of Canímar, and some boats from the Bay of Matanzas delivered it to him. From that nearby place where Guillermo Schweyer stayed, he even had his own rowboat.

When the armistice came on April 4, 1898, the entire Northeast Brigade was camped at Mogote. Schweyer installed himself at the head of the Betances Regiment as colonel. The commanding officer had been Martín Duen, a man as brave as he was black, and he was dark as ebony.

I should also cite the second commander of the Regiment of Matanzas. After the war, Vicente Jorge presented himself as lieutenant colonel of the regiment without ever having fought in the war at that rank!

This is how it was at almost every rank, with the exception of Colonel Diago, Clemente Gómez, the Mayato brothers, Daniel Tabares (Canario), and some others: General Clemente Dantin, the Romero brothers, Pedro Gómez, and Rafael Águila. Most of the officers who survived the war were white officers who managed to avoid fighting in the province of Matanzas. Although they were in the war, when Weyler invaded Matanzas, he didn't see them or any sign of them.

The courageous escort squadron, with which I rode, had sixteen riders; after four months we had grown to one hundred men, fully equipped and all heroic in our providential machete charges. In the charge of San Ignacio, for example, we had eighteen men[1] attack thirty, and none of the enemy survived.

In the charge of Josefita,[2] thirteen of us set out to attack two hundred. In that battle we killed a sergeant and took twenty-eight useful horses that all at once increased our numbers in the escort; what's more, we took eighty head of cattle for the infantry.

Another example is our machete charge on the guerrillas of Jovellanos. There, we took five useful horses, seventy head of cattle, and killed two guerrillas. I killed one myself, just as I did at Josefita.

I must point out that the escort that undertook these charges and others consisted of thirty men often against one hundred, and that the record of the Liberation Army shows that none of us had a rank higher than corporal or sergeant. This shows that the officer positions we deserved

---

1. Eighteen men: In chapter III he states that sixteen men charged at San Ignacio.
2. Josefita: A town seventy-five miles east of the city of Matanzas.

for the battles we waged and won were given just after the war to the increasing number of sons of distinguished families, and therefore only because of their color. They are imposters who falsify the history of the Liberation Army, especially in my own province that I know so well. They were honored and feted after the war, those very same *majases* who only gorged themselves on oxen during the war. This, while we gave life to Cuba Libre shot by shot, machete stroke by machete stroke.

~

When the war ended I was eighteen years old, and, as I said before, I couldn't read or write. I weighed all of the sacrifices and hardships that I had endured in the war, and I realized that in order to be truly respected in our society, it was imperative that I learn to read and write. So I locked myself up in a house for six months without involving myself in the tumult of Cuba Libre. After those six months, I was able to make some modest scribbles that with effort could be understood. In order to know with more certainly if my writing could be read, I gave some of it to my protector and commanding officer, Colonel Fernando Diago. He was amazed at my accomplishments and told General Pedro E. Betancourt about them. They visited me to congratulate me and to encourage me to continue with the self-sacrifice of my studies. To show General Betancourt's reaction, I have enclosed a letter from my dear commander and friend.

Pedro E. Betancourt
Civil Governor of the
Province of Matanzas
Particular

For Ricardo Oviedo,

Dear Ricardo,

I received your kind letter of the 28th, made up of your very affection-
ate writings which you dedicate to me, and I thank you for it. You
know that I have always loved my soldiers, and more, those like you,
who were so brave and who have conducted themselves so well.

I suppose that you have already been freed because I have written to the Judge of [unidentified word], and the prosecutor for this court is a good man and very fair; so you will be able to be freed on a provisional basis until the oral case is heard in court. And because in this case you are innocent, as I said to the court, you can be sure that you will certainly leave without fear of being incarcerated again.

I see that you have greatly improved your writing, and that it is pretty clear. Continue to work on it and write every day one hour or two so that you can perfect your writing in cursive.

Some days ago I wrote to you. I suppose that you received the letter. Continue to be a good Cuban, and always count on the support and love of your commanding officer.

Coronel Diago
Matanzas, March 29, 1900

(The reason for the letter was the death of a bandit on January 14, 1900. While I was in the cavalry police in Sabanilla del Encomendador it was made clear that, upon cross-examination, there was a discrepancy in my companion's statement; so I was detained for fifteen days by the court.)

⌐‒

As for those parts in which the reader might think that I am being overly critical of my comrades, please keep in mind that my only motivation is to lay bare the events and deeds that ignited a civil war like the war for Cuba's independence. And more, I want to be a guide to the new generation of Cubans, so that they can get at least a general idea of what this type of war is like, one in which human beings, with rare exception, turn cruel.

Also, I want those who read these notes to see the excessive cruelty that still persists in these fights. If that cruelty isn't punished by man, then there is something secret and invisible, a supreme force, that leaves its mark, its judgment, without violence, but without pardoning a single case of cruelty. Indeed, consider the events of Prendes.

Colonel Cervantes also had a sad end, although later he appeared for the occasion of the sale of his property as a prisoner of war.

General Avelino Rosa could not have been surpassed in cruelty even by those same liberators in the province of Matanzas. It has already been seen that his glories in five different wars have been eclipsed by the last war of independence of Cuba. I believe that could have ended his own cruelty because he did go a year and some months without any fighting. But it seems as if he couldn't control himself during his command in that terrible province. When the war ended in Cuba, he returned to his own country, Colombia or Venezuela, and immediately took part in a revolt that was going on there. We received cables from newspapers reporting that in that same year, 1899, he had been taken prisoner and dragged to death from the tail of a horse. That monster had done things in the war that, reader, you wouldn't believe if I were to describe them. It would sound like a nightmare for those who were fighting to redeem their country from the yoke of tyranny and defending their cause and lives. It would be a strange story indeed, where Cubans allowed a foreigner, in a position to help them, to take advantage of his rank to kill Cubans under his command. In the end, Commander in Chief Máximo Gómez had to relieve Rosa of his command of the province and replaced him with General Pedro E. Bentancourt.

Also, reader, take notice of the end suffered by the *presentado* who took the Spanish column to Cubilinganga in order to kill all the sick and wounded there. By chance he was brought to us so that he would die by the hands of the same men whom he was freely directing in order to kill those who had done him no wrong.

I cite these events in order to make them more visible and as a reminder, because if the reader heeds their example, he will see other similar injustices in different contexts. These events prove to humans that there is a higher power. So those who feel moved by the spirit of injustice should resist the impulse. God will send them a sign to help them, even though in their hour of need they might not realize it.

It was because of a lack of security on every date that each one of these cruel and bloody events occurred. I ask for the reader's benevolence, because in this, as in no other theaters of redemptive revolution, there was no time to stop and to worry about dates, for several reasons.

One, because of the lack of communication with the towns, and also because the commanders were so preoccupied with the constant fights with the enemy that they lost all of the records.

To Colonel Fernando Diago y de Cárdenas, my commander in the war and my loyal friend in peace, I dedicate this book.

Ricardo Batrell

LOOKING FOR RICARDO BATRELL IN HAVANA

An Appendix Essay

IN AUGUST 2006, I had the privilege of spending a week at the Archivo Nacional de Cuba in Havana, reading Ricardo Batrell's papers and any additional material I could find on black soldiers in the Cuban War of Independence. Armed with Aline Helg's and Ada Ferrer's respective notes that list most of the items to be found in Batrell's papers, along with Fernando Heredia's and Blanamar Rosabal's respective essays that describe the content of most of the papers, I arrived at the Archivo with a fairly good sense of what I was looking for; but in retrospect, I really had no idea what to expect.

It's a bit of an oddity in Havana that very few people outside the researching community, so it seems, actually know where the Archivo Nacional is. Tucked away on Compostela Street in a sleepy corner of Old Havana, the building is a good distance away from the typical tourist attractions. So, every morning I went through the same ritual: I hail a cab as I make my way down the Malecón from Vedado toward Old Havana. Getting in, I show the cabby the map, point to my destination, and say "El Archivo Nacional, por favor." Invariably, my request is met with a quizzical look; he examines the map until I ask him to drive down the Malecón past the Castillo de Real Fuerza. Once we pass all of the tourist buses from Varadero pulled up to see the Cathedral of Havana, and pass the big curve at the Armadores de Santander Hotel, then pass the docks, the driver glances at me nervously, and I respond, "Más allá, más allá," waving forward, and we drive on. Then, as we round the last curve and come to the intersection of Compostela and Desamparados, the building seems to leap out of nowhere. Sitting nearly kitty-corner to the street, its massive structure muscles up to the corner, taking up an entire city block and dwarfing the surrounding apartment buildings. I say to the cabby, "Para aquí, por favor, el edificio está allá" (Stop here, please; the building is right there), pointing to the massive structure. He stops, looks up, and smiles. Sometimes he says, "No sabía que este edificio estaba aquí" (I didn't know that this building was here). Handing him his money, I thank him for the ride, grab my backpack, and start up the street toward the entrance in the middle of the block. The building is in a residential section of the old city, so there are children playing in the street and people standing in doorways staring at the *extranjero*. Nothing could scream "foreigner" more loudly than a grown man wearing shorts and carrying a backpack.

Founded in 1840, the Archivo Nacional is an impressive example of colonial-era neoclassicism. Its weighty stone facade, the ionic columns, so many straight lines pointing to the heavens, nearly overstate Spanish colonial power, which, of course, by the mid-nineteenth century was in rapid decline. As the official custodian of national memory, the Archivo Nacional houses numerous documents and artifacts pertinent to the colonial and republican eras. Practically any project on Cuban history or culture requires some time there. And so I have come too, on a pilgrimage of sorts, to try to reconstruct a life that Cuba's national narrative and the hemisphere's racial narrative can't seem to accommodate.

I first read his voluminous set of letters to Juan Gualberto Gómez, the secretary of war, the secretary of the provincial government, and other government officials. These letters help to provide some information about Batrell's life after the war, but more important, they provide insights into his thoughts concerning the development of the fledgling republic, particularly his views on race. After spending a full day on his letters, the archive staff brought me the much-anticipated file labeled "Relato escrito y firmado por Ricardo Batrell" (Account written and signed by Ricardo Batrell). I was particularly focused on this file, which no one had commented on in any detail, because it seemed to promise material for the second volume of his autobiography. (Toward the end of *Para la historia,* Batrell includes a photograph of himself in his officer's uniform when he was in the Constitutional Army. Beneath the photo he

Appendix

writes: "In 1906 in the August Revolution: with this photograph will come the second volume about my civilian life and my participation in the August Revolution.")

I knew that there might be something quite special here, and so I brought my digital camera so that I could photograph all of this particular file. But even though I knew that the content of the file was important, I wasn't prepared for the impact the physical reality of his papers would have on me. Batrell wrote on lined paper about eight inches wide by five inches long, about half the size of a standard 8½ by 11 sheet of paper. After nearly one hundred years, the paper itself was still in very good condition, with few tears and no crumbling at the edges. Indeed, I was entirely unprepared for how beautiful this manuscript was. The paper had deepened in color over time, transforming from what I assumed was its original white or beige to a deep golden brown, nearly a burnt orange. Batrell wrote in black ink, with an elegant hand that complemented the aesthetics of the paper. To the extent to which good penmanship connotes a certain command of literacy, the aesthetics of his script suggested to me the long, hard work of mastery. I sat and imagined the meticulous pains he must have taken to develop his hand, yet another piece of ammunition in his arsenal, another tactic in the larger war for black civil rights. Like so many other blacks who acquired literacy in order to tell their own story, he was born into nothing; he was told that he would amount to nothing, yet here was the palpable evidence in my own hands of his presence in the world. Over the span of a century, he was still telling his story, still making his case to those who would listen.

The pages are numbered, beginning at 665, and go through 758— ninety-three handwritten pages in all, some 8,236 words. Page 665 begins with the date February 12, 1910, then launches into the description of a battle in mid-sentence: ". . . what gunfire! The Northern Brigade had never fired on us like that before . . ." Although the context for the first page is unclear, the pages that follow, for the most part, describe events in 1898, ostensibly additional material for the final chapter. Although the episodes do not strictly follow a chronology of movements across Matanzas, many allude to the armistice that is either about to be signed or has just been signed; and most of the episodes concern operations after formal hostilities have ceased, yet while lingering tensions, before the Spanish evacuation, continue to threaten the outbreak of violence. This material also sharpens the discussion of Batrell's selection for his memoir, and thus the metaphoric and political work his volume seeks to perform. By comparing material ultimately left out of his published account, we might see more clearly how he uses his wartime experiences to address specific postwar polemics. To this end, this material falls into four broad categories: polemical statements, nearly identical episodes he includes in the published version, one substantially altered episode, and episodes not included in the published narrative.

First, the polemical statements are essentially the same in content as many of those made in the published version, but approached slightly differently. For example, on the page immediately following his comments on the Northern Brigade, he reiterates the theme of discrimination against black soldiers, here being denied the promotions that they deserve:

Alberto and I were, in effect, the commanding officers of our little squadron. We were to go on the mission with the escort until it was completed.

This responsibility was important because this was an opportunity to prove that we deserved the promotions that we had been denied in the escort. Because of our feats in battle, not one of us should have finished the war with a rank less than lieutenant.

Despite the fact that we were small in number, we nevertheless deserved an officer's rank. In fact, the Spanish never saw those who were given the officer's rank, while we were the authors of the historic *danzón*. Betancourt's men were brave, proven through our repeated machete charges in those three months. We were going to the town called Pacífico, almost all of us only as corporals, while those officers couldn't even see from so far away our "operations" with those Spanish soldiers and guerrillas.

So those who have a higher rank, it is because of us. We fought without rest and without any concern for promotion. We only thought about liberating Cuba, our beloved homeland.

We had the great satisfaction that in the theater of the War of Independence that was our province, with the difficult terrain and in the most populous province of Cuba, we were the true liberators. Not because of our names, but because we got up every morning in the midst of those Spanish soldiers, and we went to bed firing the last shot. We did this day after day, month after month, and year after year until we were crowned at the summit of liberty, until the flag of our country, with its solitary star, flew clean and with our honor as witness, as its firm defenders![1]

We have seen this protest against the lack of promotion for black soldiers across all three chapters, but particularly in chapter III. The protest is, in fact, closely linked to all of the major themes the introduction identifies, and the protest points directly to the larger jeremianic implications of the text. In fact, the final sentence above seems to echo a striking line in the epilogue: "This, while we gave life to Cuba Libre shot by shot, machete stroke by machete stroke"—the line ending his final jeremiad.

And, as one might expect, the extant papers actually include an additional jeremiad:

at that time, for those of us who were creating this our homeland selflessly, there was no personal ambition, just the desire to climb that hill, to make Cuba Libre real. We wanted nothing more than to redeem our country. We knew nothing but the days and hours waiting to fall under the bullets or blades of the enemy on the altar of idolized Cuba, the altar that afterwards politics has desecrated, and has made it so that the guerrillas of yesterday are worth more than the saints and fathers of the homeland. (757–58)

Following yet another passage of the denial of promotions to black soldiers, this diatribe invites a comparison between what Batrell regards as the very worst of Cuban society and what should be its best. Because of postwar intrigue, the worst and best are inverted, as he implicitly calls for the restoration of the proper social and moral order, again a return to the ideals of Cuba Libre.

In addition to material that revisits established polemics, the bulk of the archival material consists of episodes included in the published narrative, nearly verbatim; thus, they might be read as near-final versions and particularly important in that Batrell drafted them several times. That the episodes pursue many of the dominant themes of the narrative proper further underscores Batrell's attention to their metaphoric possibilities. For example, the archival material includes the episode in chapter III in which Batrell, his brother, and three comrades approach what turns out to be a mobile fort hitched to oxen. Because some of his comrades do not heed his suspicion, one gets shot. The archival material includes this episode nearly exactly as it appears in the published account, perhaps further emphasizing Batrell's concern for the portrayal of his forbearance and leadership. Likewise, the episode in chapter III in which he falls asleep on his horse and wakes up in front of a Spanish fort is part of the archival material, as is the episode in chapter III with General Menocal in which Batrell's escort attempts to prove its valor to skeptics by riding out to attack the approaching Civil Guard. Again, a concern for the portrait of devotion and exemplary valor may well inform the multiple drafting of these episodes.

Strikingly different from these duplicate passages, the archival material does include one longer episode that appears in the published version, but is substantially different in manuscript. Toward the end of chapter III, after the armistice has been signed, Batrell is charged with policing the countryside and with rounding up outlaws still victimizing the civilian population. In doing so, he captures a guerrilla, but prevents his men from killing him. This act of kindness leads to a great deal of trouble for him, in that his comrades accuse him of cowardice, his commanding officer reprimands him, and finally the guerrilla returns to the rebel camp in disguise in an attempt to frame one of his comrades. While this episode in the published version ends with the recapture of the guerrilla and Colonel Diago hitting him, the manuscript version, below, ends with guerrilla's death by machete:

> It was according to Providence that during those two days the guerrillas from Cabezas were freed and came with the *pacíficos* to visit our camp. Among them was the guerrilla of the previous

controversy; he had been ordered by the Spanish to go to the headquarters disguised as one of the most miserable among the visitors.

If it weren't for his perverse intentions, no one would have noticed him; even I wouldn't have recognized him. He went to tell the general that a commission of his escort that had been through the town of Cabezas had taken two centenes. To say this was to level a serious accusation, because he knew it would be punished by the Wartime Tribunal. It almost resulted in the accused being hanged. When he made this accusation, Colonel Diago summoned Porfirio, the soldier the guerrilla accused, to see if he knew the *pacífico*. Porfirio, who was from that town, could identify the *pacífico*. Porfirio knew that "bird" from before the war, because he was from the same town. Despite the guerrilla's disguise, Porfirio knew him no matter how he dressed. He said that he was the guerrilla whose life I'd spared. The colonel didn't let him beg for mercy; he hit the guerrilla four or six times with the flat of his machete blade, and this alarmed us because we had never seen Colonel Diago get so mad. Seeing him so enraged, I realized the seriousness of the situation; that damned guerrilla had cost me two arguments for having saved his life— when I took him prisoner, and later when Colonel Diago gave me my first and only reprimand in the war. What's more, that same miscreant came to make accusations against my comrades after I had saved his life; he should have thanked all of us, but instead he did the opposite. He disguised himself in tattered clothing to evoke sympathy, he who three or four days before was a guerrilla in his vile striped uniform.

I mounted my horse and I caught up with him on the road from Mogote going up the hill called Vera Bocoy. He saw me, machete in hand, and begged me not to do it. But because my comrades wanted to kill him, I started to give him several blows with the flat of my machete. As I raised my machete (Paraguayo) to hit him, he yelled so much that he couldn't pronounce a single word. Because we were close to the camp, the infantry from the hill of their camp could see what I was doing with that villain who looked for his death in his perverse intentions. I beat him until he fell down on the ground out of breath. He already had bruises on his sides. And I heard my comrades yelling, "Kill him, Ricardo!" as Catalino arrived to help me. He was the hero of three years of war and hadn't been separated from me for one moment in all those hours of danger. Because he didn't have full control over his machete, when he tried to hit him, the machete glanced off and cut off the ear of that perverse guerrilla.

I couldn't stop Catalino from killing him with his blows. I didn't kill that guerrilla myself because I wanted to avoid an even bigger problem with the general, given the original controversy with the infantry. When I arrived at the camp, General Betancourt was there and was angry; he reprimanded me, saying "Why have you done this?" (751–57)

That Batrell changes the published version to omit the final killing of the guerrilla may further emphasize a tension or ambivalence that marks the entire text. At several moments, Batrell pauses to lament the cruelty of war, and in his epilogue he asks his reader not to judge his fellow *mambises* and him for being too cruel. Indeed, on the one hand, he needs to develop fully the theme of black bravery, one that largely depends on killing, often by machete. Yet, on the other hand, he does not want to alienate his postwar audience, one that may feel further removed from the brutality of war, and thus less inclined to sympathize with figures who take joy in hacking the enemy to death. Perhaps this tension leads Batrell to change the episode in order to modify the brutality. In the published version, the episode ultimately delivers Batrell as an infinitely patient figure willing to endure reprimands and betrayal in service to a higher purpose, while the manuscript delivers Batrell and his compatriots as war-hardened soldiers more than willing to kill the enemy at every opportunity.

As for the three episodes ultimately omitted from *Para la historia,* although we do not know exactly why they were not included, or indeed who ultimately made the decision to excise them, their absence does shed some additional light on the ultimate shaping of the volume. First, pages 675–77 describe an additional example of Batrell's skill and bravery:

We camped that night at Tobaco. And there my friendship with Garino came to a sad end. He was in Sanguily's mounted escort that rode the horses taken at Josefita. He was one of the unarmed, and so had never fought before. But at Viajaca, he fought and had fired on the fort. Afterward, I said that even though the war was almost over, we would make a fighter out of him yet.

The rest of my comrades thought that this was funny, and they mocked him in the way that young soldiers do. So Garino, who was the oldest and largest of all of us, was embarrassed and assumed that I had started all of the joking. He pulled out his machete and we exchanged thrusts and parries while the rest of the troop tried to intervene to stop us. They thought Garino would get hurt, despite the fact that he was older and twice my size.

They thought that he'd be wounded because I had already shown in our jousts that I could handle a machete with the best fighters in the camp. The fight ended without incident mainly because I didn't fight very hard so that I wouldn't injure my furious comrade. I could see that he was so angry that he couldn't appreciate how good I was with a machete. (675–77)

As we've seen in the narrative proper, Batrell paints himself as the most courageous of the group, the most mature in his ability to protect his comrades from unnecessary danger, and here he is the most skilled sword-fighter. Typical too, he points out his youth and small stature and younger age, again throwing his superior attributes into further relief.

The second excised episode involves an act of altruism. Having discovered a cavalryman with no horse, Batrell seeks to remedy the situation:

We stayed there almost ten days resting our horses and waiting for all of the regiments of the brigade to meet there where the general could review all of the forces.

On the fourth day that we were there, I saw a young soldier named Gervacio. In 1896, he had come from Bridagier Francisco Pérez's forces; he was the commander of that same brigade. He had come to our unit with Captains Juan Sardiña and Victoriano Montes de Oca down to our force, and he had spent eight months with Sanguily's force, until we came to the same place accompanying General Juan Ruiz. And there he had become ill. He was brave and a cavalryman, but because his horse had been rendered useless in that rocky area, I noticed that he was there unarmed. We had a horse left over from the ones captured at Josefita; so I said to the general that I wanted to give it to Gervacio so that he could ride with the escort. The general asked me just one question, if I could guarantee that Gervacio was a brave soldier. I replied in the affirmative, and Gervacio was given the remaining horse. We saddled it and left. And the new soldier become a part of the escort.

This happened in the month of July in 1898. (678–80)

Where the first episode may have been omitted because Batrell felt the theme of his own valor had been fully developed through other material, the omission of this short passage may be explained similarly, in that this display of his altruism and kindness is well developed, largely through his relationship with his brother. Furthermore, to the extent to which this episode illustrates Batrell's affinity for fellow freedom fighters—he recognizes a kindred soul and thus goes out of his way to help him—his dedication to others who fight for the cause as passionately as he does is also well established in the text.

In sharp contrast, the final omitted episode relates a mutiny that Batrell foments. Where the published account goes to great lengths to illustrate Batrell's bravery and defiance of authority in service to the cause, none push the issue of insubordination quite as far as the following episode:

Following the 19th, there was a mutiny in the escort that I caused because there had been a breakdown in discipline the day before in a battle. So, it was ordered that we drill in fencing. I ignored the order because I was already fully prepared to use my machete. . . .

I didn't like Andrés Martínez because he tried to hit my brother with the flat of his machete just because he made a mistake in the drills. In just one of my moves I was so much better. My brother had gone to so many battles, and Martínez had just made excuses not to go into battle, excuses that all of us had heard many times. So, when they ended the drill, I was waiting at a distance, and I went to ask him for an account of the exercise that my brother had to participate in. But because Martínez just wanted to avoid the issue by alluding to his higher rank, we had a fight. It got pretty dangerous when he pulled out his machete. I grabbed my Mauser and I yelled, "I'll shoot!" Almost everyone in the escort had a great love for me, especially those in the vanguard, because we were the boldest in the battles with the enemy. In the face of this rebellion or mutiny, Andrés's authority was compromised, so he left to go to headquarters, which was close to the infantry camp.

He told all of this to General Betancourt and Colonel Diago, in the hope that they would impose order and respect for discipline. When they arrived, they were confused by the situation and spoke to almost the entire escort that was on my side. They ordered all of the men into formation, all of those who were part of the mutiny, and that was the entire vanguard made up of thirty men called "the mambiza flower." Even though at first the general refused to talk to the men in the mutiny, there was a good chance that he would change his mind. He called me over and asked me what was it that I wanted. I said that I wanted to go to the escort of the infantry. He asked me why, and I told him what had happened, and I finished saying that I couldn't be under the orders of a man like Andrés Martínez who, when facing the enemy, didn't measure up to even our weakest man. Regardless of his ineptness as a soldier, he tried to impose a discipline and respect that he hadn't earned. In the camps and in the hours when there was no enemy, he committed acts like the one against my brother. So I refused to recognize his authority, and so I wanted to leave and go to the escort of the infantry.

My arguments were having an effect on the general, but he didn't want to weaken discipline further or to decide in favor of those in the mutiny. So he only responded, "And your brother, isn't he older than you? He hasn't protested what you say Andrés has done?"

"General," I replied, "even under great pressure, my brother may seem passive or indifferent to the situation. But I can't wait or simply witness unjust things. And more, if something wrong is done to my brother, whom I admire, it is as if it were done to me."

But, as I said before, the general didn't want to give in to my arguments, and he said, "You say that you want to transfer to the escort of the infantry. Go, then!"

When I told him that I wanted to go, they took back my horse and all the equipment I had taken from the guerrillas I had killed the day before.

Meanwhile, he was asking the rest of the soldiers who were on my side, "What do you want?" All of my good comrades said, "Yes, all of us want to go with Ricardo to the infantry." Among them who said this was Gervacio, he who a few days before in Prendes began to ride with us.[2] He did it to show his gratitude, but before the general arrived, I had told him to remain neutral because he had been in the escort just a few days, and the general was going to say that he didn't have anything to complain about.

So that's how it went. Everyone said that they wanted to go with me to the escort of the Remington Betances infantry.

In the midst of all of this, the general singled out poor Gervacio; he made him step out of formation, and said to him, "You too, you are complaining?"

To which he replied, "Yes."

We never saw General Betancourt become so angry and violent, either before or after that day. Our loving commander was so overcome with fury that he took out his revolver, and Colonel Diago had to intervene. Then, in a reflex action, he drew his machete . . . ; he was about to hit Gervacio, but he just lost the will. Then he just said, "Go to the infantry."

And then he turned to me, and said, "You can go if it is your choice, Ricardo."

I then went to the infantry that was close by.

And to the rest he said, "You all can break formation." And

everyone did. But he couldn't let everyone go, because he didn't have riders whom he could trust to replace us.

Everyone complied, given the fact that the general was so angry; but after two hours some went to the headquarters. And when they saw that the general had calmed down, they insisted that they no longer stay in his escort. Then the general readily admitted that they were right. This, among other things, my good comrades told me. And later the general summoned me to talk alone. He was very good to us during the war. (Although after the war he changed. But the official record declares, "Render unto Caesar what is Caesar's.")

They said that to him. Then he said, "If some of you want to leave because he has left, you weren't really a part of the escort before he came."

They replied, "Yes, but the escort was never as big and in such good condition, with seventy or more men, before Ricardo joined."

Just one operation, made successful because of my leadership and fearlessness, led eighteen men to mount and ride in the escort. And more than that, I was very well prepared in the battles, from the beginning to the end in retreat.

Our own general knew all of this very well, despite the denial of rank that took place at that time, as it does in all revolutions. But true patriots are not interested in rank, or don't know the benefits that rank can bring. For when wars end, what is done is to show off one's rank so that one can receive twice the benefits. First, civilians don't interest themselves in who was truly the bravest for the sacred cause of liberty to triumph. Second, those with higher rank receive higher pay, and show off their higher pay even though they know that they were paid off. It's not fair since they receive greater benefits and positions from names validated by the official record, because of the ranks they held without having won them through facing enemy fire. This is a threat to the very justice and liberty we fought to defend.

Let's return to General Betancourt's side when he ordered me to look for a solution to this state of rebellion that reigned over the escort. When I arrived at his tent, situated on one of the hills of San Miguel de los Baños, he made us follow him to a place away from his tent. And he told me that I was to return to the escort of the cavalry. And everyone complied. After a few days, he said that he would transfer Andrés Martínez to the command of a small group of guerrillas who were *pasados*. With those guerrillas' horses, Sanguily had a little group of cavalry. And he would make Andrés commander of this little group of riders. We were all satisfied with this decision.

As I said before, Sanguily was a very good commander in the war, even though he didn't give us the officers' positions that we rightly deserved. But he was fair in his treatment of the courageous soldiers.

I returned to the escort, and a few days later they threw Martínez out of the escort. (710–26)

Perhaps the longest episode in the archival material, this section revisits now standard poses for Batrell: Batrell the fearless fighter, Batrell as beloved comrade, Batrell as chosen son, Batrell as exemplar of military honor, and so on. We also see in the published text Batrell committing acts of insubordination. Yet, where in *Para la historia* his insubordination is limited to himself, and thus does not threaten the larger military order essential for the success of the revolution, here he describes the revolt of an entire unit. Perhaps the extent of the revolt, were it included in the published version, might undermine Batrell's claim of loyalty to the cause of Cuba Libre. Here Batrell acts on impulse and with clear disdain for a superior officer; though his contempt is linked to Martínez's cowardice, the larger revolt Batrell inspires never establishes a clear link with any of the noble ideals that Batrell claims as motivation. The men follow his lead, according to the account, out of love and personal loyalty, not out of devotion to a free and independent Cuba.

If in fact Batrell excised this episode because it tends to destabilize the metaphoric foundation of the text, then such an episode further underscores the care and deliberateness with which Batrell created his text. At first glance, both the text and the archival material appear rough, perhaps rushed in their preparation and assembly. The non sequiturs, ambiguous references, grammatical errors, and the like seem to suggest a text still beyond the control of its author. But a closer examination of Batrell's tropic vocabulary reveals an author quite self-conscious about the construction of his rhetorical self and the larger signifying field that self will inhabit. Some of these episodes suggest that excessive killing or unrestrained self-interest are features that limit rather than enhance the metaphoric capabilities of his hero, while others may reveal a sensitivity to overstatement—that certain episodes simply repeat ideas and themes already well developed.

At this point my scholarship gives itself over to speculation. We have Batrell's published memoir and his papers, yet we still know so little about him—indeed, nothing about his life after *Para la historia* was published, about how the book was received, or about his thoughts on the 1912 massacre, and so much more. But as I took the final photographs of his papers and began to think of the black farmhand-cum-freedom fighter teaching himself to write these very pages, I thought that perhaps at the limits of empirical data, speculation and imagination are the least that Batrell deserves. If he can reach across a century to us and still dare to rewrite the official history of his day, we can reach back to imagine how an allegedly subhistorical subject might go about reclaiming his own country, how he might marshal the rhetoric to tell his own story.

ACKNOWLEDGMENTS

With the publication of *A Black Soldier's Story: The Narrative of Ricardo Batrell and the Cuban War of Independence,* we take yet another step toward the fuller recovery of vital yet neglected black voices, pivotal in the development of the Western Hemisphere. This step has been made possible by the collective efforts and inspiring generosity of many friends, colleagues, and institutions. Any success this volume may achieve is the direct result of their contributions, and all errors and shortcomings are entirely my own.

First and foremost, I thank my wife, Kimberly Wallace-Sanders, for her support and patience throughout the development of this project: once again, thank you for a love supreme.

I also thank my dear friend and wonderful colleague Rudolph P. Byrd. The loving attention given to the manuscript and your insightful suggestions were of critical importance and truly motivational. But perhaps more important, thank you for the steadfast encouragement to cross disciplinary boundaries and to take risks, and for the constant reminder that the port would be well worth the cruise.

My colleagues in the African American studies and English departments at Emory University deserve my sincerest thanks for their interest in the project and for their words of encouragement.

I extend lasting gratitude to my colleagues and friends in the Department of Spanish and Portuguese at Emory University: María Carrión, Lisa Dillman, José Quiroga, and Karen Stolley. María, for making me feel like a member of the larger Caribbean family; Lisa, for her timely advice on theories of translation; José, for his contacts in Cuba and his enthusiasm for the project; and Karen, for showing me how one can, in midcareer and with small children, learn a second language and have fun doing it.

Acknowledgments

I thank my friends and colleagues in Havana without whose help this project would have been impossible: Roberto Zurbano Torres, Tomás Fernández Robaina, Rafaela Curbelo, Julio López Valdés, Anaisis Pereira, and Peter Semanat Martínez, along with his mother, Emelia Martínez Larduet, and his family. Zurbano was a great help in navigating the Cuban bureaucracy and in gaining access to the Archivo Nacional; more important, his friendship and those long, searching conversations about race and Cuba informed all of my thinking on the subject. Thanks to Tomás, for helping me find books at the Biblioteca Nacional, for his support of the project, and for his insights into Afro-Cuban culture. Thanks to Rafaela, Julio, and Anaisis for their help in the Archivo Nacional; they were the first to show me the Batrell papers and were tireless in finding additional materials germane to the project. And thanks too to Peter and his family for taking me in and giving me home-cooked meals—indeed, for a home away from home.

I owe a tremendous debt of gratitude to my Spanish tutors: Ryan Prendergast, Julia Carroll, Katherine Ford, María Rosa-Rodríguez, and Margarita Pintado-Burgos. Thank you for your patience and expert instruction, and for the emotional support to stick with it. Julia, Katherine, and Margarita proofread the translation, saving me from more than one embarrassing mistake.

The graduate students in my seminar on Afro-Cuban culture in spring 2008 helped to shape this project in crucial ways. Thank you to Jessie Dunbar, Omar Granados, Keme Hawkins, Jessica Hinton, Kathryn Juergens, Noelia Martín-García, Guirdex Masse, Sarah Prince, Roopika Risam, Gilberto Ruiz, and Anastasia Valecce: your honest criticism of the manuscript was invaluable, your capacity for hard work affirming, and your enthusiasm for Afro-Cuban culture infectious.

The tireless and timely work of my research assistants in finding books and vital information dramatically improved the quality of this book. Ángel Díaz and Adrienne Rotella, thank you for all of your help.

I express my appreciation to the anonymous reader who made meticulous corrections to the translation; thanks to these suggestions, the translation has been much improved.

John Chasteen has been a steadfast supporter of the project from nearly the beginning: thank you for your advice and your example as a scholar and translator.

It goes without saying that financial support is crucial for any research project. I owe a great debt to the Center for Teaching and Curriculum, the International Research Program, the University Research Committee, and the Bill and Carol Fox Center for Humanistic Inquiry, all at Emory University. Without the grants and fellowships these institutions provided, this project would never have come to fruition.

To the Oberlin College group—Lawrence Buell, Calvin Hernton, and Kathie Linehan: thank you for your lasting example of engaged scholarship and teaching.

I express the sincerest thanks to my editors at the University of Minnesota Press, Richard Morrison and Adam Brunner. Thank you for your patience for this long overdue project, for your belief in its potential, and for your enlivening vision for its design.

As always, Tony Dixon is in these pages and in our lives.

Thanks to Steve Saltzman for a love and appreciation of Cuba that always serves as inspiration.

I thank my extended family: Earl and Arthrell Sanders, Claire Sanders and Burton Balfour, Rose Wallace, Raymond Wallace, Gregory Wallace and Jeff Weiser, and Christopher Wallace, Kimberly Hall Wallace, Christian and little Kameron.

Finally, I thank our sons, to whom this volume is dedicated. Though I don't provide a translation of the dedication, the sentiment is self-evident, and I'm sure you will come to read it in your own time and in your own way.

TRANSLATOR'S NOTES

Introduction

First epigraph: This quotation, attributed to Juan Gualberto Gómez, appears on a billboard just outside of Sabanilla (recently renamed Juan Gualberto Gómez), the hometown of Gómez and Batrell.

1. Ferrer, *Insurgent Cuba*, 3; Foner, *Antonio Maceo*, 172.

2. Several black soldiers dictated their accounts of the War of Independence. See Herrera, *Impresiones de la Guerra de Independencia*, and Montejo, *Biography of a Runaway Slave*. Several black officers, including Antonio Maceo, wrote campaign diaries. See Maceo, *Antonio Maceo*.

3. Pérez, *Cuba*, 30–63.

4. Foner, *A History of Cuba and Its Relations with the United States*, 1:62–63; Dubois, *Avengers of the New World*, 21; Davis, "He Changed the New World," 54; Pérez, *Cuba*, 77. Subsequent references to Pérez, *Cuba*, are given in the text.

5. Corzo, *Runaway Slave Settlements in Cuba*, 117–67.

6. Paquette, *Sugar Is Made with Blood*, 209–32; Pérez, *Cuba*, 100.

7. Quoted from Bell, *Toussaint Louverture*, 287.

8. Pérez, *Cuba*, 106, 111.

9. Ferrer, *Insurgent Cuba*, 15.

10. Pérez, *Cuba*, 121.

11. Ferrer, *Insurgent Cuba*, 23.

12. Pérez, *Cuba*, 124.

13. Ferrer, *Insurgent Cuba*, 95.

14. Quoted from ibid., 126.

15. Ibid., 122–27.

16. Quoted from Pérez, *Cuba*, 148.

17. Foner, *A History of Cuba and Its Relations with the United States*, 2:354.

18. Foner, *Antonio Maceo*, 198.

19. Ferrer, *Insurgent Cuba*, 2.

20. Montejo, *Biography of a Runaway Slave*, 161.

21. Flint, *Marching with Gomez,* 39.

22. Quoted from Pérez, *Cuba,* 164.

23. Tone, *War and Genocide in Cuba, 1895–1898,* 223.

24. Boza, *Mi diario de la guerra,* 21.

25. Pérez, *Cuba,* 178.

26. Quoted from de la Fuente, *A Nation for All,* 40.

27. Pérez, *Cuba,* 179.

28. Ibid., 182.

29. Ibid.

30. Montejo, *Biography of a Runaway Slave,* 195.

31. Ricardo Batrell Oviedo to Juan Gualberto Gómez, January 5, 1906, ANC, Adgilisiciones, box 12, no. 484.

32. Smart, *Nicolás Guillén,* 75.

33. Ibid., 53.

34. Lane, *Blackface Cuba, 1840–1895,* 29.

35. Ibid., 72.

36. Ibid., 92–93.

37. Helg, *Our Rightful Share,* 138.

38. De la Fuente, *A Nation for All,* 54.

39. Ibid., 23–53.

40. Helg, *Our Rightful Share,* 156.

41. Ibid., 156; de la Fuente, *A Nation for All,* 69.

42. Helg, *Our Rightful Share,* 149. Subsequent references are given in the text.

43. De la Fuente, *A Nation for All,* 72.

44. Helg, *Our Rightful Share,* 222.

45. Ibid., 225.

46. Ibid., 7.

47. Bergad, *Cuban Rural Society in the Nineteenth Century,* 67.

48. Ibid., 68.

49. Ferrer, *Insurgent Cuba,* 160; Bergad, *Cuban Rural Society in the Nineteenth Century,* 309.

50. Heredia, "Ricardo Batrell empuña la pluma," 300n10.

51. Paquette, *Sugar Is Made with Blood,* 214.

52. Heredia, "Ricardo Batrell empuña la pluma," 300.

53. Bergad, *Cuban Rural Society in the Nineteenth Century,* 309.

54. Ibid., 307.

55. Rosabal, "Ricardo Batrell, un expediente inconcluso," 317; Heredia, "Ricardo Batrell empuña la pluma," 300.

56. Heredia, "Ricardo Batrell empuña la pluma," 301n12.

57. Rosabal, "Ricardo Batrell, un expediente inconcluso," 316.

58. Ibid., 315.

59. Helg, *Our Rightful Share,* 213.

60. Ricardo Batrell Oviedo to Secretario de Gobernación, December 4, 1909, ANC, AD, box 54, no. 4129; Rosabal, "Ricardo Batrell, un expediente inconcluso," 317; Heredia, "Ricardo Batrell empuña la pluma," 300–301.

61. Rosabal, "Ricardo Batrell, un expediente inconcluso," 321.

62. Ricardo Batrell Oviedo to Juan Gualberto Gómez, February 1, 1922, ANC Adgilisiciones, box 12, signatura no. 484.

63. Heredia, "Ricardo Batrell empuña la pluma," 298.

64. Omar Granados, "Seminar Comments," February 28, 2008, Emory University, Atlanta, Georgia.

65. Heredia, "Ricardo Batrell empuña la pluma," 303–4.

66. Ibid., 306.

67. Ibid., 306–7.

68. Batrell to Secretario de Gobernación.

69. Ricardo Batrell Oviedo, "Relato escrito por Ricardo Batrell, sobre la Guerra de Independencia–Incompleto," ANC, AD, box 70, no. 4242, 758.

70. Ricardo Batrell Oviedo and Alejandro Neninger, "Manifesto al pueblo de Cuba y a la raza de color," *La Discusión,* August 11, 1907.

71. Ibid.

72. Pérez, Ferrer, and Helg are the first U.S.-based historians to cite Batrell.

73. Flint, *Marching with Gomez,* 85–88.

74. Prados-Torreira, *Mambisas,* 63–66.

75. Ibid., 152.

76. Sierra Madero, "Mambises y Homosexuales," 3.

77. Howard-Pitney, *The Afro-American Jeremiad,* 20, 5.

78. Bercovitch, *The American Jeremiad,* 10.

79. Ibid., xi.

80. Radillo y Rodriguez, *Autobiographía del Cubano Luis de Radillo y Rodriguez ó episodios de su vida histórico-politico-revolucionaria, desde el 24 de febrero de 1895 hasta el 1 de enero 1899,* 11.

81. Ibid., 12.

82. Ibid., 93.

83. Andrews, *Afro-Latin America, 1800–2000,* 4.

84. Gates, "Literary Theory and the Black Tradition," 25.

85. For a fuller discussion of the privileged social space Manzano tries to reserve for himself, see Jerome Branche, "'*Mulato entre negros'* (y blancos): Writing,

Race, the Antislavery Question, and Juan Francisco Manzano's *Autobiographía,*" *Bulletin of Latin American Research* 20, no. 1 (January 2001): 63–87.

86. See Rama, *The Lettered City*. "To advance the systematic ordering project of the absolute monarchies," Rama explains, "to facilitate the concentration and hierarchical differentiation of power, and to carry out the civilizing mission assigned to them, the cities of Latin America required a specialized social group" (16). This "priestly caste," of which blacks were a part, comprised "the lettered city."

87. De Jesús, *The Souls of Purgatory,* 100.

88. Ventura de Molina, *Jacinto Ventura de Molina y los caminos de la escritura negra en le Río de la Plata,* 41.

89. Andrews, *To Tell a Free Story,* xi.

90. Ibid.

91. Douglass, *Narrative of the Life of Frederick Douglass, an American Slave,* 153.

92. Ibid., 157.

93. Moses, *Black Messiahs and Uncle Toms,* 5.

94. Ibid., 226–27.

Appendix

1. Ricardo Batrell, "Relato, escrito y firmado por Ricardo Batrell," Archivo Nacional de Cuba, Adquisiciones, box 70, no. 4242, 666–69. Subsequent references are given in the text.

2. Gervacio: This figure seems to be the same Gervacio whom Batrell supplied with a horse in the previously cited episode.

WORKS CITED

Andrews, George Reid. *Afro-Latin America, 1800–2000.* New York: Oxford University Press, 2004.

Andrews, William. *To Tell a Free Story: The First Century of Afro-American Autobiography, 1760–1865.* Urbana: University of Illinois Press, 1988.

Baquaqua, Mahommah Gardo. *The Biography of Mahommah Gardo Baquaqua: His Passage from Slavery to Freedom in Africa and America.* Ed. Robin Law and Paul E. Lovejoy. Princeton, N.J.: Wiener Publishers, 2007.

Batrell Oviedo, Ricardo. *Para la historia: Apuntes autobiográficos de la vida de Ricardo Batrell Oviedo.* Havana: Seoane y Alvares Impresores, 1912.

Bell, Madison Smartt. *Toussaint Louverture: A Biography.* New York: Pantheon Books, 2007.

Bercovitch, Sacvan. *The American Jeremiad.* Madison: University of Wisconsin Press, 1978.

Bergad, Laird W. *Cuban Rural Society in the Nineteenth Century: The Social and Economic History of Monoculture in Matanzas.* Princeton, N.J.: Princeton University Press, 1990.

Boza, Barnabé. *Mi diario de la guerra: Desde Baire hasta la intervención americana.* Havana: Editorial de Ciencias Sociales, 2001.

Branche, Jerome. "'*Mulato entre negros*' (*y blancos*): Writing, Race, the Antislavery Question, and Juan Francisco Manzano's *Autobiographía.*" *Bulletin of Latin American Research* 20, no. 1 (January 2001): 63–87.

Bueno, Maria de los Reyes Castillo. *Reyita: The Life of a Black Cuban Woman in the Twentieth Century.* Durham, N.C.: Duke University Press, 2000.

Castillo y Zúñiga, José Rogelio. *Para la historia de Cuba: Autobiographía del General José Rogelio Castillo y Zúñiga.* Havana: Impenta y Papeleria de Rambla y Bouza, 1910.

Corzo, Gabino La Rosa. *Runaway Slave Settlements in Cuba: Resistance and Repression.* Trans. Mary Todd. Chapel Hill: University of North Carolina Press, 2003.

Davis, David Brion. "He Changed the New World." *New York Review of Books* 54, no. 9, May 31, 2007.

Works Cited

de Jesús, Ursula. *The Souls of Purgatory: The Spiritual Diary of a Seventeenth-Century Afro-Peruvian Mystic, Ursula de Jesús*. Ed and trans. Nancy E. van Deusen. Albuquerque: University of New Mexico Press, 2004.

de la Fuente, Alejandro. *A Nation for All: Race, Inequality, and Politics in Twentieth-Century Cuba*. Chapel Hill: University of North Carolina Press, 2001.

Douglass, Frederick. *Narrative of the Life of Frederick Douglass, an American Slave*. New York: Penguin Books, 1986.

Dubois, Laurent. *Avengers of the New World: The Story of the Haitian Revolution*. Cambridge: Harvard University Press, 2004.

Ferrer, Ada. *Insurgent Cuba: Race, Nation, and Revolution, 1868–1898*. Chapel Hill: University of North Carolina Press, 1999.

Flint, Grover. *Marching with Gomez: A War Correspondent's Field Note-Book Kept during Four Months with the Cuban Army*. New York: Lamson, Wolffe and Company, 1898.

Foner, Philip S. *Antonio Maceo: The "Bronze Titan" of Cuba's Struggle for Independence*. New York: Monthly Review Press, 1977.

———. *A History of Cuba and Its Relations with the United States*. Vol. 1. New York: International Publishers, 1962.

———. *A History of Cuba and Its Relations with the United States*. Vol. 2. New York: International Publishers, 1963.

Gates, Henry Louis, Jr. "Literary Theory and the Black Tradition." In *Figures in Black: Word, Signs, and the "Racial Self."* New York: Oxford University Press, 1987.

Helg, Aline. *Our Rightful Share: The Afro-Cuban Struggle for Equality, 1886–1912*. Chapel Hill: University of North Carolina Press, 1995.

Heredia, Fernando Martínez. "Ricardo Batrell empuña la pluma." In *Espacios, silencios y los sentidos de la libertad: Cuba entre 1878 y 1912,* ed. Fernando Martínez Heredia, Rebecca J. Scott, and Orlando F. García Martínez. Havana: Ediciones UNIÓN, 2001.

Herrera, José Isabel. *Impresiones de la Guerra de Independencia*. Havana: 1948.

Howard-Pitney, David. *The Afro-American Jeremiad: Appeals for Justice in America*. Philadelphia: Temple University Press, 1990.

Lane, Jill. *Blackface Cuba, 1840–1895*. Philadelphia: University of Pennsylvania Press, 2005.

Maceo, Antonio. *Antonio Maceo: Diarios de campaña*. Ed. Aisnara Perera Díaz. Havana: Editorial de Ciencias Sociales, 2001.

———. *El Pensamiento Vivo de Maceo*. Ed. José Antonio Portuondo. Havana: Biblioteca Básica de Cultura Cubana.

Works Cited

Manzano, Juan Francisco. *The Autobiography of a Slave*. Trans. Evelyn Picon Garfield. Detroit: Wayne State University Press, 1996.

Montejo, Esteban. *Biography of a Runaway Slave*. Ed. Miguel Barnet. Trans. W. Nick Hill. Willimantic, Conn.: Cubstone Press, 1994.

Moses, Wilson Jeremiah. *Black Messiahs and Uncle Toms: Social and Literary Manipulations of Religious Myth*. Rev. ed. University Park: Pennsylvania State University Press, 1993.

Paquette, Robert L. *Sugar Is Made with Blood: The Conspiracy of La Escalera and the Conflict between Empires over Slavery in Cuba*. Middletown, Conn.: Wesleyan University Press, 1988.

Pérez, Louis A, Jr. *Cuba: Between Reform and Revolution*. 2d ed. New York: Oxford University Press, 1995.

Prados-Torreira, Teresa. *Mambisas: Rebel Women in Nineteenth-Century Cuba*. Gainesville: University of Florida Press, 2005.

Radillo y Rodríguez, Luis de. *Autobiogaphía del Cubano Luis de Radillo y Rodríguez ó episodios de su vida histórico-politico-revolucionaria, desde el 24 de febrero de 1895 hasta el 1 de enero 1899*. Havana: Imp. La Tipografía, de M. Sarlara Rodríguez, 1899.

Rama, Ángel. *The Lettered City*. Trans. John Charles Chasteen. Durham, N.C.: Duke University Press, 1996.

Rosabal, Blancamar León. "Ricardo Batrell, un expediente inconcluso." In *Espacios, silencios y los sentidos de la libertad: Cuba entre 1878 y 1912,* ed. Fernando Martínez Heredia, Rebecca J. Scott, and Orlando F. García Martínez. Havana: Ediciones UNIÓN, 2001.

Seacole, Mary. *Wonderful Adventures of Mrs. Seacole in Many Lands*. New York: Penguin Books, 2005.

Sierra Madero, Abel. "Mambises y Homosexuales," *Semonario "El Veraz."* www.elveraz.com.

Smart, Ian Isidore. *Nicolás Guillén: Popular Poet of the Caribbean*. Columbia: University of Missouri Press, 1990.

Tone, John Lawrence. *War and Genocide in Cuba, 1895–1898*. Chapel Hill: University of North Carolina Press, 2006.

Ventura de Molina, Jacinto. *Jacinto Ventura de Molina y los caminos de la escritura negra en el Río de la Plata*. Ed. William G. Acree Jr. and Alex Borucki. Montevideo, Uruguay: Linardi y Risso, 2008.

INDEX

Index

Index

Index

Mark A. Sanders is professor of African American studies and English at Emory University.